CSWE's Core Competencies in This Text

P9-APO-508

Competency	Chapter
Professional Identity	
Practice behavior examples of professional identity help students to:	
Serve as representatives of the profession, its mission, and its core values	1, 4, 9, 12, 19
Know the profession's history	1, 2, 19
Commit themselves to the profession's enhancement and to their own professional conduct and growth	1, 3, 4, 5, 9, 18, 19
Advocate for client access to the services of social work	9, 12, 13, 16, 19
Practice personal reflection and self-correction to assure continual professional development	3–7, 18, 29
Attend to professional roles and boundaries	2, 4, 15, 18
Demonstrate professional demeanor in behavior, appearance, and communication	2–7, 9, 18
Engage in career-long learning	3–6, 9, 18, 19
Use supervision and consultation	2, 4–6,15, 18
Ethical Practice	
Practice behavior examples of ethical practice help students to:	
Encourage to conduct themselves ethically and engage in ethical decision making	2, 3, 5, 8, 13
Know about the value base of the profession, its ethical standards, and relevant law	2, 3, 8, 12, 13, 15
Recognize and manage personal values in a way that allows professional values to guide practice	5, 7, 13, 19
Make ethical decisions by applying standards of the National Association of Social Workers *Code of Ethics* and, as applicable, of the International Federation of Social Workers/International Association of Schools of Social Work Ethics in Social Work, Statement of Principles	5, 12, 13, 15
Tolerate ambiguity in resolving ethical conflicts	13
Apply strategies of ethical reasoning to arrive at principled decisions	5, 12–14
Critical Thinking	
Practice behavior examples of critical thinking help students to:	
Know about the principles of logic, scientific inquiry, and reasoned discernment	10, 13–15, 17
Use critical thinking augmented by creativity and curiosity	4–6, 8, 10, 13, 14, 18, 19
Requires the synthesis and communication of relevant information	1, 2, 4–6, 8, 10, 13, 14
Distinguish, appraise, and integrate multiple sources of knowledge, including research-based knowledge, and practice wisdom	3, 4, 8, 10–14, 16, 17
Analyze models of assessment, prevention, intervention, and evaluation	5, 6, 8, 10, 13, 17
Demonstrate effective oral and written communication in working with individuals, families, groups, organizations, communities, and colleagues	4–8, 12, 13

Adapted with the permission of Council on Social Work Education

Competency	Chapter
Diversity in Practice	
Practice behavior examples of diversity in practice help students to:	
Understand how diversity characterizes and shapes the human experience and is critical to the formation of identity	3, 6, 7, 9, 12
Understand the dimensions of diversity as the intersectionality of multiple factors including age, class, color, culture, disability, ethnicity, gender, gender identity and expression, immigration status, political ideology, race, religion, sex, and sexual orientation	3, 6, 8, 9, 12, 16
Appreciate that, as a consequence of difference, a person's life experiences may include oppression, poverty, marginalization, and alienation as well as privilege, power, and acclaim	8, 9, 10, 12
Recognize the extent to which a culture's structures and values may oppress, marginalize, alienate, or create or enhance privilege and power	7, 8, 9, 11, 12
Gain sufficient self-awareness to eliminate the influence of personal biases and values in working with diverse groups	3, 7, 8, 12
Recognize and communicate their understanding of the importance of difference in shaping life experiences	6, 8, 9, 12, 14
View themselves as learners and engage those with whom they work as informants	3, 6, 7, 9, 12
Human Rights & Justice	
Practice behavior examples of human rights and justice help students to:	
Understand that each person, regardless of position in society, has basic human rights, such as freedom, safety, privacy, an adequate standard of living, health care, and education	3, 6, 8, 10–14, 19
Recognize the global interconnections of oppression and are knowledgeable about theories of justice and strategies to promote human and civil rights	10–13, 19
Incorporate social justice practices in organizations, institutions, and society to ensure that these basic human rights are distributed equitably and without prejudice	6, 8, 10–13, 15, 19
Understand the forms and mechanisms of oppression and discrimination	3, 6, 8, 10–13, 19
Advocate for human rights and social and economic justice	8, 10–12, 14, 19
Engage in practices that advance social and economic justice	8, 10–12, 14, 19
Research-Based Practice	
Practice behavior examples of research-based practice help students to:	
Use practice experience to inform research, employ evidence-based interventions, evaluate their own practice, and use research findings to improve practice, policy, and social service delivery	3, 6, 8, 10, 13, 17
Comprehend quantitative and qualitative research and understand scientific and ethical approaches to building knowledge	8, 17
Use practice experience to inform scientific inquiry	8, 16, 17
Use research evidence to inform practice	3, 8, 11, 16, 18

Competency	Chapter
Human Behavior	
Practice behavior examples of human behavior help students to:	
Know about human behavior across the life course, the range of social systems in which people live, and the ways social systems promote or deter people in maintaining or achieving health and well-being	3, 6, 7, 10, 12, 16
Apply theories and knowledge from the liberal arts to understand biological, social, cultural, psychological, and spiritual development	3, 10, 12, 16
Utilize conceptual frameworks to guide the processes of assessment, intervention, and evaluation	3, 10, 12, 16
Critique and apply knowledge to understand person and environment	6, 10, 12, 16
Policy Practice	
Practice behavior examples of policy practice help students to:	
Understand that policy affects service delivery and they actively engage in policy practice	3, 8, 11, 15
Know the history and current structures of social policies and services, the role of policy in service delivery, and the role of practice in policy development	8, 10–12, 15
Analyze, formulate, and advocate for policies that advance social well-being	11–15
Collaborate with colleagues and clients for effective policy action	8, 11, 13, 15, 19
Practice Contexts	
Practice behavior examples of practice contexts help students to:	
Keep informed, resourceful, and proactive in responding to evolving organizational, community, and societal contexts at all levels of practice	3, 4, 6, 8–11, 13, 15, 16, 19
Recognize that the context of practice is dynamic, and use knowledge and skill to respond proactively	4–6, 8, 9, 11, 13, 16, 19
Continuously discover, appraise, and attend to changing locales, populations, scientific and technological developments, and emerging societal trends to provide relevant services	6, 8–11, 14, 16, 19
Provide leadership in promoting sustainable changes in service delivery and practice to improve the quality of social services	6, 9, 11, 17, 19

Competency	Chapter
Engage, Assess, Intervene, Evaluate	
Practice behavior examples of engage, assess, intervene, evaluate help students to:	
Identify, analyze, and implement evidence-based interventions designed to achieve client goals	3–5, 8, 12, 16
Use research and technological advances	5, 8, 12, 16
Evaluate program outcomes and practice effectiveness	3–5, 8, 9, 12, 16
Develop, analyze, advocate, and provide leadership for policies and services	8, 9, 12, 16
Promote social and economic justice	8, 9, 12, 16
A) ENGAGEMENT	
Substantively and effectively prepare for action with individuals, families, groups, organizations, and communities	
Use empathy and other interpersonal skills	3–16
Develop a mutually agreed-on focus of work and desired outcomes	3–16
B) ASSESSMENT	
Collect, organize, and interpret client data	3–17
Assess client strengths and limitations	3–16
Develop mutually agreed-on intervention goals and objectives	3–16
Select appropriate intervention strategies	3–17
C) INTERVENTION	
Initiate actions to achieve organizational goals	3–16
Implement prevention interventions that enhance client capacities	3–17
Help clients resolve problems	3–16
Negotiate, mediate, and advocate for clients	3–16
Facilitate transitions and endings	3–17
D) EVALUATION	
Critically analyze, monitor, and evaluate interventions	3–17

SIXTH EDITION

Social Work Practicum

A Guide and Workbook for Students

Cynthia L. Garthwait
The University of Montana

PEARSON

Boston   Columbus   Indianapolis   New York   San Francisco   Upper Saddle River
Amsterdam   Cape Town   Dubai   London   Madrid   Milan   Munich   Paris   Montréal   Toronto
Delhi   Mexico City   São Paulo   Sydney   Hong Kong   Seoul   Singapore   Taipei   Tokyo

Editorial Director: Craig Campanella
Editor-in-Chief: Ashley Dodge
Editorial Product Manager: Carly Czech
Editorial Assistant: Nicole Suddeth
Vice President/Director of Marketing: Brandy Dawson
Executive Marketing Manager: Kelly May
Marketing Coordinator: Courtney Stewart
Senior Digital Media Editor: Paul DeLuca
Production Project Manager: Liz Napolitano
Manager, Central Design: Jayne Conte
Cover Designer: Suzanne Behnke
Cover Image: ©Nicolas Nadjar/Alamy
Interior Design: Joyce Weston Design
Editorial Production and Composition Service: Hema Latha/Integra Software Services, Ltd.
Printer/Binder: Edwards Brothers/Malloy
Cover Printer: Lehigh-Phoenix Color/Hagerstown
Text Font: 10/12 Melior

Credits and acknowledgments borrowed from other sources and reproduced, with permission, in this textbook appear on the appropriate page within text.

Copyright © 2014, 2010, 2006 by Pearson Education, Inc. All rights reserved. Manufactured in the United States of America. This publication is protected by Copyright and permission should be obtained from the publisher prior to any prohibited reproduction, storage in a retrieval system, or transmission in any form or by any means, electronic, mechanical, photocopying, recording, or likewise. To obtain permission(s) to use material from this work, please submit a written request to Pearson Education, Inc., Permissions Department, One Lake Street, Upper Saddle River, New Jersey 07458 or you may fax your request to 201-236-3290.

Library of Congress Cataloging-in-Publication Data
Garthwait, Cynthia L.
   Social work practicum : a guide and workbook for students / Cynthia L. Garthwait.—6th ed.
      p.   cm.
   Includes bibliographical references and index.
   ISBN-13: 978-0-205-84893-5
   ISBN-10: 0-205-84893-1
   1. Social work education—United States—Outlines, syllabi, etc.   2. Social work education—United States—Examinations, questions, etc.   I. Title.
   HV11.7.H67 2014
   361.3076—dc23

                                                                              2012034137

10 9 8 7 6 5 4 3 2 1

                                                             Student Edition
                                                             ISBN-10: 0-205-84893-1
                                                             ISBN-13: 978-0-205-84893-5

                                                             Instructor's Review Copy
                                                             ISBN-10: 0-205-84907-5
                                                             ISBN-13: 978-0-205-84907-9

Contents

Foreword

The practicum experience is so central to social work education that it is a mandated component of preparation for both BSW and MSW students. However, the very nature of practicum—as something that happens outside the classroom—means that potential exists for disconnect between the academic content of social work education and the experiential learning that takes place in practicum. *The Social Work Practicum: A Guide and Workbook for Students* addresses this disconnect, and invites clear and well-articulated linkages between the essential components of social work education.

The successful integration of practicum with classroom learning is both challenging and necessary. Social work students in practicum function in a variety of settings, serve diverse populations, and work with various client configurations. As an instructor, it can be challenging to help students with such diverse practice experiences integrate and apply essential knowledge, skills, and values to their very different practicum experiences. However, such integration is critical to the developing professional, and to the clients they will serve in practicum and in their future careers.

The ability to both thoughtfully and purposefully integrate and apply appropriate concepts to practice is a skill that must be taught, and this is best done in the context of practicum. However, the skills of integration and application are not developed simply by being placed in practicum after having received classroom instruction. Rather, students need and deserve well-articulated guidance to thoughtfully combine their learning experiences, and *The Social Work Practicum: A Guide and Workbook for Students* continues to meet that critical need.

Through *The Social Work Practicum: A Guide and Workbook for Students*, Professor Garthwait provides an intentional common experience for students to explore the integration and application of knowledge, skills, and values to diverse practicum experiences. It is a book that blends experiential learning and academic content, thereby serving as both an instruction guide and a model for what we expect students (and practitioners) to do with the various components of their social work education.

The Social Work Practicum: A Guide and Workbook for Students reflects Professor Garthwait's strong student-focused approach to social work education, and her extensive experience as an educator and clinician. The skillfully crafted exercises and resources support students as they work through the process of becoming more self-aware, and developing the skills needed to practice truly integrated social work. The book is balanced, providing enough content but also empowering students to be the authors of their own experiences, now and in the future.

The benefit of experience is reflected in the sixth edition of *The Social Work Practicum: A Guide and Workbook for Students*. It carries on the tradition of excellence from previous editions but with improvements that can only come from current, relevant understanding of students, their experiences, and the profession of social work. For example, the sixth edition of this book includes additional content designed to support the Council on Social Work Education's EPAS Core Competencies and many new resources designed to facilitate discussion about integration of classroom learning with practicum. With each new edition, *The Social Work Practicum: A Guide and Workbook for Students* becomes an even stronger resource for students, instructors, and practicum supervisors.

Appropriate for use at the bachelors and masters level of social work education, *The Social Work Practicum: A Guide and Workbook for Students* is an invitation to settle into the space between the classroom and practicum. Even more, *The Social Work Practicum* provides the tools needed to ensure that the space between the classroom and practicum forms a crucible, creating exceptional opportunities for student-centered learning, creative application of concepts, and thoughtful integration of social work education.

Mary-Ann Sontag Bowman, Ph.D., LCSW
Associate Professor
University of Montana

Preface

Social work educators know very well that the practicum is an exciting opportunity to watch their students integrate theory and practice in real social work settings. Social work students like you who are prepared for this challenge will find that the professional perspectives, theories, and models you learned about in class can really come to life. In the practicum, you will bring your academic learning to the practicum site, provide services to very real clients in very real settings, see that ethical issues are no longer hypothetical, and move from the status of student to the role of professional.

This book was written to support the vital purpose of the practicum, which is to help you link theory and practice and build competency at each stage of the practicum. To that end, each chapter focuses on a discrete topic of great importance to both practicum and social work professional practice. Each chapter builds on previous ones, and offers sections such as Background and Context, Guidance and Direction, Workbook Activities, graphics to facilitate the integrating of classroom learning and practicum experience, and additional suggested learning activities.

Building upon your school's practicum seminar and the supervision offered by faculty members and agency supervisors, this book will provide all parties involved in your practicum with a number of valuable resources to help you understand how theory connects to practice, that critical thinking is needed in professional practice, how broad competencies and specific practice behaviors become part of your professional repertoire, and that ongoing professional development is not completed when the practicum concludes, but only begins at another level.

Knowing that the world needs committed, caring, and competent professionals like you are about to become, my hope is that you will use this book to its fullest, which no doubt you will also do with the actual experiences you are about to have.

Acknowledgments

This edition is dedicated to Gary, Nathan, and Benjamin, who have always supported my commitment to students and the clients they are learning to serve. The knowledge contained in this book has as its source the numerous, varied, and valuable experiences I have had in both social work practice and social work education. Clients and client systems have taught me about themselves and their perspective on social issues, about myself as a change agent, and about the way the world can be. Both BSW and MSW students have taught me about enthusiasm, commitment, and responding to one's professional calling. My colleagues at The University of Montana School of Social Work have provided insight and supports in my development as an educator. Thanks also go to Kristin Jobe, Integra; Ashley Dodge, Editor in Chief; Carly Czech Editorial Product Manager; Nicole Suddeth, Editorial Assistant; and Liz Napolitano, Production Project Manager at Pearson.

1

©Iqoncept/Dreamstime

The Purpose of a Practicum

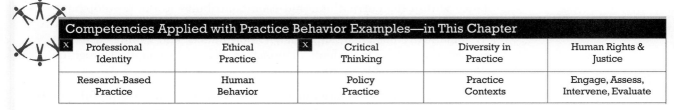

Competencies Applied with Practice Behavior Examples—in This Chapter				
x Professional Identity	Ethical Practice	x Critical Thinking	Diversity in Practice	Human Rights & Justice
Research-Based Practice	Human Behavior	Policy Practice	Practice Contexts	Engage, Assess, Intervene, Evaluate

CHAPTER PREVIEW

This introductory chapter presents the concept of practicum as a unique learning experience which offers you the opportunity to review classroom **knowledge**, integrate this knowledge with the professional **skills** required in the social work profession, and support all interventions with the **values** of the social work profession. This chapter also provides a Student Self-Assessment of Practicum Strengths tool you can use now to identify the strengths you bring to the social work practicum so that you can build on them throughout your learning experience and then measure them again at the end of the practicum.

You are to be congratulated for embarking on your exciting social work practicum experience and applauded for reaching this stage in your professional education. You have been approved for a practicum based on your academic achievements and your readiness for professional experience. The practicum offers a unique opportunity to apply what you have learned in the classroom, expand your knowledge, develop your skills, and hone your use of professional values. It is time for you to move from the role of a student to that of a professional social worker.

BACKGROUND AND CONTEXT

Almost universally, students of social work at both the BSW and MSW levels describe their practicum as the single most useful, significant, and powerful learning experience of their formal social work education. It is during the practicum that the concepts, principles, theories, and models discussed in the classroom come to life. During the practicum, students work with real clients and have the opportunity and responsibility to use and enhance the skills and techniques they previously rehearsed in classroom role-playing and simulations. It is also during the practicum that students make considerable progress in developing self-awareness and come to a better understanding of their individual strengths and limitations as well as the influence of their personal values, attitudes, and life experiences on their practice. The practicum can and should be a time when classroom theory is integrated with social work practice and when students merge with the values and fundamental principles of their chosen profession.

Educational Policy 2.3 of the Council on Social Work Education's (CSWE) Educational Policies and Academic Standards (2008) states thus:

> In social work, the signature pedagogy is field education. The intent of field education is to connect the theoretical and conceptual contribution of the classroom with the practical world of the practice setting. It is a basic precept of social work education that the two interrelated components of curriculum—classroom and field—are of equal importance within the curriculum, and each contributes to the development of the requisite competencies of professional practice. Field education is systematically designed, supervised, coordinated, and evaluated based on criteria by which students demonstrate the achievement of program competencies. (p. 8)

For many students, the practicum is a very positive and meaningful experience, but for some the practicum can fall short of expectations. The quality of every practicum experience can be enhanced if students are provided with guidance in identifying and making use of learning opportunities. A practicum structure that helps students to examine and analyze their settings in ways that build on their prior classroom learning is of critical importance. In addition, some of the most meaningful learning occurs as a result of having to deal with unexpected events and frustrations during the practicum.

In order to ensure a positive learning experience and minimize the chances of having negative experiences, you should remember to:

- Clarify your ***professional goals*** while remembering that your school and agency will also have goals for the time you spend in practicum.
- Develop a ***positive professional relationship*** with your agency field instructor and your faculty supervisor while also seeking to learn from others working in your agency.
- Approach your ***responsibilities*** as professionally as possible while also remembering that you are a student who has much to learn.
- Strike a balance between structuring your practicum for maximum learning with maintaining an ***openness to learning*** experiences that are not planned.

HOW TO USE THIS BOOK

This book is designed to provide you with guidance and structure during the social work practicum. If used in a thoughtful manner throughout the practicum, it will help you make the best of whatever your practicum setting has to offer. Needless to say, this will not happen without effort. It requires a real commitment and a willingness to invest time in the learning process.

HOW THE CHAPTERS ARE STRUCTURED

Although the chapters in the book are numbered in the conventional manner, this is not to suggest that you are to necessarily move through the book sequentially, one chapter after another. Rather, it is expected that you will be gathering information to complete the workbook activities in several of the chapters at the same time. It is expected that you will move back and forth between sections and will also revisit the same section several times as you gain experience in the practicum and begin to look at various questions and issues from new perspectives. The chapters may also be read in a different order to accommodate the structure and outline of your school's program.

Each chapter begins with a section titled ***Chapter Preview***, which presents a short capsule of the chapter content and reasons why the content and focus of the chapter is essential. It also describes the relationship between this chapter and previous ones, while also linking it to chapters that follow. The first major section of each chapter, ***Background and Context***, presents selected concepts and principles related to the topic addressed by the chapter. The concepts and definitions presented in this section are not a substitute for a textbook or assigned readings, but rather should act as a

Critical Thinking

Practice Behavior Example: Social workers distinguish, appraise, and integrate multiple sources of knowledge, including research-based knowledge, and practice wisdom.

Critical Thinking Question: How can you learn from a broad range of sources?

review of key ideas that set the stage for what follows. The ideas in the **Background and Context** section of each chapter will stimulate creative thinking and raise important questions that need to be considered as you work your way through the practicum. These sections offer you general suggestions, guidance, advice, and sometimes even a few specific do's and don'ts intended to encourage and facilitate learning in relation to the chapter's objectives and particular focus.

In most of the chapters, several pages have been cast into a workbook format and titled **A Workbook Activity**. You will be asked to engage in critical thinking activities and answer questions that will help you integrate knowledge, skills, and values needed for the professional competencies for social work practice.

A section titled **Suggested Learning Activities** lists several specific tasks and activities that provide additional opportunities and experiences for learning as well as a few additional ideas, words of encouragement, and specific cautions that may be important to you in the practicum experience.

Each chapter is followed by a **Chapter Review**. Chapters 5–19 contain Practice Test, which resembles a social work licensing examination in form and content.

The bibliography, provided at the end of the book, lists several books and articles related to the topics addressed in the book. These suggestions serve as resources for additional information and help in an in-depth examination of the topics presented. Using textbooks and readings from courses you have taken as reference guides will also help you understand how social workers continue to build on their previous knowledge and skills as more advanced practice is expected over time.

Professional Identity

Practice Behavior Example: Social workers practice personal reflection and self-correction to assure continual professional development.

Critical Thinking Question: Although you are just beginning your practicum, you have some of the strengths a social worker will need. As you complete this self-assessment, identify the strengths you already have.

Student Self-Assessment of Practicum Strengths: A Workbook Activity

Student Self-Assessment of Practicum Strengths

Areas of Competence	Practicum Strengths					
	Prepracticum Self-Assessment of Strengths			Postpracticum Self-Assessment of Strengths		
	Yes	In Progress	No	Yes	In Progress	No
Attitudes						
1. Empathetic, caring, and concerned for clients	X					
2. Personal values, beliefs, and perspectives that are compatible with the agency's mission	X					
3. Personal values, beliefs, and perspectives that are compatible with the NASW Code of Ethics						
4. Committed to achieving social justice			X			

Areas of Competence	Practicum Strengths					
	Prepracticum Self-Assessment of Strengths			Postpracticum Self-Assessment of Strengths		
	Yes	In Progress	No	Yes	In Progress	No
5. Respectful of diversity among clients and communities	X					
6. Nonjudgmental toward clients and colleagues		X				
Motivation to Learn						
7. Open to new learning experiences	X					
8. Willingness to take on new responsibilities		X				
9. Open to building self-awareness and professional competence		X				
10. Adequate time and energy to devote to the practicum			X			
11. A sense of "calling" to the profession	X					
12. Commitment to using supervision		X				
General Work Skills						
13. Writing skills (reports, letters, professional records, using technological tools)		X				
14. Ability to quickly process information, understand new concepts, and learn new skills	X					
15. Ability to read rapidly, grasp ideas quickly, and pull meaning from the written word	X					
16. Ability to organize, plan, and effectively manage time	X					
17. Ability to meet deadlines and work under pressure	X					
18. Ability to follow through and complete tasks		X				
Social Work Skills						
19. Ability to listen, understand, and consider varied views, perspectives, and opinions		X				
20. Verbal communication skills		X				
21. Ability to make thoughtful and ethical decisions under stressful conditions		X				
22. Assertiveness and self-confidence in professional relationships with clients and colleagues		X				
23. Ability to identify a need and formulate a plan to meet that need	X					
24. Ability to solve problems creatively and effectively		X				

(continued)

(*continued*)

Areas of Competence	Practicum Strengths					
	Prepracticum Self-Assessment of Strengths			Postpracticum Self-Assessment of Strengths		
	Yes	In Progress	No	Yes	In Progress	No
Knowledge						
25. Self-awareness of how one's values, beliefs, experiences impact work and other persons	X					
26. Knowledge of laws, rules, regulations, and policies of agency			X			
27. Knowledge of the assessment tools, methods, and techniques used by agency			X			
28. Knowledge of theories and interventions used by agency			X			
29. Understanding of the process of planned change						
30. Knowledge of the community context of agency			X			
Prior Experience Related to Practicum						
31. Experience in setting similar to agency						
32. Experience with clients or client systems similar to those served by agency			X			
33. Experience applying theory to practice	X					
34. Experience working with professional teams	X					
35. Experience playing social work roles	X					
36. Training in professional skills related to those needed in practicum						

Social workers are committed to taking a strengths perspective on their clients, helping them to address their problems and enhance their social functioning by building on their strengths. By applying that approach to your own learning and professional growth, you can use your professional strengths and assets as building blocks for the professional skills you will need. The following exercise will help you take a strengths perspective on yourself.

1. List the most significant strengths that you bring to the practicum based on the preceding checklist.

Sensitivity to other cultures and a deep love of getting to know clients, build upon their strengths, + motivate them. Team player, enthusiastic, used to high stress environments

2. What strengths not on this list do you bring to your practicum experience?

A deeper love and connection with clients – I see the ability to trust and care for each other as friends as a strength.

3. What can you do to secure learning experiences that will build on your strengths?

Ask for some time doing direct service / interacting with participants

4. What are the most significant limitations that you bring to the practicum experience?

Time and energy - already doing so much.

How Do We Learn? A Workbook Activity

The social work practicum is a unique opportunity in which you are offered the opportunity to prepare for professional social work practice by integrating your classroom knowledge and skills into professional competencies in a real social work setting with real clients. Your experience will be enhanced if you are aware of how you learn.

Learning is a type of change, which can be exciting and exhilarating, or difficult and painful. Basically, we learn when we take risks—when we begin to think in a different way, when we view the familiar from a different angle, when we try out new behavior, or even when we confront our biases and unlearn some things we assumed were true. Openness to this type of learning can bring unexpected insights and unanticipated growth. Learning to face our hesitancies to venture into the professional world, take risks, challenge ourselves beyond our current competencies, and then be open to supervision and feedback will always result in an enriching learning experience. This new learning will excite and inspire you. It may create some discomfort, but that is the price of learning.

When the learning is about us—our biases, prejudices, and emotional hang-ups—the experience can be especially challenging. However, this can free us from attitudes and behaviors that limit personal growth and effectiveness. Because clients deserve the highest quality of services possible, the profession of social work is committed to identifying competencies needed for practice, developing best practice standards, and adhering to evidence-based practice that measures the effectiveness of interventions.

Answer the following questions about your learning style and learning goals, and think ahead about how you can maximize your learning experience. Your practicum will stretch your thinking, so open yourself up to this experience so that you do not miss a significant learning opportunity.

1. What learning experiences do you hope will help you acquire knowledge and develop social work practice skills?

—shadowing an experienced social working
—sitting in on agency-wide meeting
—seeing how funding problems are solved

2. What are you most excited and enthusiastic about?

– seeing an agency w/ MSWs and how that changes the quality of work.

3. What are your greatest fears or worries?

– That I'll be asked to do something I can't deliver on.

4. Given what you know about yourself and how you learn, what types of assistance, guidance, or structure would help you lower your defenses and be open to learning in the areas that cause you some level of anxiety or worry (e.g., demonstrations, shadowing, reading client records, watching videos)?

– definitely shadowing
– a supervisor who is open to questions and gives positive feedback ; increasing responsibility over time ,

5. If you have a learning disability, what accommodations will you request in your practicum agency?

Suggested Learning Activities

- Conduct a cursory examination of each chapter in this book. Note the topics addressed and how the content is organized. Try to identify the links between chapters, since they are designed to build on each other.
- Keep this book with you while at your practicum agency and try to answer all of the workbook questions.
- Collect the textbooks you used in your social work courses and use them to help you integrate your classroom learning with your practicum experience.

References

Alle-Corliss, Lupe, and Randy Alle-Corliss. *Advanced Practice in Human Service Agencies.* 2nd ed. Boston: Brooks/Cole, 2006.

Barker, Robert. *The Social Work Dictionary.* 5th ed. Washington, DC: NASW Press, 2003.

Berg-Weger, Marla, and Julie Birkenmaier. *The Practicum Companion for Social Work: Integrating Class and Field Work.* 3rd ed. Boston: Allyn and Bacon, 2011.

Commission on Accreditation. *Handbook of Accreditation Standards and Procedures, Educational Policies and Accreditation Standards.* Alexandria, VA: Council on Social Work Education, 2008.

Grobman, Linda May, ed. *The Field Placement Survival Guide: What You Need to Know to Get the Most from Your Social Work Practicum.* 2nd ed. Harrisburg, PA: White Hat Communications, 2011.

Mizrahi, Terry, and Larry Davis. *The Encyclopedia of Social Work*. 20th ed. Washington, DC: NASW Press and Oxford University Press, 2010.

Rogers, Gayla, Donald Collins, Constance Barlow, and Richard Grinnell. *Guide to the Social Work Practicum*. Itasca, IL: Brooks/Cole, 2000.

Royse, David, Surjit Singh Dhooper, and Elizabeth Rompf. *Field Instruction*. 6th ed. White Plains, NY: Longman, 2010.

Sheafor, Bradford, and Charles Horejsi. *Techniques and Guidelines for Social Work Practice*. 9th ed. Boston: Allyn and Bacon, 2012.

Sweitzer, H. Frederick, and Mary A. King. *The Successful Internship: Transformation and Empowerment in Experiential Learning*. 3rd ed. Florence, KY: Cengage Learning, 2009.

CHAPTER 1 REVIEW

1. After completing the "Student Self-Assessment of Practicum Strengths" in the activity section of this chapter, identify and prioritize the strengths you wish to acquire in terms of (1) attitudes, (2) motivation and desire to learn, (3) abilities and skills, and (4) knowledge and experience.

©Hjalmeida/Dreamstime

2

School, Agency, and Student Expectations

Competencies Applied with Practice Behavior Examples—in This Chapter				
X Professional Identity	X Ethical Practice	Critical Thinking	Diversity in Practice	Human Rights & Justice
Research-Based Practice	Human Behavior	Policy Practice	Practice Contexts	X Engage, Assess, Intervene, Evaluate

CHAPTER PREVIEW

This chapter will help you understand the similar yet unique expectations of the three stakeholders involved in your practicum. They include you the student, your agency, and your university social work program. It also provides a framework for understanding the skill-building process in which you are about to be engaged. Finally, it describes the progression of professional development from student to advanced practitioner.

A key to making your social work practicum a quality learning experience is the clarification of expectations. What do **you** really expect? What does the **agency** expect of you? What does your **school** expect of you and your practicum agency? Identifying and clarifying expectations will ensure a smooth and positive practicum experience, and not doing so may lead to problems. The purpose of this chapter is to encourage and facilitate a clarification of expectations.

BACKGROUND AND CONTEXT

You will quickly learn that there are many expectations for you and your practicum. Both clients and professionals with a variety of points of view, experiences, and roles to play will have a stake in your learning. This includes you, your university social work program, your agency, and your clients. This combination of people and groups who have a stake in your learning is similar to actual social work practice, so while you are still a student, it is helpful to understand what those expectations are.

The specific objectives associated with a practicum can be found in your school's practicum manual, in official descriptions of your social work curriculum, and in other documents issued by the social work program. All parties to the practicum are expected to adhere to the National Association of Social Workers (NASW) *Code of Ethics* as well as the expectations for social work programs accredited by the Council on Social Work Education (CSWE). General expectations of all the parties that will be involved in your practicum are given in Table 2.1.

Given the fact that you are in the process of learning to become a social worker and you generally lack experience, you must consider how this lack of skill and experience might affect your clients and the quality of the services provided to them. Even though you are a student, you will have a great deal to offer your clients, and when the work expected of you is beyond your level of knowledge and skill, consult with your field instructor for guidance and suggestions. Review your classroom learning, drawing upon theory and any skill-building exercises in which you have participated. The clients served by a student social worker are to be made aware that they are being served or assisted by a student. However, most clients will see you as a developing professional and will be cooperative and trusting of you, your knowledge, and your skills.

Professional Identity

Practice Behavior Example: Social workers engage in career-long learning.

Critical Thinking Question: A professional social worker needs to learn throughout his or her career. Watch for social workers engaging in this important practice.

Table 2.1   **Practicum Stakeholder Expectations**

As a student, you have much at stake in the quality of your practicum. You have worked and studied a long time in preparation for this experience in an agency with real clients, and no doubt have hopes that this experience will prepare you for professional social work practice. Below are common expectations of all stakeholders, organized by the areas in which expectations have been assumed or explicitly written. Notice how the secondary and primary roles expected of you by the various stakeholders vary between the parties based on their role in the practicum.

Student Expectations	Primary Role	Secondary Role	Preparation of Student	Organization of Work	Supervision	Evaluation
Prior to, during, and following practicum experience	Learn and integrate theory and practice	Provide services to clients and client systems	Classroom content and experience Orientation by agency field instructor	Assignments given by agency field instructor Learning goals required by university	Daily tasks supervised in agency Integration of theory and practice supervised by university	Ongoing evaluation by agency field instructor Academic grade given by university

Your agency and agency field instructor also have much at stake in your practicum. They serve real clients facing real life challenges, and expect you to engage in activities with those clients that are ethical, professional, and effective. Their expectations for you and the practicum experience include the following.

Agency Expectations	Primary Role	Secondary Role	Preparation of Student	Organization of Work	Supervision	Evaluation
Prior to, during, and following student placement	Provide services to clients and client systems	Supervise practicum student	Orientation by field instructor	Task assignments given by field instructor	Daily tasks supervised in agency Supervision training provided by university	Ongoing and final evaluation by field instructor

Your university social work program has invested itself in developing curriculum, designing learning experiences, and building a partnership with your agency, and expects that you will be able to use this experience to integrate classroom learning with practicum learning opportunities.

University Expectations	Primary Role	Secondary Role	Preparation of Student	Organization of Work	Supervision	Evaluation
Prior to, during, and following student placement	Learn and integrate theory and practice	Provide services to clients and client systems	Classroom content and experience Orientation by field instructor	Learning goals required by university	Integration of theory and practice supervised by university	Academic grade given by university

Although your clients do not yet know that you will be working with them, they will expect to receive professional services from you and your agency, and that you will be prepared to help them address their needs and concerns ethically, under supervision, and with respect.

Table 2.1   **Continued**

Client or Client System Expectations	Primary Role	Secondary Role	Preparation of Studen	Organization of Work	Supervision	Evaluation
Prior to, during, and following intervention	Receipt of services by competent social workers and students	Allowing self to be served by student	Not aware of services to be provided by student	Tasks designed to meet client needs and goals	Ongoing supervision by social worker	Professional-level services expected Effectiveness defined by client

GUIDANCE AND DIRECTION

Three major factors will determine the overall quality of your social work practicum experience:

- *Your motivation to learn*, including your career goals, the level of effort you are willing to put into this experience, your level of openness to learn about yourself, and your motivation for selecting social work as a career.
- *Your capacity to learn*, including your strengths, limitations, learning style, experiences upon which to build, academic ability, and ability to integrate theory and practice.
- *Your opportunity to learn*, including adequate time to devote to the practicum, your ability to minimize distractions from other parts of your life, the availability of experiences in your agency, and the presence of mentors and supervisors.

Social work requires that practitioners develop many skills needed to play various social work roles, improve competence at all levels of practice, and design interventions based on a broad range of perspectives, theories, and models. You will not yet be expected to possess these skills, and will be taught and supervised as you acquire them through the process described in Figure 2.1. This figure represents the process of skill building through didactic classroom learning, rehearsal of skills, observations of others performing the skills, attempts to develop the skill under supervision, reflection on performance, successive attempts at performing the skill, ongoing skill development, and advanced skill performance. Not only do practicum students use this process as they develop skills but professional social workers also go through a similar process each time they acquire a new skill.

Ethical Practice

Practice Behavior Example: Social workers make ethical decisions by applying standards of the National Association of Social Workers.

Critical Thinking Question: What are the ethical situations you expect to encounter in your agency?

Engage, Assess, Intervene, Evaluate

Practice Behavior Example: Social workers select appropriate intervention strategies.

Critical Thinking Question: How will you know what theories and models are being used in your agency in daily practice?

Didactic Learning

(factual information, theory base, liberal arts foundation, profession of social work)

⬇

Rehearsal of Skills in Controlled Setting

(classroom, practicum, practicum seminar)

⬇

Observation in Practice Setting

(practicum, media practice examples)

⬇

Supervised Attempt at Performing Skill

(using skill, initial integration of theory and practice)

⬇

Reflection on Performance of Skill

(self-reflection, supervisor feedback)

⬇

Successive Attempts at Performing Skill

(incorporating supervisor feedback, understanding of integration of theory and practice)

⬇

Ongoing Skill Development

(deepened level of ethical reasoning in application of skill, developing increased proficiency)

⬇

Advanced Skill Level

(teaching skill to others, supervising others, contributing to evidence-based practice)

Figure 2.1

Skill Building Continuum: From Student to Advanced Practitioner

Clarifying Expectations: A Workbook Activity

1. You will be spending hundreds of hours in your practicum setting. What do you expect from this investment of your time in the following areas?

Skills

_____

_____

Knowledge

_____

_____

Competencies

_____

_____

Values

_____

_____

Generalist experiences

_____

_____

Specialized experiences

_____

_____

Job preparation

_____

_____

2. Knowing that what you are willing to invest in the practicum determines what you will get out of it, list the key things you can commit to during the practicum.

_____

_____

_____

3. Are there any expectations of yourself, your agency, or your university that you are concerned about meeting? What can you do to successfully meet those objectives?

_____

_____

_____

4. If you were a client of your practicum agency, what would you expect of your social worker? What would you expect of your practicum student?

_____

_____

_____

Skill Building Across a Social Work Career: A Workbook Activity

Examine the table below and consider how the professional levels of practice build upon each other over time. Think about how each of the domains of skill building evolve over time for social work students and practitioners alike.

Skill Building Across a Social Work Career

Skill-Building Domains	Levels of Practice			
	BSW Student	MSW Student	Entry-Level Practitioner	Skilled Practitioner
Level of experience in using a skill or practice behavior	First attempt in using of a skill	Building on previous experience in using a skill	Using a skill for entry-level practice, independently but with supervision	Using a skill for advanced practice, independently while teaching the skill to others
Learning context of professional development	Classroom and practicum as learning context	Classroom, practicum, and previous experience as learning context	Agency practice as context for professional development	Agency practice and leadership role as context for professional development
Values base of professional development	Identification and acquisition of professional and personal values	Deepening understanding and use of professional values	Ongoing examination, development, and use of professional values	Advanced development, use, and teaching of professional values
Theory base of professional development	Understanding and beginning application of orienting/ explanatory theories and practice theories	Understanding, critiquing, and application of orienting/ explanatory theories and practice theories	Application of orienting/ explanatory theories and practice theories and measuring effectiveness of practice theories	Application of orienting/explanatory theories and practice theories, measuring effectiveness of practice theories, theory building
Evaluation of professional development	Supervisor and faculty evaluation with self-evaluation encouraged	Supervisor and faculty evaluation with self-evaluation encouraged	Supervisor evaluation with self-evaluation required	Self-evaluation, peer review, self-evaluation required, and expectation to evaluate others

Suggested Learning Activities

- Read your school's practicum manual. Pay special attention to descriptions of what is expected of the practicum student.
- Ask your field instructor if there is a job description for social work practicum students. If there is, read it carefully to understand what your agency expects.
- Carefully examine the practicum evaluation form and specific criteria that will be used to evaluate your performance so you can see what level of performance will be expected by your university social work program.
- Talk to former students who have completed a practicum in your agency. Ask them for advice and guidance on what to expect and about learning opportunities available. Also ask if they have any suggestions for you.
- Listen carefully to other students in your practicum seminar. Are their concerns similar to or different from yours? What can you learn from them, and what can you share with them that will enhance their learning?

References

Baird, Brian. *The Internship, Practicum, and Field Placement Handbook: A Guide for the Helping Professions.* 6th ed. Upper Saddle River, NJ: Prentice Hall, 2011.

Birkenmaier, Julie A., and Marla Berg-Weger. *The Practicum Companion for Social Work: Integrating Class and Field Work.* 3rd ed. Boston: Allyn and Bacon, 2011.

Bogo, Marion, and Elaine Vayda. *The Practice of Field Instruction in Social Work.* 2nd ed. New York: Columbia University Press, 1998.

Commission on Accreditation. *Educational Policies and Accreditation Standards.* Alexandria, VA: Council on Social Work Education, 2008.

Doel, Mark, Steven Shardlow, and Paul Johnson. *Contemporary Field Social Work: Integrating Field and Classroom Experience.* Los Angeles: Sage Publications, 2011.

Grobman, Linda May, ed. *More Days in the Lives of Social Workers: 35 "Real-Life" Stories of Advocacy, Outreach, and Other Intriguing Roles in Social Work Practice.* Harrisburg, PA: White Hat Communications, 2005.

National Association of Social Workers. *Code of Ethics.* Washington, DC: NASW Press, 1999.

Sheafor, Bradford, and Charles Horejsi. *Techniques and Guidelines for Social Work Practice.* 9th ed. Boston: Allyn and Bacon, 2012.

CHAPTER 2 REVIEW

1. Expectations are placed on practicum by students, agencies, and schools of social work. Although these expectations overlap and resemble each other, they are also distinct because of the unique nature of each interested party. How might this be like the variety of expectations a client and social worker have at the beginning of an intervention? What can you learn from this comparison?

3

Developing a Learning Plan

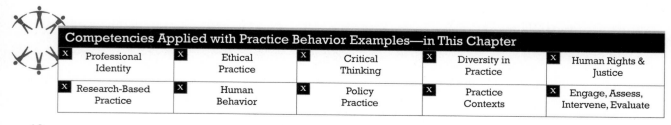

Competencies Applied with Practice Behavior Examples—in This Chapter				
X Professional Identity	X Ethical Practice	X Critical Thinking	X Diversity in Practice	X Human Rights & Justice
X Research-Based Practice	X Human Behavior	X Policy Practice	Practice Contexts	X Engage, Assess, Intervene, Evaluate

CHAPTER PREVIEW

This chapter offers a framework for understanding how a learning plan for practicum can help to structure and enhance the integrative learning experience. It outlines a set of generalist competencies which can serve as a template for a learning plan, and highlights the core competencies of the Council on Social Work Education. Finally, it explains the process of integration of theory and practice, which is a fundamental goal of practicum experiences.

Good learning experiences in practicum are usually the result of a well-planned learning agreement. For the most part, a good practicum experience is usually one that has been well conceived and outlined. In addition, you may have some very valuable unplanned learning experiences. Overall, you will increase your chances of success if you design a clear learning plan, but will also do well if you watch for opportunities to participate in learning opportunities that present themselves along the way. You may also have some challenging and even negative experiences, and although you might wish to avoid negative learning experiences, they may very well be the best teachers.

BACKGROUND AND CONTEXT

As you begin your practicum, it is important to list your desired outcomes for learning and then identify and arrange activities and experiences that will help you reach those goals. A ***learning goal/competency*** is a broad description of what you plan to learn, and is not easily measurable. Such a goal is often stated in terms such as the following: *to acquire, to understand, to explore, to become familiar with, to analyze,* and *to synthesize.*

A ***learning objective***, also called a learning activity, is what you hope you will know or be able to do following your practicum and is usually measurable. Such an objective is usually stated in terms such as the following: *to arrange, to compile, to conduct, to define, to demonstrate, to discuss, to write,* and *to obtain.* These activities might include conducting assessments, observing staff meetings, visiting agencies, designing and implementing treatment plans, writing report or grants, facilitating groups, conducting training, participating in community committees, and providing legislative testimony.

Learning outcomes or practice behaviors are what you gain, achieve, become familiar with, or master as you work toward overall professional competency. Outcomes might be described in terms such as ability to do the following: link theory to practice, utilize community resources, practice at all levels, utilize social work roles, evaluate effectiveness of agency program, influence social policy, and engage in ongoing professional development.

Assessment techniques, also known as evaluation tools, are the ways in which learning and performance are measured. These techniques include supervisory sessions, observations by supervisor, videotaped sessions, review of written documentation, client feedback, and pre- and post-tests.

As you plan your practicum experience, it is important to include experiences that will help you acquire the professional competencies identified by the profession. The core competencies of the CSWE provide a guide for developing your learning plan, as do the Generalist Social Work Competencies identified in the following section of this chapter.

A plan for learning will incorporate educational goals and anticipated outcomes from three sources: the university school of social work, the practicum agency and its field instructor, and the student. These goals for each of these stakeholders will usually fall into three categories: knowledge, skills, and values, all of which contribute to your competency as a social worker.

Social work **knowledge** is an understanding of professional terminology, facts, principles, concepts, perspectives, and theories. No doubt you have spent many hours learning about individuals and families, communities, research, and social policy. This knowledge will be used in the practicum as you apply it in real-life situations.

Critical Thinking

Practice Behavior Example: Social workers distinguish, appraise, and integrate multiple sources of knowledge, including research-based knowledge, and practice wisdom.

Critical Thinking Question: Social workers possess knowledge, skills, and values for practice. What do you see as the relationship between them?

Social work **skills** are the behaviors of practice. They are the techniques and procedures used by social workers to bring about desired change in the social functioning of clients or in social systems with which clients interact. For the most part, skills are learned by watching and following the lead of skilled practitioners. You can learn about skills from a textbook, but you cannot acquire skills simply by reading about them. Your practicum experience will afford you the opportunity to acquire and enhance your social work skills.

A **value** is a strong preference that affects one's choices, decisions, and actions and that is rooted in one's deepest beliefs and commitments. Values determine what a person considers important, worthwhile, right, or wrong. Social work values (e.g., service, social justice, integrity) can be learned or "caught" from others, but it is doubtful that they can be taught by others in a systematic and deliberate way. Typically, our values arise from our deepest beliefs about the way the world ought to be. Your practicum will undoubtedly be a time for you to more clearly understand what your values are, and you will also begin to see how your values may at times be in conflict with the values of others, including your clients.

It is possible to separate social work knowledge, skills, and values for purposes of discussion and analysis, but in the actual practice of social work, they are interwoven. For example, one's skill grows out of one's knowledge and values. Likewise, the possession of social work knowledge and values is of little use unless they both are expressed in action. Finally, knowledge and skills can be used to harm or manipulate clients unless guided by an ethical value base of services to clients.

Preparing a Plan for Learning

A form for preparing a written learning plan using this approach can be found in the Appendix. This sample learning agreement and the ideas behind it can be modified to fit the requirements of a particular school of social work. This learning agreement lists the learning goals (Generalist Competencies) in the left-hand column. The next column provides space for the overall learning objectives (Activities) for the practicum. The field instructor and student select additional goals specific to the practicum setting and include them in this column. The third column is to be completed by entering a timeline for the completion of the learning objectives. The fourth column provides space for a listing of learning outcomes. The fifth column is to be completed by specifying the method and criteria to be used in evaluating progress toward achieving the generalist competencies.

The Generalist Perspective and the Plan for Learning

The curricula for BSW programs and the first year of MSW programs are built around the concept of generalist social work practice. Thus, the practicum is expected to reflect a broad range of experiences in order to prepare them for generalist practice.

The ***generalist perspective*** is a way of viewing and thinking about the process and activities of social work practice. It is a set of ideas and principles that guide the process of planned change at all levels of practice, in a wide variety of settings, and as you practice a number of social work roles. One of the unique characteristics of the generalist social worker is commitment and ability to adapt his or her approach to the needs and circumstances of the client or client system, rather than expecting the client to conform to the methods of the professional or the agency. The generalist avoids selecting an intervention method or approach until after he or she and the client have worked together to complete a careful assessment of the client's concern or problem and have considered various ways in which the client's problem or concern can be defined, conceptualized, and approached. Finally, the generalist is prepared to draw on and use a wide range of intervention techniques and procedures, and is not bound to a single theory or model.

Keeping that definition in mind, Table 3.1 lists ***generalist competencies***. The table, building on these competencies, also provides a rationale for the use of each competency in social work and a list of specific practice behaviors required for the demonstration of that competency.

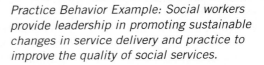

Practice Contexts

Practice Behavior Example: Social workers provide leadership in promoting sustainable changes in service delivery and practice to improve the quality of social services.

Critical Thinking Question: Generalist social workers practice at the micro, mezzo, and macro levels. How do you see the levels as connected?

Table 3.1   Generalist Competencies for Social Work Practice

Generalist Competency	Rationale for Competency	Practice Behaviors Related to Generalist Competency
Generalist Competency 1 The generalist social worker practices at multiple levels (micro, mezzo, and macro) individually and simultaneously and moves between systems and levels of practice based on client/client system needs, resources, and likelihood of success to enhance social functioning and facilitate social change.	Generalists practice at multiple levels because of the complex nature of social problems, and because social functioning, social change, and social justice are supported by interventions at all levels of practice.	**Micro Practice Behaviors** Interpersonal helping skills, communication skills, relationship building, and interviewing. **Mezzo Practice Behaviors** Coordination, group facilitation, advocacy, education, consulting, and mediation. **Macro Practice Behaviors** Planning, community development, program management, research, social policy formation, and administration.

(*continued*)

Table 3.1   Continued

Generalist Competency	Rationale for Competency	Practice Behaviors Related to Generalist Competency
Generalist Competency 2 The generalist social worker plays a broad range of professional roles individually and simultaneously to promote social justice, enhance social functioning, and promote social change. Generalist social workers may play several roles in any given situation, and can move between these roles as needed.	Generalists play a broad range of professional roles because of the variety of client/client system needs and resources, as well as to enhance social functioning, promote social justice, and promote social change at multiple levels of practice. They see the connections between professional roles and understand the importance of using them prescriptively, matching roles with need.	Selects social work role based on client/situation needs, conceptualization of the location of the problem being addressed, and targets for change. Plays roles at all levels of practice, including some roles specific to one level of practice and others which can be played at all levels of practice.
Generalist Competency 3 The generalist social worker uses a variety of discreet yet interacting lenses, conceptual frameworks, and paradigms to guide practice, including the strengths, ecosystems, and diversity perspectives.	Generalists understand that clients, groups, organizations, communities, and social systems cannot be understood in isolation, and that understanding the interaction between these entities is essential to effective interventions.	Incorporates a variety of professional perspectives into all phases of the helping process. Uses professional perspectives to identify targets for enhancing social functioning and improving the fit between clients and social systems.
Generalist Competency 4 The generalist social worker uses a variety of orienting (explanatory) theories to guide practice, including social systems theory, human development theory, group theory, organizational theory, community development theory, social movements theory, and social development theory.	Generalists need to understand the development of individuals, families, social systems, groups, organizations, and societies in order to comprehend the social conditions faced by clients and to implement effective interventions.	Incorporates orienting (explanatory) theories into all phases of planned change (engagement, assessment, planning, intervention, and evaluation at all levels).
Generalist Competency 5 The generalist social worker uses a variety of practice theories and models to guide practice and address client needs and resources, including task-centered casework, crisis intervention, client-centered casework, empowerment model, family systems model, mutual aid model, structural model, organizational development model, community organization model, and social change model.	Generalists use practice theories and models to design individualized interventions that are empirically based, grounded in best practices, methodologically sound, creative, and matched to the situation at hand. These theories and models provide practitioners with a versatile repertoire of techniques, help them avoid limiting themselves to a single approach, and afford the opportunity to combine approaches for effective interventions.	Incorporates practice theories and models into interventions at all levels of practice based on client need and resources. Combines practice theories and models creatively to address multiple social issues faced by clients and client systems.

Table 3.1   Continued

Generalist Competency	Rationale for Competency	Practice Behaviors Related to Generalist Competency
Generalist Competency 6 The generalist social worker, in partnership with client systems, uses the planned change process of assessment, planning, intervention, termination, and evaluation at all levels of practice.	Generalists use the planned change process to enhance social functioning and promote social change because a sound assessment creates the basis for an intervention plan that can be implemented and evaluated based on identified goals and objectives.	Engages clients, builds productive professional relationships, assesses client problems and strengths, designs sound intervention plans, implements effective intervention plan, and evaluates outcomes.
Generalist Competency 7 The generalist social worker is guided by the National Association of Social Workers' *Code of Ethics*, incorporates social work values into interventions at all levels, and uses a process for ethical decision making and resolving ethical dilemmas.	Generalists understand how personal and professional ethics and values underlie codes of conduct, client choices, community development, societal attitudes, definitions of social problems, development of social policy, and research.	Incorporates social work and client values into all interventions. Uses NASW *Code of Ethics* in ethical decision making and to resolve ethical dilemmas.

"List of Seven Generalist Competencies" from BSW COMPETENCY CATALOGUE. Copyright © 2008 by the University of Montana. Reprinted with permission.

The Educational Policy and Accreditation Standards of the Council on Social Work Education (2008, 3–7) also identify ***core competencies*** for social workers.

1. Identify as a professional social worker and conduct oneself accordingly.
2. Apply social work ethical principles to guide professional practice.
3. Apply critical thinking to inform and communicate professional judgments.
4. Engage diversity and difference in practice.
5. Advance human rights and social and economic justice.
6. Engage in research-informed practice and practice-informed research.
7. Apply knowledge of human behavior and the social environment.
8. Engage in policy practice to advance social and economic well-being and to deliver effective social work services.
9. Respond to contexts that shape practice.
10. Engage, assess, intervene, and evaluate with individuals, families, groups, organizations, and communities.

The list of ***Generalist Competencies*** in Table 3.1, in combination with the ***Core Competencies of the Council on Social Work's Educational Policies and Accreditation Standards***, can guide the structure of your practicum, so identify ways in which you can acquire those competencies vital to the practice of social work. All of these competencies are integrated throughout this book in multiple ways, showing you how they are acquired over time and in a variety of ways. Watch for reference to these core competencies and work to integrate them into your professional repertoire. The generalist competencies are incorporated into the learning agreement and practicum evaluation in the Appendix.

GUIDANCE AND DIRECTION

As you prepare your learning agreement in light of generalist competencies and core competencies of the social work profession, incorporate learning experiences that will help you develop these competencies. Your learning contract is negotiated between you, your field instructor, and your faculty supervisor. They understand what you must learn to become a competent generalist social worker. Most learning agreements are working documents that are modified throughout the practicum as additional learning needs are identified and new learning opportunities arise. Your plan should be exciting and ambitious to stretch and expand your knowledge and skills. It must also be realistic given your practicum setting, your abilities, your prior experience, and the time available to you.

Each of us has a unique approach to learning or a particular learning style. As you develop your plan, consider your preferred method of learning. For example, you may be inclined to jump into the middle of an activity or opportunity because you learn best by doing. Perhaps you learn best by first observing others and then later trying your hand at the activity. Maybe you need to first understand the theory or rationale behind an activity before you are ready to take action. No one learning style is best or most effective in all situations. You may want to use a learning styles inventory or assessment instrument to better understand your preferred method of learning. (See, for example, Kolb, 1981.) Give your field instructor as much information as possible about how you learn. That information will help him or her select assignments and responsibilities as well as determine your readiness for certain experiences.

If you have a learning disability or a condition that, without accommodation, may in some way limit your learning or performance, be sure to share this information with your field instructor and faculty supervisor. Such conditions need to be considered in developing a plan for practicum learning. If you suspect that you have a learning disability, consult with a learning specialist who can assess the nature of the disability, recommend ways of compensating for the limitation, and guide you toward a program of remediation and accommodation. Your university may also have services available to students with disabilities, and may have professionals skilled in adapting practicum experiences to meet individual needs as well as those who would advocate for reasonable accommodations in practicum settings.

Include in your plan the experiences and activities that will help you to integrate theory with practice. Classroom concepts and ideas should come alive during the practicum. You will be expected to integrate what you learned in the classroom with the real-life experiences in your practicum. Strive to identify the beliefs, values, and theories behind your decisions and your selection of an intervention. Seek exposure to social work practice and programs based on various beliefs about how, when, and why people and social systems are able to change.

Ethical Practice

Practice Behavior Example: Social workers recognize and manage personal values in a way that allows professional values to guide practice.

Critical Thinking Question: What personal and professional values do you bring to the practicum?

Even though your practicum learning experience will be specific to your practicum agency, remember that you are developing knowledge and skills that can be generalized to other social work settings. Secure a breadth of experience while also finding ways to go into depth in your particular area of interest. By doing so, you will prepare yourself for work in another setting while immersing yourself in practice issues about which you care deeply.

Describe your desired outcomes for learning in ways that permit the monitoring and measurement of progress. However, also recognize that many important outcomes such as developing a commitment to social work values, growing in self-awareness, acquiring self-confidence, and using a variety of perspectives and theories are inherently difficult to quantify and measure. Describe your desired outcomes as precisely as possible, but remember that not everything will be measurable. It is better to describe outcomes in general and imperfect ways than to not mention them at all, even if you have a hard time showing how you will measure them. Consider how your attempts to measure your learning parallel your clients' attempts to demonstrate their growth. Your struggle to grow and to measure that growth will hopefully increase your sensitivity to your clients' hard work.

If your school requires you to complete a professional portfolio or final professional paper as part of the practicum experience, build into your learning plan as many of the elements of the portfolio or paper as possible and appropriate. Because a portfolio is usually focused on the demonstration of your knowledge and skills in a variety of areas, the practicum is an ideal opportunity to structure your learning and then to showcase the ways in which you integrated academic classroom learning with practicum activities. If your school requires a summative capstone paper, project, or presentation based on your practicum experiences, plan now to acquire the learning experiences that will help you successfully complete that assignment and demonstrate your competence.

Once you have completed your plan and it has been approved by your field instructor and faculty supervisor, follow it. Review it often and modify it as needed, but resist the temptation to abandon a part of the plan simply because it calls for a learning opportunity that is difficult to arrange. Do everything possible to obtain the experiences you need to advance your learning. Become assertive in asking for meaningful learning experiences. If you need help to arrange these because of agency reluctance to offer them to you, ask your faculty supervisor to advocate on your behalf. In addition, be alert to learning experiences that become available to you unexpectedly during your practicum, and find ways to integrate these experiences into your learning plan. You will be asked to perform tasks and take on responsibilities for which you feel unprepared. That may cause anxiety, fear, and embarrassment, which is understandable and normal. You must be willing to take on tasks and responsibilities even when you do not feel ready. If you wait until you feel confident and certain that you would not make mistakes, you might miss opportunities to learn something new.

As you formulate your learning plan, give careful thought to your personal plans for the next five years. For example, if you are a BSW student hoping to go on to graduate school, what can you do during the practicum to prepare yourself for graduate study or to increase your chances of being accepted into graduate school? If you expect to enter the job market immediately after graduation, what can you build into your plan that will prepare you for the job you seek? What specific licensing or certification

Diversity in Practice

Practice Behavior Example: Social workers view themselves as learners and engage those with whom they work as informants.

Critical Thinking Question: Because it is important to learn how to work with diverse clients and coworkers, how can you acquire experience in learning from both?

may be required for you to practice social work in your state or to become certified in a specialty area? If you are an MSW student, what learning goals can you set for yourself that will adequately prepare you for advanced practice?

During your practicum, you may learn some things that are surprising or even discouraging. For example, you will probably discover that not all clients are motivated, that some are difficult to like and respect, and that some will not make use of needed and available services. You will probably learn that client, agency, or social changes can be slow, that social problems are more complex than you realized, that you must be skillful in the art of politics, and that not all professionals are competent and ethical. Your faculty supervisor can help you gain perspective on such matters, so be sure to share these experiences and observations with him or her.

In addition to the formal learning plans you develop, consider using a professional journal. This exercise can help you in many ways. A journal can document your progress in learning, show your professional growth over time, allow you to express your doubts and questions without sharing them with your supervisors, and offer you the chance to reflect on the very personal nature of your work. Many students report that journal keeping is very useful because it serves as a written record of growth that is encouraging and reinforcing.

Do not be surprised if much of what you actually learn during your practicum was not anticipated and could not have been written into your plan. Expect some surprises. Perhaps your agency's funding will be drastically cut, and you may end up working in a different unit or service area. Your field instructor may take another job and you will have to adjust to a successor with a different supervisory style. Although such experiences can be stressful, they can also be valuable learning opportunities. They will certainly teach you to be flexible and open to new experiences. You can also gain invaluable perspective on how agencies and the social workers in them cope with change and stress, capitalize on funding or policy shifts, and turn problems into opportunities.

Planning to Learn: A Workbook Activity

Your responses below will help you identify desired outcomes and prepare a plan that can guide and enhance your practicum. Respond honestly and with as much precision as possible.

1. Ask your field instructor what skills and knowledge are most needed by social work students in the agency and record them here.

_____

_____

2. Review the program objectives of your school's social work program, and record them here. They will be included in various ways in the practicum activities in which you engage.

_____

_____

3. Look at your school's practicum evaluation form to see how your learning agreement relates to the evaluation. Make a note of any questions you have.

_____

_____

4. What orienting/explanatory theories (e.g., those that explain human development and behavior, family systems, group dynamics, organizational development, community development, and social development) will you try to apply in your practicum? See Chapter 16 (Planned Change Process), for a definition of orienting theories.

_____

_____

_____

5. What practice theories and models (e.g., those that provide guidance in developing interventions) will you try to apply in your practicum that address client and client systems needs? See Chapter 16 (Planned Change Process), for a discussion of practice theories and models.

_____

_____

_____

6. As you think about your learning agreement, what parallels do you see between your learning needs and the experiences of clients when they identify their needs for social work intervention?

_____

_____

_____

7. Reflect on the differences between these terms which describe the levels of learning and performing on the basis of this learning.

Understand _____   Compare _____

Utilize _____   Integrate _____

Synthesize _____   Critique _____

Suggested Learning Activities

- Consult your school practicum manual and various descriptions of the curriculum in search of specific learning goals and objectives for the practicum.
- Work with a group of other students to brainstorm possible tasks, activities, and projects that might be pursued in your practicum agency as a way of expanding learning opportunities.

- If your practicum agency cannot provide the learning experience that you need, ask your field instructor to help you gain that experience by working several hours each week in another agency.
- Read your school practicum evaluation form or rating instrument to better understand what you are expected to learn during the practicum and how you are expected to demonstrate that you have acquired specific knowledge and skills.
- If you have a specific career goal such as chemical dependency certification, school social work certification, social work licensing, or graduate school, identify the requirements for this goal and seek practicum experiences related to that goal.
- Ask social workers in your agency what they wish they had known or were able to do when they started their social work position. Find ways to learn this for yourself while in practicum.
- If at any time you feel disappointed with your field experience, discuss this concern with your field instructor. Do not delay or avoid this discussion and let your negative feelings build up inside.

References

Baird, Brian. *The Internship, Practicum, and Field Placement Handbook: A Guide for the Helping Professions*. 5th ed. Upper Saddle River, NJ: Prentice Hall, 2011.

Commission on Accreditation. *Educational Policy and Accreditation Standards*. Alexandria, VA: Council on Social Work Education, 2008.

Kolb, David. *Learning-Style Inventory*. Boston: McBer and Company Training Resources Group, 1981.

Kolb, David. *Experiential Learning: Experience as the Source of Learning and Development*. Upper Saddle River, NJ: Prentice Hall, 1984.

Sheafor, Bradford, and Charles Horejsi. *Techniques and Guidelines for Social Work Practice*. 9th ed. Boston: Allyn and Bacon, 2012.

University of Montana School of Social Work. *BSW Competency Catalogue*, 2008.

CHAPTER 3 REVIEW

1. You will need to prepare yourself for generalist practice even if at some point in your career you specialize in one area. Refer ahead to Chapter 13 (Professional Social Work) where generalist competencies are listed. How can you make sure you have the learning experiences you will need to function as a generalist?

4

Getting Started

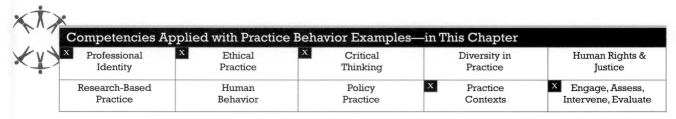

Competencies Applied with Practice Behavior Examples—in This Chapter				
x Professional Identity	x Ethical Practice	x Critical Thinking	Diversity in Practice	Human Rights & Justice
Research-Based Practice	Human Behavior	Policy Practice	x Practice Contexts	x Engage, Assess, Intervene, Evaluate

CHAPTER PREVIEW

This chapter focuses on the importance of getting your practicum off to a good start, providing suggestions and guidance for ensuring that this will happen. Included is information designed to help you understand the ways in which your reactions to being supervised, both positive and negative, parallel the reactions of clients to being observed and evaluated. In addition, a tool is provided to help you identify the factors which influence the successful application and integration of theory to real-life situations. Additional guidance is given on how to monitor the development of professional skills and practice behaviors.

Previous chapters have helped you to learn about what will be expected of you in the practicum and what you can expect of the practicum. They have underscored the importance of formulating learning goals and identifying activities that can facilitate your learning and help you reach those desired outcomes. This chapter focuses on questions and concerns that are common during the first weeks and months of the practicum.

Beginning a practicum is similar to starting a new job because it is a time of excitement and confusion. There are many new people to meet and much to learn, so the first few weeks can feel overwhelming. Entering an unfamiliar organization is something like entering an unfamiliar culture where you encounter a new set of norms, rules, and customs. You will probably feel some anxiety about your knowledge and skills, and you will wonder if you will be able to perform competently. However, within a matter of weeks you will be familiar with the setting and will be much more comfortable. There are a number of concrete steps you can take now to make certain that your practicum gets off to a good start.

BACKGROUND AND CONTEXT

Initial experiences are pattern setting. If the first days and weeks of contact with a new student are positive for the field instructor and other agency staff, the field instructor will likely conclude that the student can be trusted and given responsibilities. If, on the other hand, these first contacts give the field instructor cause to doubt whether the student is capable and responsible, he or she may hesitate to assign meaningful work to the student. In order to get the practicum off to a good start, you must anticipate how you might be perceived by the field instructor and what he or she might be thinking and feeling about your presence in the agency. Among the field instructor's thoughts about supervising students might be the following:

- I am glad that we have a practicum student because we're understaffed and have too much work to do. The student can do some of our work.
- I look forward to having a student. Practicum students usually have a lot of enthusiasm, and they tend to look at the work of this agency from a fresh perspective.
- I hope this student works out. I remember one student who did not do well in this agency because she was too insecure and immature.
- I wonder if I can find the time necessary to properly supervise this student. I hope he or she catches on quickly, because I am too busy to provide a lot of supervision.

- I worry about students overstepping the bounds of their assignments and responsibilities and dislike having to clean up messes made by others.
- I hope this student is ready for a taste of reality.
- I like having students here because their questions encourage me to think critically about what I do and why.

Practicum students universally have ambivalent reactions and emotions to the challenges of the practicum, such as excitement about learning from a mentor versus anxiety about being observed and evaluated. This is normal, and very similar to the experiences of the client when entering a professional relationship with a social worker. Monitoring your own reactions to supervision, both positive and negative, will help you become more empathetic to your clients. The workbook section of this chapter contains a tool designed to help you identify those ambivalent reactions, and compare them to client reactions.

Practicum students need to shift from their university's focus on education to the agency's focus on training. The faculty members of a social work program emphasize the learning of general knowledge, theory, and broad principles that can be applied in many practice settings. By contrast, agency administrators and supervisors are concerned mostly with training that emphasizes the learning of policies, procedures, and skills specific to their agency. ***Professional education*** encourages discussion, debate, and the consideration of alternative ways of assessing and responding to a problem or situation. It is related to the mission and purpose of the social work profession, and focuses on learning outcomes. By contrast, ***professional training*** is designed to teach what the agency has established as the standard or typical responses to given situations. This training is agency-specific and related to the mission of the agency. It is measured through work outcomes rather than learning only. Because these responses reflect the agency's purpose, policy, and procedures, they are generally to be followed rather than challenged and debated. Hopefully you will integrate the broad knowledge obtained from the academic world with the specific training provided within the agency.

Professional Identity

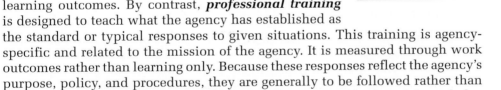

Practice Behavior Example: Social workers engage in career-long learning.

Critical Thinking Question: A professional social worker possesses knowledge, skills, and values. What do you see as the relationship between them?

All social agencies have what is often called an ***office culture***. This term refers to the general ways of operating that are based on history, agency values, theoretical underpinnings of services provided, morale, policies and procedures, and staff interaction. Hopefully the office culture is positive and optimistic, as this will allow you to see an organization at its best and learn how a healthy, learning, and functional organization operates.

All organizations, including human services agencies, have a political dimension. For example, an agency's managers must make difficult and unpopular decisions, and thus must use their power and authority to accomplish the agency's goals. Some conflict and power struggles are inevitable in organizational life, and these will soon become apparent to you. You need to be aware that aligning yourself with one side or another in these conflicts can undermine the success of your practicum.

The term ***office politics*** refers to the undercurrent of power struggles created by factors such as conflict between various factions within an organization, personal ambition, jockeying for greater power, and efforts to lobby on behalf of a certain opinion. Larger organizations have more complex internal politics. Even though office politics are normal and difficult to avoid, if you become caught up in these power struggles and conflicts, learning opportunities may be closed and some agency staff may withdraw their support. As a general rule, the larger and more political an organization, the more active the office grapevine is. Rumors, gossip, and speculations are common within organizations having many bureaucratic layers, and are especially frequent during times of uncertainty, conflict, and rapid change. Participating in agency gossip can be another major pitfall for you.

GUIDANCE AND DIRECTION

First impressions have a powerful impact on personal and professional relationships. Because of that, it is vital that you make a favorable first impression on your field instructor and the other staff members in your practicum agency. Make a deliberate effort to get the practicum off to a good start.

As suggested previously, there are a number of reasons why a field instructor will feel confident about assigning challenging responsibilities to a student. To make these assignments, the field instructor must trust the student and believe that he or she is capable of doing the work and not likely to make significant mistakes. Very often, the field instructor makes this decision on the basis of patterns he or she sees in the student's ordinary behavior (i.e., on the basis of the little things he or she notices about the student). Thus, you should strive to display behaviors that can assure your field instructor that you can and will perform in a responsible manner. For example, do your best to develop the following learning behaviors and work behaviors.

Learning Behaviors

- Demonstrate your enthusiasm for learning and applying your knowledge in the agency.
- Inform your field instructor of your prior work and volunteer experiences to help him or her better understand your abilities.
- Demonstrate initiative and a willingness to take on responsibilities and assignments.
- Take all assignments seriously, no matter how trivial and unimportant they may seem.
- Keep your field instructor informed about what you are doing, why you are doing it, and what you plan to do next.
- Consult with your field instructor immediately if you encounter an unusual or unanticipated problem or difficulty, especially one that has legal ramifications or one that might create a public relations problem for the agency.
- Be a good listener and be attentive to your field instructor and to other staff members during supervisory conferences and staff meetings.
- Demonstrate the ability to accept and use constructive criticism of your work, skills, and attitudes.
- Ask questions that reveal a desire to learn and to understand the work of the agency and its policies and procedures, but avoid asking in a manner that appears to challenge or criticize the agency.

Practice Contexts

Practice Behavior Example: Social workers provide leadership in promoting sustainable changes in service delivery and practice to improve the quality of social services.

Critical Thinking Question: Which of the practice theories that you learned in class are used in your agency?

- Volunteer to take on tasks that are not attractive to regular agency staff.
- Make friendly overtures to others in the agency.
- Demonstrate a capacity to build relationships and get along with a variety of different people.

Work Behaviors

- Prepare all letters, reports, and client records with great care, according to the agency's prescribed format, and in a timely manner.
- Meet all deadlines. Be on time for all scheduled appointments and meetings. Remain on the job for all the hours you are expected to be in the practicum agency.
- If you must make a change in your work schedule, or if you discover that you will not be able to keep an appointment, contact your field instructor immediately and work out an alternative plan.
- Be well prepared for all meetings with your field instructor and for agency staff meetings.
- Demonstrate that you have read agency manuals and other materials and are therefore familiar with your agency's mission, programs, policies, and procedures.
- Do your best to understand a new assignment or responsibility the first time it is explained to you. If you are unclear about something, ask for clarification rather than pretending you understand.
- Keep your desk and work space neat and organized.
- Pay attention to your personal grooming, and dress appropriately for the practicum.
- Do not engage in gossip, spread rumors concerning other agencies or professionals, or criticize other students, agency staff, clients, or other agencies in the community.
- Be extremely careful to protect your clients' rights to privacy and the confidentiality of agency records.

Engage, Assess, Intervene, Evaluate

Practice Behavior Example: Social workers select appropriate intervention strategies.

Critical Thinking Question: Although generalist social workers practice at various levels, they understand the connections between these levels of practice. How do you see them as connected?

As you enter your agency, recognize that there are both formal and informal aspects to the structure and function of your setting. There are the official policies and procedures, the formal organizational chart, and the chain of command, all of which serve to describe the work of your agency, show who is responsible for what, and provide written guidelines for employees. There are also the informal workings of the agency, and they may differ greatly from what is shown in organizational charts or policy manuals. You may discover that official titles and actual job descriptions do not match, that those with official power may not be the ones to whom others look for guidance, and that exceptions may be made to official policies under certain circumstances.

As you encounter office politics, make very thoughtful decisions about how you can respond in ways that will protect your practicum experience and avoid offending others. Although it is difficult to offer guidance on how to handle office politics because every situation is different, here are some general guidelines for you to consider:

- Use the first several weeks and months in the practicum to carefully observe how staff members interact, maneuver, and use their power and influence.

- Be cognizant of and sensitive to the official lines of authority and to the power relationships inherent in the chain of command as described by the agency's organizational chart. Follow the chain of command. To disregard those established power relationships will cause confusion and may put your practicum in jeopardy.
- Do not jump to conclusions concerning who is most valued and respected within the agency and who has the most power and influence. Power relationships are often more subtle and complex than they appear at first. Consequently, your first impressions may be erroneous.
- Cultivate relationships with those in the agency who command the respect of most fellow professionals and the support staff and who are respected and valued by their administrative superiors. Longtime office staff members are often very powerful in an organization.
- Do not align yourself with someone in the agency who has a reputation for being a complainer, a loose cannon, a troublemaker, a back stabber, or who has little loyalty to the agency.

Every organization has many unwritten rules. It is likely that no one will think to tell you about them until after you ask about or have broken one. For example, you might be breaking a rule if you bring food or drink to a staff meeting, or if a certain report is submitted late even though it is permissible to be a little late on other types of reports. The best way to learn about these informal rules and procedures is to observe the work of others in the agency and ask why things are done a certain way.

Remember that there is no such thing as a stupid question. Your field instructor expects you to ask many questions, especially in the beginning, but he or she also expects you to remember the answers that you are given. Thus, record the answers so you do not ask the same questions over and over. Your field instructor expects that you will make some mistakes, but he or she expects you to learn from each mistake and not make it a second time.

Finally, it is important to learn how the process of **integrating academic content and actual practicum experiences** works and sometimes does not work. Practicum students who are excited to apply what they have learned in the classroom may find that what works in theory and in rehearsal may not work as easily or effectively in real-life situations. Instead of concluding that theory is not useful, consider the numerous factors which impact the way in which the application of theory is influenced in real people's lives. Real practice is more complicated than classroom examples, and it is important to learn how to anticipate what will influence outcomes and interventions. Real life is messy, people don't change in a linear fashion, there are many unknowns at the outset of an intervention, and each client or client system is unique. Table 4.1 demonstrates some of the most important factors which may account for the application and integration of theory to real practice.

Ethical Practice

Practice Behavior Example: Social workers make ethical decisions by applying standards of the National Association of Social Workers Code of Ethics.

Critical Thinking Question: Although you are a student and not a social worker, what is your ethical obligation to provide effective services to clients?

Table 4.1   Factors Which Influence Application and Integration of Theory and Practice

Client Characteristics	Social Worker Characteristics	Contextual Characteristics
Motivation of Client • Enthusiasm level • Voluntary/involuntary • Willingness to engage in intervention • Level of hope	**Knowledge of Social Worker** • Understanding of client situation • Awareness of resources • Understanding of explanatory theories • Understanding of practice theories and models	**Timing** • Too soon • Too late • Interference of life circumstances • Waiting lists
Ability of Client • Cognitive understanding • Coping skills • Confidence level • Self-efficacy	**Skill of Social Worker** • Skill in planned change • Practice skills at all levels • Use of evidence-based practice • Broad repertoire of techniques	**Social Support** • Family support • Friend support • Informal resources • Formal resources
Client Diversity • Attitude toward seeking and receiving help • Client values and beliefs • Cultural differences • Varied life experience	**Values of Social Worker** • Client-centered focus • Empowerment and strengths approach • Compatible personal and agency values • Compatible personal and professional values	**Social Policies and Programs** • Accessibility • Eligibility criteria • Effectiveness level • Cultural competence
Experience with Social Workers • Positive or negative • Voluntary or involuntary • Effectiveness • Partnership-focus	**Practice Experience** • Entry or advanced level • Practice wisdom • Depth and breadth of experience • Professional growth	**Social Environment** • Community resources • Institutional support • Economic environment • Political environment

---

Student Self-Monitoring of Practice Behaviors: A Workbook Activity

Student Self-Monitoring of Skill Development

Instructions: This tool is to be used by practicum students as well as supervisors as a way of critically analyzing the ongoing process of skill development from the student's perspective. Micro, mezzo, and macro skills can all be self-monitored using this tool.

This tool shows the stages through which students proceed as they attempt to perform a skill for the first time until they develop competence in the skill. These stages are:

Preparation → Attempt → Reflection/Adaptation → Refinement.

(*continued*)

The tool also shows the professional areas in which students can monitor themselves, including

- Knowledge Necessary for Skill Development
- Relationship of Skill to Intervention Plan
- Professional Use of Self
- Self-Evaluation of Effectiveness and Professional Growth.

Student _____

Supervisor _____

Micro Skill Being Monitored _____

Mezzo Skill Being Monitored _____

Macro Skill Being Monitored _____

	Professional Areas to be Monitored			
Stage of Skill Development	**Knowledge Necessary for Skill Development**	**Relationship of Skill to Intervention Plan**	**Professional Use of Self**	**Self-Evaluation of Effectiveness and Professional Growth**
Preparation for Initial Attempt at Performing Skill	What academic learning will help me develop this skill? What social work role applies to this skill? What agency policies and procedures guide the use of this skill? What if I don't know what to do?	What orienting or explanatory theories apply? What practice theories or models apply? What ethical issues are involved? How does this skill relate to the goals of the intervention plan?	Am I ready? What professional gifts can I bring to the development of this skill? Do I have any biases or preconceived notions? Will my inexperience influence the outcome?	How will I know how I am doing? Will my client let me know if I am making a mistake? How does my agency evaluate the effectiveness of its social workers? Is there evidence that this skill works for clients like mine?
Initial Attempt at Performing Skill	Am I abiding by agency policies and procedures? Does my client expect the same ability from me as from a social worker? What classroom knowledge can I remember and use? What knowledge does my client have about this?	What is my client's behavior telling me? What might my client not be saying that is important? Am I connecting with my client? Is this intervention plan suited to my client?	Can my client tell I am inexperienced? Can I adjust my approach during a session? Can I trust my judgment? What part does the client play in the selection of the intervention plan?	Is it fair to "practice" on clients? What is my client's reaction telling me? Did my preparation help? What is my intuition telling me?

(continued)

Reflection and Adaptation of Skill	How can I answer questions better? Did I know enough? How can I learn more to do this better? Who can help me prepare for the next time?	What should I do differently? Did my client seem motivated? Did my performance fit with the plan? Does the intervention plan or goals need to change?	How can I better use my skills next time? Will my increased confidence help my client? How can I perform less mechanically? Am I able to focus on my client's issues rather than my own?	How can I help my client succeed? How can I evaluate my professional growth? How would my client define success? How can I adapt techniques and practice models to meet my client's needs?
Refinement of Skill	What will I need to know to work with more challenging situations? What can my colleagues and supervisors teach me? What is the best way to get feedback? How does continuing education work?	Will this skill work with diverse clients? How can I individualize intervention plans? What is the client's responsibility to use my skills? How do I use my skills with involuntary or unmotivated clients?	What biases or stereotypes have I become aware of? How can I adapt my interactions with clients during a session rather than after a session? What are my professional gifts? How can I become more open to learning and evaluation?	What have I learned from self-evaluation? What have I learned from my client? What level of competence is required at different levels of practice? How can I teach this skill to others?

Parallel Processes of Supervision: A Workbook Activity

Parallel Processes of Ambivalence: Client Interventions and Student Supervision

The term **parallel process** has been used to describe the similarities between a social work student who is being supervised in a learning environment and a client who is engaged in an intervention.

Using the matrix below, identify the responses and emotions (columns 2–5) you have about the domains of supervision (column 1). Compare them with the similar reactions that a client might have to social work intervention in what is called a parallel process or reaction. Use this throughout your practicum to remind yourself of the similarities between you as a student being supervised and them as a client working with a social worker.

(*continued*)

Domains of Intervention and Supervision	Responses to Intervention and Supervision			
	Positive Client Responses to Intervention	*Positive Student Responses to Supervision*	*Negative Client Responses to Intervention*	*Negative Student Responses to Supervision*
Matching	Hoping for a good match	Hoping for a good match	Worrying about a poor match	Worrying about a poor match
Building Working Relationship	Willing to engage in professional relationship	Excited to engage in professional relationship	Reluctance to share personal information	Reluctance to show inexperience or gaps in knowledge
Assessing Needs	Relieved to have needs validated	Glad to have learning needs validated	Worrying about being judged	Worrying about being judged
Identifying Strengths	Glad to have strengths recognized	Glad to have strengths recognized	Worried that too much will be expected	Worried that too much will be expected
Setting goals and Objectives	Wanting to set own goals	Wanting to set own goals	Not wanting to have goals set without input	Not wanting to have goals set without input
Implementing Plan	Relieved to be starting on a plan	Relieved to be starting on a plan	Nervous about ability to complete plan satisfactorily	Nervous about ability to complete plan satisfactorily
Monitoring Performance	Glad to have short-term, reasonable goals	Glad to have short-term, reasonable goals	Self-conscious about being observed	Self-conscious about being observed
Dealing with Barriers	Glad to have social worker to help with problems implementing intervention plan	Glad to have supervisor to help with problems implementing learning plan	Discouraged about barriers and unexpected events	Discouraged about barriers and unexpected events
Supporting Efforts and Work	Appreciative of support and encouragement	Appreciative of support and encouragement	Wishing progress could be made quicker	Wishing that progress could be made quicker
Dealing with Mistakes	Learning from mistakes	Learning from mistakes	Embarrassed and worried about impact of mistakes	Embarrassed and worried about impact of mistakes
Addressing Power	Respectful of position of social worker	Respectful of position of supervisor	Worried about power of social worker to impact personal life	Worried about power of supervisor to impact professional life

(*continued*)

Evaluating Performance	Understanding the value of constructive evaluation	Understanding the value of constructive evaluation	Worried or resentful about possible negative evaluation	Worried or resentful about possible negative evaluation
Making Recommendations	Hopeful for positive recommendation of social worker	Hopeful for positive recommendation of supervisor	Worried about negative recommendation of social worker	Worried about negative recommendation of supervisor
Terminating Relationship	Ready to move out of professional relationship	Ready to move out of supervisory relationship	Mixed feelings about ending relationship	Mixed feelings about ending relationship

Suggested Learning Activities

- Read agency manuals and visit websites that describe agency policy and procedures.
- Request opportunities to be introduced to a variety of staff members so you can learn from a number of people and observe their professional approaches and skills.
- Attend any staff or committee meetings open to you to observe employee interaction.
- Establish a mechanism for maintaining an up-to-date calendar that includes appointments, staff meetings, and other obligations.
- Walk around the office and agency building. Locate potentially critical features such as emergency exits, fire alarms, and fire extinguishers.

References

Baird, Brian. *The Internship, Practicum, and Field Placement Handbook: A Guide for the Helping Professions.* 6th ed. Upper Saddle River, NJ: Prentice Hall, 2011.

Dolgoff, Ralph. *An Introduction to Supervisory Practice in Human Services.* Boston: Allyn and Bacon, 2005.

Healy, Karen. *Social Work Theories in Context: Creating Frameworks for Practice.* New York: Palgrave Macmillan, 2005.

Royse, David, Surjit Singh Dhooper, and Elizabeth Lewis Rompf. *Field Instruction: A Guide for Social Work Students.* 6th ed. Boston: Allyn and Bacon, 2012.

Sweitzer, Frederic H., and Mary A. King. *The Successful Internship: Transformation and Empowerment in Experiential Learning.* 3rd ed. Pacific Grove, CA: Brooks Cole, 2009.

CHAPTER 4 REVIEW

1. How might the characteristics of clients, social workers, and the context of practice interact to influence whether or not theory and practice are combined in a way that will result in successful interventions?

©Ginasanders/Dreamstime

5

Learning from Supervision

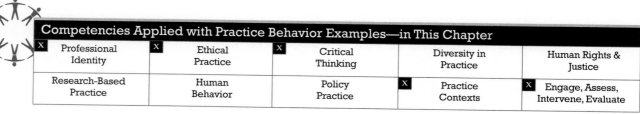

Competencies Applied with Practice Behavior Examples—in This Chapter				
X Professional Identity	X Ethical Practice	X Critical Thinking	Diversity in Practice	Human Rights & Justice
Research-Based Practice	Human Behavior	Policy Practice	X Practice Contexts	X Engage, Assess, Intervene, Evaluate

Diversity in Client Behavior: A Workbook Activity
From Cynthia Garthwaite, <u>The Social Work Practicum</u>

1. **A low-income couple with six children lives in a small and crowded house and has great difficulty financially. They choose to have additional children, which will strain the family even more financially.**

   A. What diverse beliefs, values, minority status, or customs may be operating in this situation?

   B. How might this situation be misunderstood if you are not familiar with the clients' beliefs and customs?

   C. What else would you need to know in order to be competent in this situation?

   D. What individual, family, or cultural strengths might be identified in this situation?

CHAPTER PREVIEW

This chapter provides information on the nature, functions, and context of professional supervision, including a variety of styles, perspectives, and approaches to supervisory activities. It shows how students can use supervision when integrating theory and practice as well as in as how to use supervision to ensure ongoing professional growth. The stages of practicum from both a student and supervisory point of view are presented, accompanied by recommendations for supervision. Additionally, the forms and types of supervision commonly used by field instructors are described.

The quality of your practicum is closely tied to the nature and quality of the teacher–student relationship you develop with your field instructor. Learning from a skilled and caring supervisor can enrich a practicum experience and provide a positive model of staff interaction. Every supervisor or field instructor, like every student or every client, has both strengths and limitations. You will need to identify your field instructor's strengths and plan your practicum to take advantage of them.

BACKGROUND AND CONTEXT

In order to understand practicum supervision and how to make good use of it, it is necessary to examine the purpose and functions of supervision within an organization. Although the word **supervision** has its roots in a Latin word that means "to look over" or "to watch over," modern supervisory practice places less emphasis on the supervisor being an overseer of work and more emphasis on the supervisor being a skilled master of the work to be done, a leader, a mentor, and a teacher.

There are few jobs more challenging than that of a supervisor in a social service agency. It is a job that requires sensitivity, skill, common sense, commitment, good humor, and intelligence. Supervisors are mediators and conduits between line-level social workers and higher-level agency administrators. They frequently represent the agency in its interactions with other agencies and the community. In addition, they are often faced with the challenging tasks of responding to the concerns and complaints of clients who are dissatisfied with the agency's programs or with the performance of a social worker or other staff member. The responsibility of supervisors to clients, staff, funding sources, and administration is a broad and demanding expectation, and supervising students is only one aspect of their job description.

Although being a supervisor can be demanding, it can also be a satisfying job, especially for those who understand and appreciate the teaching aspect of supervision. Watching a new social worker or social work student learn and develop on the job can be a satisfying and inspiring experience. That is one reason why many busy agency supervisors choose to serve as field instructors to social work students. Hopefully your field instructor is highly motivated to teach you about social work practice because he or she wants to give back to the profession.

Practice Contexts

Practice Behavior Example: Social workers continuously discover, appraise, and attend to changing locales, populations, scientific and technological developments, and emerging societal trends to provide relevant services.

Critical Thinking Question: How will the issues facing your practicum agency influence your supervisor?

Kadushin and Harkness (2002) identify three functions of agency-based supervisory practice: the administrative function, the supportive function, and the educational function. The ***administrative function*** of supervision includes such responsibilities as recruiting, selecting, and orienting new staff; assigning and coordinating work; monitoring and evaluating staff performance; facilitating communication up and down within the organization; advocating for staff; serving as a buffer between staff and administration; representing the agency to the public; and encouraging needed agency change.

The ***educational function*** of supervision focuses on providing informal training and orientation and arranging for formal in-service staff training. Basically, the supervisor is responsible for ensuring that staff members receive all of the initial training needed to perform well in their positions. In addition, the supervisor is responsible for recognizing training needs and providing ongoing in-service training.

The ***supportive function*** of supervision has to do with sustaining staff morale, cultivating a sense of teamwork, building commitment to agency goals and mission, encouraging workers by providing support, and dealing with work-related problems of conflict and frustration. This aspect of supervision is extremely important in human services agencies in which stress and burnout can be common risks. The supervisor must strive to create a work environment that is conducive to the provision of quality services to clients, while also supporting staff who may at times feel stressed and unappreciated.

Professional Identity

Practice Behavior Example: Social workers use supervision and consultation

Critical Thinking Question: As you consider what your field instructor will expect of you, how does each expectation contribute to the delivery of effective and ethical social work services?

Your field instructor will be concerned with these three functions as they relate to practicum students. He or she will pay attention to whether you are performing the work of the agency in an appropriate manner and in keeping with agency policy and procedure. He or she will be sensitive to your fears and insecurities, and to the fact that you have personal responsibilities in addition to those related to the practicum. Your field instructor will want to do everything possible to facilitate your learning but, in the final analysis, his or her primary obligation must be to the agency's clients or consumers and to the agency that serves those clients.

There are many types of supervision, all of which serve an important purpose, and all of which are valuable in specific ways. Each type of supervision addresses a certain need or situation, and it is recommended that you expose yourself whenever possible to as many forms of supervision as you can, as each one teaches different things and uses different approaches. You may receive the following types of supervision and teaching.

- ***Individual supervision*** (regular meetings between field instructor and student)
- ***Group supervision*** (meetings between field instructor and a group of students)
- ***Peer supervision*** (meetings attended by a small group of social workers who assume responsibility for providing guidance and suggestions to each other and to students)
- ***Formal case presentations*** (meetings at which one or more social workers describe their work on a specific case and invite advice and guidance on how it should be handled)

- **Ad-hoc supervision** (brief, need-based, unscheduled meetings to discuss a specific question or issue)
- **Virtual supervision** (computer, e-mail, or Web-based supervision)
- **Role playing** (rehearsal of skills in which student takes on client or social work role)
- **Modeling** (demonstration of a technique during supervision or actual intervention)

A social worker who assumes the role of field instructor has special **ethical obligations**. Supervisors assume responsibility for the quality of work done by those they supervise. Ethically, they must have knowledge and skill in the areas in which they provide supervision. They are expected to evaluate the performance of those they supervise, use helpful and fair methods, and help supervisees gain knowledge and skills. They must also take care to manage the supervisory relationship, maintaining professional boundaries and avoiding dual relationships, both of which can complicate and undermine the supervisory relationship.

Your field instructor will no doubt take these obligations seriously; thus you can expect that he or she will treat the supervisory relationship in an ethical and professional manner. Occasionally certain behaviors by a field instructor may prompt your school's faculty supervisor or practicum coordinator to reevaluate the suitability and appropriateness of using a particular field instructor as a supervisor for students. This may include lack of time to supervise, and not being available to students. Supervisors may lack genuine interest in supervising students, resulting in minimal commitment to teaching and mentoring. Hopefully you will not encounter a supervisor who is incompetent or unethical, but it is possible. If your field instructor exhibits any of these behaviors or attitudes, consult with your faculty supervisor or practicum coordinator to determine a course of action in order to ensure the quality of supervision available to you.

Social workers have a number of **legal obligations** when taking on the responsibility of field instructor. Those obligations are based on the principle of **vicarious liability,** which essentially means that a supervisor may be held liable for the actions, good or bad, of those he or she supervises. Field instructors, in their role as trainers, mentors, and supervisors, must in the end do whatever they can to make sure that students avoid making decisions that could be considered **malfeasance** (commission of an unlawful or wrongful act), **misfeasance** (commission of a proper act in a way that is injurious or wrongful), or **nonfeasance** (failure to act in accordance with one's responsibility). Further, field instructors and students are also held to the concepts of **standards of care** (the type, level, and specific type of treatment or intervention that is indicated and appropriate for a specific client with a particular condition) and **standards of practice** (professional expectations that are based on what has been termed a reasonableness standard, which is the manner in which an ordinary person who is reasonable and prudent would have acted under similar circumstances).

Supervisors have a variety of styles or preferred ways of doing their jobs, all of which will affect the student's experiences in the agency. No one style or approach is necessarily better or more right than others. Varying supervisory styles are more or less effective depending on the nature of the work to be done and the level of training and experience of those being supervised. Table 5.1 illustrates the various approaches to supervision to which the student will generally need to adapt.

Table 5.1	**Supervision Dimensions and Approaches**	
Process orientation	**Orientation**	Task/Outcome orientation
Rapid completion of tasks	**Pace of Work**	Methodical pace to complete tasks
Retention of power and authority	**Authority and Power**	Sharing of power and empowering of others
Independent decision making	**Decision making**	Collaborative decision making
Written agreements	**Format of Agreements**	Verbal and written agreements
Focuses on details to achieve goals	**Attention to Detail**	Leaves details to others and focuses on overall mission
Close monitoring of work to avoid mistakes	**Overseeing and Directing of Work**	Allows autonomy and assumes success
Separation of professional and personal lives	**Worker Relations**	Views personal lives as impacting professional lives
Delegates tasks when needed	**Work Assignments**	Delegates tasks readily
Views professional growth as worker responsibility	**Professional Development**	Secures, encourages, and arranges professional growth opportunities

GUIDANCE AND DIRECTION

Learning to use supervision is of central importance to the success of a practicum. Because social work is challenging and sometimes stressful, and also because your work directly affects clients' lives, you will need guidance, direction, support, and feedback from your field instructor. Social workers use supervision to help them deal with challenging situations, to provide performance feedback, and to give support. Learning to use supervision for professional development is an important part of your practicum.

Engage, Assess, Intervene, Evaluate

Practice Behavior Example: Social workers develop a mutually agreed-on focus of work and desired outcomes.

Critical Thinking Question: What parallels do you see as the similarities between a client/social worker setting of goals for intervention and a student/supervisor setting of goals for learning?

Strive to use supervision in a purposeful and responsible manner. Arranging a regularly scheduled supervisory meeting time each week will help you avoid the difficulties of constantly having to arrange a suitable meeting time. Prepare for each meeting and do not expect your field instructor to do all of the talking. Bring questions, observations, and requests for input and feedback to the meeting. Use this time to examine your performance and explore new ideas.

The conscious building of professional social work skills and competencies is directly related to the conscious use of professional supervision. This is why social work programs and practicum agencies collaborate so closely in the design and implementation of practicum programs. Both entities understand the developmental stages of professional development, and because of that choose to structure the practicum experience in a way that other experienced social workers lead students through the skill-building process of integrating theory and practice. It is the responsibility of both the supervisor and the student to discuss the following questions in supervisory sessions. They will assist students to engage in a reflective process that enhances the acquisition of professional skills and practice behaviors. Students who actively engage in the supervisory relationship will gain much knowledge about practice and about themselves.

You and your field instructor will discuss many things during your scheduled time together, and two main categories of supervision will become apparent. The first of these is **supervision about the work that you are doing, and the interventions with clients** in which you are engaged. Following is a list of questions that will arise in discussions about interventions. The second category is **supervision about professional development**, and a list of discussions questions about that area is also included below.

Discussion of Interventions

- What **professional role** is expected of the social worker in a practice situation?
- What determines the most **appropriate level of practice** at which to intervene?
- What **theories of orientation/explanation** help to explain the development of individuals, families, groups, organizations, communities, and societies?
- What **theories of orientation/explanation** help to explain the etiology of a social problem or condition?
- What **theories and models of practice** help to guide the development of an intervention plan?
- What is involved in the process of **matching client need with an intervention plan**?
- What is the role of **practice wisdom** in interventions?
- What is the role of **intuition** in interventions?
- What is the role of **social work research** in interventions?
- How can **diverse clients** be served in a culturally competent manner?
- What can be **learned from mistakes**?
- How can **academic information be applied** in real-life situations?

Discussion of Professional Development

- How can a student **acquire basic and advanced skills** in practice?
- How can a student maximize his/her **learning style** to grow professionally?
- How can a social worker use **supervision over a professional career**?
- What professional skills and practice behaviors can be used **at all levels of practice**?
- Why is it important to gain **generalist skills** to address social problems?
- What can **clients teach us**?
- What is used as the **measurement of professional growth**?
- What skills and practice behaviors can be **transferred between fields of practice**?

- What *level of performance* will be expected for BSW and MSW level practice?
- When is a social worker *ready to supervise others*?

Take these questions with you to supervisory sessions with your field instructor and engage in professional conversations about them over time. It is good to learn how to utilize supervision for both consultation on interventions and for professional growth while you are a student. Continuing to use and give supervision to others is an element of sound social work practice. Expect your field instructor to ask some very pointed, thorough, and thoughtful questions in order to learn about and monitor your work in the agency. Supervisors ask these questions in order to be of support to you and to ensure that clients are well served. They will help you analyze your performance, understand why an intervention was successful or not, and develop your critical thinking skills. In regard to specific cases you have been assigned to, the following questions may be addressed in order to help you reflect and purposefully grow professionally. They are grouped together in the phases of the helping process.

Critical Thinking

Practice Behavior Example: Social workers analyze models of assessment, prevention, intervention, and evaluation

Critical Thinking Question: How are the stages of learning and developing competency similar to those that clients experience when they participate in interventions?

The role of a supervisor is to give both instruction and feedback, and you will increase your chances of success if you seek and are open to input about yourself and your work. You may be anxious because your field instructor will be evaluating your performance. However, that is his or her responsibility, having been asked by your school to guide your learning and offer constructive criticism in order that you might learn about yourself and develop your knowledge and skills. In order for you to develop your knowledge and skills over time, your field instructor should evaluate your performance in an ongoing and continuous manner. You should receive feedback, suggestions, and constructive criticism during all phases of your practicum so that you can continue to grow professionally. If this is not happening, discuss the matter with your field instructor and ask for an ongoing critique of your performance. Your supervisor may use questions similar to those in Table 5.2.

Table 5.2	**Supervisory Questions Regarding the Planned Change Process**

Engagement
Was the client voluntary or involuntary?
What skills did you use to engage the client in the planned change process?
What problem(s) were identified?
What was the client's level of motivation?

Assessment
What data did you gather and how did you interpret them?
What problems and strengths did you identify?
What goals and objectives were set?
What intervention plan was designed?

Table 5.2   **Continued**

Intervention
What roles and responsibilities did the client have in the intervention plan?
What roles and responsibilities did you have in the intervention plan?
What orienting/explanatory theories informed the intervention plan?
What practice theories/models guided the intervention plan?

Evaluation
What process was used to monitor progress on the goals and objectives?
To what degree were the plan's goals and objectives met?
What evaluation methods and tools were used to measure outcomes?
How was termination handled?

Your field instructor is responsible for conducting a comprehensive evaluation of your learning and performance at the end of the academic term, and this will likely translate into a final grade in your practicum. You can expect that this evaluation will be based on direct observation of your work by your field instructor or other social workers, your verbal or written descriptions of your work and your learning, feedback from clients, and observations and input from social workers in the community who have worked with you.

As you begin your practicum and take on new responsibilities, you may be afraid of making a serious mistake or in some way hurting your clients. Such worries are to be expected. In fact, your field instructor will become concerned if you do not have these concerns, because that could mean that you are overconfident or that you do not understand the seriousness of your situation. Do not hesitate to express your fears. Your field instructor can help you with these issues and help prepare you for any tasks assigned to you. Take heart in the knowledge that most rookie student errors tend to be those related to not doing enough because students are tentative, rather than actually doing harm to clients.

Your field instructor will likely view any errors or omissions that you make not as mistakes only, but also as ways to learn and grow in your work with future clients and in more challenging future situations. Hopefully you will learn how to observe, critique, evaluate, instruct, and affirm your own practice from the constructive feedback given by your field instructor. This will teach you the value of ongoing self-monitoring of the effectiveness of your work in addition to the value of supervision.

Supervision is an interactional process that in many ways parallels the social worker–client relationship and the helping process (Shulman, 1992). In order to help you improve your performance, your field instructor will employ many of the helping skills and techniques that you and other social workers use in working with clients such as offering guidance and support, providing feedback, recognizing strengths, and confronting when necessary. Watch your supervisor model the techniques with you that are effective with clients, focusing on how they help you grow by being open to teaching and feedback. However, supervision is not counseling or therapy. If you need counseling for personal issues or those related to your practicum, seek counseling from a professional rather than from your field instructor.

Students tend to move through several stages during their practicum experience, including orientation, exploration and skill building, and beginning competency. Your field instructor will provide specific types of help at each stage, helping you move forward as a professional. As you move through the practicum, be conscious of the shifts in your experiences outlined in Table 5.3.

Many students begin the practicum with the hope that their field instructor will become a true mentor. When this happens, it is a great experience for a practicum student. Mentors can be role models and can guide and inspire students to achieve higher levels of competence. However, this may not happen

Table 5.3   Stages of Practicum: Student and Supervisor Experiences

Stage of Practicum	Student	Supervisor
Orientation stage	**Reactions** Enthusiastic, excited, anxious, unsure, overwhelmed, confused, ready, motivated, confident, worried about making mistakes, hesitant to be observed	**Reactions** Motivated to teach, hopeful that student will be competent, challenged to make time to supervise student
	Responsibilities Participate in orientation and training, become familiar with agency staff and programs, attend agency meetings, visit other agencies, develop learning plan	**Responsibilities** Provide orientation and training, offer guidance and direction, provide encouragement, assist in selection of learning activities, support initial attempts at practice behaviors, identify student competencies and limitations
Exploration and skill-building stage	**Reactions** Less anxious, more realistic, motivated, growing in confidence, willing to be observed, motivated by successes, learning from mistakes	**Reactions** Confident in allowing more student autonomy, aware of student strengths and limitations and need for supervision
	Responsibilities Take on responsibilities, implement learning plan, develop professional skills and knowledge, integrate theory and practice, gain exposure to all facets of agency practice, gain experience in all levels of practice, play variety of social work roles, identify strengths and address limitations	**Responsibilities** Monitor completion of learning activities, provide instructive and corrective feedback, help build on experiences, assist student in integrating theory and practice, help student assume more challenging tasks

Table 5.3   **Continued**

Stage of Practicum	Student	Supervisor
Beginning competency stage	**Reactions** Increased confidence in skills, enhanced insight, heightened self-awareness, motivated for professional position	**Reactions** Confidence in student as entry-level practitioner, affirming of student competence
	Responsibilities Identify own professional growth needs, experienced in most aspects of practicum experience, need less supervision and direction, identify tasks independently, integrate theory and practice, refine skills	**Responsibilities** Help student refine skills, assign broad range of tasks at all levels of practice, expect autonomous performance, help student generalize learning to other settings and populations

for a number of reasons. Even if your field instructor does not become a mentor, he or she can teach you what you need to know to be effective. When seeking a mentor, you may need to look to persons outside your practicum agency.

Conflicts may arise in the supervisory relationship. For example, you may feel that your field instructor does not devote enough time to you and your learning needs. You may feel that your field instructor is either too controlling or not structured enough. The two of you may have very different personalities. Perhaps you and your field instructor differ in terms of gender, race, ethnic background, or age, and at times these differences affect your relationship. If you have conflict, talk about it. Do not avoid the problem or circumvent your supervisor. You will be expected to find ways to deal with these issues. If the problem cannot be worked out with your field instructor, consult with your faculty supervisor.

Exercise caution on developing a dual relationship with your field instructor. He or she is to be a supervisor, not a friend or a counselor. Although there can be an element of friendship between students and supervisors, this can be problematic when supervisors need to provide feedback and students need to be able to accept it. If personal problems arise during your practicum, do not ask or expect your field instructor to provide counseling. If you need such services, arrange to receive them in another way.

Using Supervision for Learning: A Workbook Activity

1. Does your field instructor also supervise other social workers or agency staff? If so, who?

_____

_____

2. Who supervises your field instructor?

_____

3. Has your field instructor previously supervised practicum students? If yes, about how many students?

_____

4. Has your field instructor received agency-based training on staff supervision?

_____

5. Has your field instructor attended training on practicum supervision and instruction provided by your school's practicum program?

_____

_____

6. Is your field instructor known to possess some special knowledge, experience, and skills, and how can you learn from your supervisor?

_____

_____

7. In what areas of your learning do you want and welcome feedback from your field instructor?

_____

_____

8. In what areas of performance are you overly sensitive or hesitant about receiving feedback from your field instructor? What might these feelings be telling you?

_____

_____

9. Are you afraid of anything related to your practicum? What is a positive way of dealing with these fears?

_____

_____

10. It has been said that people often avoid the experiences they need most in order to learn and grow personally. Are you avoiding any practicum experiences? How can you gain these experiences in spite of your reservations?

_____

_____

11. Is it possible for you to observe and receive supervision from other social workers in your agency?

_____

_____

12. Which of the following learning experiences are available to you in your practicum? Try to find ways to participate in as many of these supervisory activities as possible.

_____ Discuss possible decisions and actions with your supervisor after you have met with your client.

_____ Discuss how your interventions fit with various perspectives, theories, or models.

_____ Observe others modeling the skills or techniques you wish to learn.

_____ Use role-play and simulations to rehearse the techniques, skills, or approaches you want to learn.

_____ Brainstorm various ways in which a situation might be handled.

_____ Watch a video or listen to an audiotape of an experienced worker's session with a client.

_____ Read and discuss an article related to the skills you wish to learn.

_____ Review and discuss the case notes and the written record of others' work with their clients.

Suggested Learning Activities

- Present a case you are working on at a peer supervisory session, asking for input from other social workers.
- If appropriate and feasible, work with a variety of social workers, supervisors, and managers in your agency so that you can observe differing supervisory styles.
- Ask your field instructor how your agency provides support to its employees, such as through an employee assistance program or continuing education.
- In Sheafor and Horejsi (2012), read the sections titled "Providing and Receiving Supervision" (438–441) and "Developing Self Awareness" (427–429).

References

Aasheim, Lisa. *Practical Clinical Supervision for Counselors: An Experiential Guide.* New York: Springer Publishing Company, 2011.

Baird, Brian N. *The Internship, Practicum, and Field Placement Handbook: A Guide for the Helping Professions.* 6th ed. Upper Saddle River, NJ: Prentice Hall, 2011.

Coulshed, Veronica, Audrey Mullender, David N. Jones, and Neil Thompson. *Management in Social Work.* 3rd ed. New York: Palgrave Macmillan, 2006.

Dessler, Gary. *Supervision and Leadership in a Changing World.* Upper Saddle River, NJ: Prentice Hall, 2012.

Dolgoff, Ralph. *An Introduction to Supervisory Practice in Human Services.* Boston: Allyn and Bacon, 2005.

Hawkins, Peter, and Robin Shohet. *Supervising in the Helping Professions.* New York: Open University Press, 2006.

Hayes, Robert, Gerald Corey, and Patricia Mouton. *Clinical Supervision in the Helping Professions: A Practical Guide.* Pacific Grove, CA: Brooks/Cole, 2003.

Kadushin, Alfred, and Daniel Harkness. *Supervision in Social Work.* 4th ed. New York: Columbia University Press, 2002.

National Association of Social Workers. *Code of Ethics.* Washington, DC: NASW Press, 1999.

Pecora, Peter, David Cherin, Emily Bruce, and Trainidad de Jesus Arguello. *Strategic Supervision: A Brief Guide for Managing Social Service Organizations.* Los Angeles: Sage Publications, 2010.

Sheafor, Bradford, and Charles Horejsi. *Techniques and Guidelines in Social Work Practice.* 9th ed. Boston: Allyn and Bacon, 2012.

Shohet, Robin, and Peter Hawkins. *Supervision in the Helping Professions.* 3rd ed. Columbus, OH: Mayfield Publishing, 2007.

Shulman, Lawrence. *Interactional Supervision*. 3rd ed. Washington, DC: NASW Press, 1992.

Weinbach, Robert. *The Social Worker as Manager: A Practical Guide to Success*. 6th ed. Boston: Allyn and Bacon, 2011.

Weisman, Daniel. *Professional Writing for Social Work Practice*. New York: Springer Publishing Company, 2012.

CHAPTER 5 REVIEW

PRACTICE TEST

The following questions will test your knowledge of the content found within this chapter.

1. In addition to state licensing requirements for social work supervision, _____ provides additional expectations for supervisors
   a. universities
   b. NASW *Code of Ethics*
   c. labor unions
   d. client advocacy groups

2. Supervisors must be informed of
   a. illegal activity discovered by social workers
   b. client complaints
   c. treatment outcomes
   d. colleague tardiness

3. The potential for dual relationships between social workers and their supervisors exists because of their close working relationship. Regarding dual relationships, social workers should know that dual relationships
   a. are inadvisable
   b. are illegal
   c. are encouraged
   d. are not covered in the NASW *Code of Ethics*

4. A supervisor's ultimate ethical responsibility is to
   a. those he or she supervises
   b. society
   c. funding sources
   d. clients

5. Supervisors' responsibility for the actions of a supervisee is referred to as
   a. tort law
   b. vicarious liability
   c. professional liability
   d. negligence

6. The main function of evaluating employee performance is
   a. to meet state laws regarding outcomes
   b. to satisfy funding sources
   c. to ensure quality of services provided to clients
   d. to promote professional development of supervisees

7. What are the similarities and differences between a social worker–supervisor relationship and a social worker–client relationship? How can this understanding be used to become more empathetic to the possible reactions of clients to social work involvement in their lives?

©Vladans/Dreamstime

6

Personal Safety

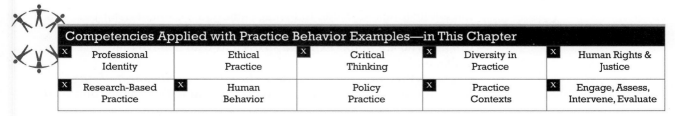

Competencies Applied with Practice Behavior Examples—in This Chapter									
x	Professional Identity		Ethical Practice	x	Critical Thinking	x	Diversity in Practice	x	Human Rights & Justice
x	Research-Based Practice	x	Human Behavior		Policy Practice	x	Practice Contexts	x	Engage, Assess, Intervene, Evaluate

CHAPTER PREVIEW

This chapter describes the potential dangers of social work practice and offers ways in which social work students can practice safely by identifying the sources and types of danger most often encountered in social work practice, becoming familiar with potential dangers and risks in practicum, and informing themselves of agency policies and procedures that can reduce risk and protect staff and clients. It also familiarizes students with precautions and preventive actions that can reduce the risk of being harmed, and provides guidance on steps and actions that can be taken to prevent violence, deescalate threatening situations, and deal with violence after it happens.

While dealing with clients in stressful and personal situations, social workers sometimes find themselves involved in emotional encounters laden with the potential to undermine the safety of both clients and social workers. Although social workers see themselves as helpers and expect most clients to be cooperative, at times they find themselves in situations in which they must deal with clients who are angry, volatile, and threatening. Accounts of violence toward social workers are increasing, due to client frustration with human service systems; cutbacks in services; increased levels of crime, drug use, and violence in society; and antiauthority or antigovernment attitudes on the part of clients. Because of potential threats and attempts at violence toward social workers, it is of the utmost importance that students learn how to avoid such danger and deal with it should it actually occur.

In addition to the physical dangers associated with certain circumstances and types of practice, exposure to job-related danger can lead to negative outcomes such as anxiety, low morale, burnout, family stress, and high staff turnover. As a social work practicum student, you must be cognizant of the dangers you face. You will need to exercise certain precautions so as to reduce risks to your safety. Moreover, you must know what steps to take when you encounter a dangerous situation rather than assume that you are not in danger or that you can handle situations without training and consideration of specific guidelines and recommendations.

BACKGROUND AND CONTEXT

Broadly speaking, the potential sources of danger to social workers include the following:

- Clients who are ***angry and feel unjustly treated*** by the agency and its staff
- Clients who present a special threat because of high-risk factors such as ***alcohol or drug use***
- Clients with extreme ***antiauthority attitudes***
- Clients with ***unstable mental health conditions***, delusions, suspicions, and impulse control problems, especially if they have discontinued the medications intended to manage emotions, thought disorders, and impulsive behavior
- Clients who are under ***extreme stress*** and who believe they have no viable options
- Clients with a ***personal history of threats, violence, or bullying behavior*** and who may have a preoccupation with violence and ready access to weapons

- Clients who are involved in ***illegal activities*** that may be discovered by a social worker
- Clients who have a ***history of being victimized*** themselves, especially over an extended period of time
- Clients who are somewhat ***socially isolated*** and without meaningful supports
- Persons with ***criminal intent and inclination*** who are found in neighborhoods near the agency or in areas where the social worker travels and works
- ***Biohazardous and toxic materials*** that may be encountered in hospitals and other health-care facilities and during visits to clients in their homes

In addition, certain practice settings present more risk to social workers than others do. Such settings include child protective agencies, programs in correctional settings, forensic units of psychiatric hospitals, shelters for the homeless, and residential facilities for youth who may be aggressive and impulsive. These settings are inherently dangerous because some of those served may have tendencies toward the use of violence. However, any practice setting can be threatening, because client–worker interactions often involve emotionally charged situations and concerns. Even clients with no previous history of violence or high-risk behaviors can, under certain circumstances, pose a threat to social workers.

Research-Based Practice

Practice Behavior Example: Social workers use research evidence to inform practice.

Critical Thinking Question: What does the professional literature tell us about the factors which put social workers at risk for violence by clients?

Certain social work practices and interventions have a greater likelihood of placing the social worker at risk. Such activities include the initial investigation of child abuse allegations, the involuntary removal of a child from a parent's home, protection of a victim of domestic violence, outreach to youth involved in gangs, treatment of aggressive youth, intervention with drug- and alcohol-involved clients, the transporting of clients who do not wish to be moved, the behavioral management of persons with certain forms of brain injury or mental retardation, and the monitoring of clients in correctional settings. In these situations, social work actions can be perceived as threatening or coercive. This may result in heightened emotion or defensiveness on the part of clients, and an inclination to use violence. Social workers who work with potentially dangerous clients face the difficult challenge of remaining humane, open, and accepting of clients while also being alert to the possibility of danger or attack. It is important not to expect every client to be a threat, but very crucial to recognize a client who might be.

Social workers in some settings experience frequent verbal abuse, and because most of these threats do not result in actual violence, these social workers may become complacent. They may come to view verbal threats as part of their job, mistakenly assuming that the clients are always bluffing and consequently fail to take reasonable precautions. Some social workers mistakenly believe that because they have been trained in basic helping skills, they will always be able to talk their way out of a dangerous situation. These overly confident workers may minimize risk, erroneously conclude that they do not need special training in how to respond in truly dangerous situations, and thus put themselves at risk. If you are doing your practicum in a hospital or other health-care setting, you should be alert to the existence of biological

Human Behavior

Practice Behavior Example: Social workers critique and apply knowledge to understand person and environment.

Critical Thinking Question: What aspects of social work practice and social agencies could contribute to strong emotional reactions by clients?

or chemical hazards and receive instruction on how to protect yourself against infectious diseases and how to avoid or properly handle biohazardous materials such as used tissues, clothing, bed sheets, or pillows that have been stained with body fluids. In some instances, you may need to wear a mask and gloves when interviewing a patient. In some cases this will be done to protect yourself from diseases and in other cases to protect a vulnerable patient. Practicum students may also be exposed to client threats over the telephone or via e-mail. You will need to be trained in agency responses to such threats in order to protect yourself, your coworkers, and your clients.

GUIDANCE AND DIRECTION

It is important to remember that much violence toward social workers can be prevented if they understand the process of escalation and how to intervene at each phase. Most dangerous interpersonal psychosocial situations are the result of tensions that have grown and intensified over time. It is vital to understand the phases of escalation, clients' needs and feelings during each phase, and what actions or interventions by the social worker might reduce the tension and level of risk.

It is preferable to intervene as early as possible in order to prevent escalation and eventual loss of control by the angry client. Remember that clients who may threaten violence are likely to be experiencing a myriad of emotions in addition to anger. Depending on the situation, they may be feeling afraid, judged, threatened by others, lonely, hopeless, wronged, misunderstood, overwhelmed, frustrated, and wanting revenge. Understanding the emotions of people who are extremely upset may serve to remind you that accurately understanding their feelings may be helpful in terms of defusing potentially dangerous situations.

Think of all potentially violent situations as having three general stages, **prevention, dealing with threats of violence,** and **dealing with violent behavior.** Hopefully such situations can be prevented, defused, or resolved without actual violence. If not, social workers must be informed about and prepared to deal with violence should it occur. Table 6.1 illustrates how social workers can protect themselves in a variety of settings and situations.

Dealing with the Potentially Violent Client

Following is a list of guidelines for anticipating potential danger, identifying situations that might put you at risk, preventing or dealing with risky situations, and resolving violent situations should they arise.

- Understand that past behavior is the best single predictor of future behavior. Before meeting with a client that you do not know and who may be dangerous, consult with agency records or the local police for information that may help you assess the risk.
- Remove all potential weapons from your office, including scissors, staplers, paperweights, and other small but heavy objects, when dealing with a potentially dangerous client.

Table 6.1   **Dealing with Potentially Violent Situations**

Stages of Potentially Violent Situations	Client Emotions and Behavior	Social Work Approaches
Escalation and prevention	Intense emotions felt and expressed, but within control of client	Recognize underlying emotions such as fear and vulnerability
	Verbal venting or unusual quietness	Offer empathy and use active listening to allow client to feel heard
	Behavior still within control of client	Work to lessen intensity and defuse emotion and resolve issue
Dealing with threats of violence	Escalation of emotions and irrational thought, no longer within control of client	Continue efforts to build rapport, move focus from client emotion to behavior
	Offensive verbal attacks, intimidation, and threats of physical violence	Set limits on speech and behavior and continue to assess danger
	Behavior potentially out of control of client without further defusing of emotions or addressing of concerns	Offer clients potential solutions and alternatives to violence while devising escape plan
Dealing with violence	Threatening actions, actual physical violence	If safety cannot be guaranteed, leave setting or escape
	Continued loss of control and escalation of violence	Call for agency assistance, security personnel, or law enforcement
	Use of weapons or body to attack social worker	Use self-defensive measures, safety plan, and escape

- Leave your office door partly open during an interview with a potentially dangerous client.
- Notify others if you are planning to meet a potentially dangerous client in your office and arrange for a way to signal for help. Arrange your office so that you are closest to the door. Place a desk or other barrier between you and the potentially dangerous client.
- Avoid meeting with clients when you are alone in the office. If you must have the meeting, turn lights on in other offices and lead clients to believe that others will be coming into the office.
- When meeting with an angry client, provide him or her with as much privacy as possible without compromising your safety.
- Make use of all safety procedures and devices available such as call devices or code systems to alert coworkers that you need help.
- Be very cautious when dealing with a person who is under the influence of alcohol or drugs, even when you know the person fairly well because such a person can be inherently unpredictable.
- Be cautious when around persons who may be involved in illegal activities such as manufacturing or selling drugs and may feel threatened by your presence or by what you have seen. They may be willing to harm you in order to protect themselves from discovery by authorities.

Engage, Assess, Intervene, Evaluate

Practice Behavior Example: Social workers use empathy and other interpersonal skills.

Critical Thinking Question: What interpersonal helping skills can you use to decrease the chances that you will be involved in dangerous situations with clients?

- Because worker attitudes play a role in either controlling or provoking threatening behavior, maintain a positive, nonjudgmental attitude toward clients.
- Minimize the sharing of personal information such as phone numbers or addresses, and take precautions in the use of social media that might put you at risk.

Personal Safety

- Remember that clients use threats and violence when other forms of communication fail them, so utilize skills that facilitate communication and help clients express themselves in words.
- Recognize that both increased structure and decreased stimuli may help clients remain calm and regain self-control.
- Remember that an attack by a client is almost always the reaction of someone who is afraid and feeling threatened. Thus, strive to demonstrate empathy and speak and act in ways that lessen the client's need to be afraid of you.
- Address the person by name. Do not argue with or criticize an angry person. Avoid doing anything that might be perceived as ridiculing or embarrassing the person.
- Trust your instincts. Assume that you have a built-in unconscious mechanism that can recognize danger more quickly than your rational thought processes. If you feel afraid, assume that you are in danger, even if you cannot clearly identify why you feel this way.
- Avoid standing above angry people because this position can appear authoritarian and threatening.
- Attacks are most likely when clients feel trapped or controlled, either psychologically or physically. To the extent possible, give clients options and choices such as allowing them to escape without having to come close to you.
- Be alert to signs of an imminent attack such as rapid breathing, teeth grinding, dilated pupils, flaring nostrils, loud speech, clenched fists, and threatening movements.
- Allow angry persons to vent their feelings because most angry persons will begin to calm down after two or three minutes of venting or name calling. However, some people are stimulated by their own words and grow even angrier because of what they are saying. If that occurs, the level of risk is increasing.
- Do not touch an angry person, especially if they may be under the influence of a substance, and do not move into their personal space. Remain at least four feet away from the person.
- Remember that an angry or dangerous person is more likely to attack someone who appears weak and unsure. Present yourself as calm and self-confident, but not haughty.
- If an individual threatens you with a gun or other weapon, assure him or her that you intend no harm and slowly back away. Do not attempt to disarm the person. Leave that to the police or security staff with special training.

Handling the Potential Dangers of a Home Visit

- Do not enter a situation that could be dangerous without first consulting with others and formulating a plan to reduce risk. Do not hesitate to seek the assistance of other social workers or the police.
- When visiting clients in their homes, keep your agency informed of your plans and itinerary and check in by phone on a prearranged schedule. Carry a means of calling for help (e.g., cellular phone, push-button emergency signals, or radio).
- Assign two staff members for potentially dangerous home visits whenever possible.
- Unless there is a good reason to visit a home unannounced, call ahead to schedule a visit.
- Consider meeting a client in a neutral location unless the home needs to be visited.
- Do not enter a home or apartment building until you have taken a few minutes to determine its level of danger. Listen for sounds of violence or out-of-control behavior. Consider whether other people are nearby and if they would respond to a call for help.
- Identify possible escape routes.
- Be aware that guns are most often kept in bedrooms and that kitchens contain knives and other potential weapons. Leave immediately if a threatening person appears to be moving toward a weapon.
- Be aware that clients who leave a room could return with a weapon.
- Do not sit in an overstuffed chair or couch from which you cannot quickly get to your feet. Select a hard and movable chair. If necessary, it can be used as a shield or barrier between you and a threatening person.
- Park your car in a way that allows for a quick escape if necessary.
- Keep your vehicle in good running order and full of gasoline so that you will not find yourself stranded in a dangerous or isolated area.
- Educate yourself about drugs and illegal drug labs so that you can recognize the dangers inherent in entering such a place.
- Learn as much as you can about the people living in the home you are visiting in order to anticipate negative attitudes toward authorities, previous history of violence, or previous experiences with social service agencies.
- If you are being followed, go immediately to a police or fire station or to a public place. Do not go to your home if you believe someone is following you or watching your movements.
- If you are likely to encounter dangerous situations, wear shoes and clothing that permit running. Avoid wearing long earrings or jewelry that could easily be grabbed and twisted to inflict pain and prevent your escape.
- Consider carrying a defensive device such as pepper spray, and learn to use it before making home visits.
- Have an escape plan ready in case you need to flee, including an escape excuse.

Handling an Intense Argument between Two or More People

- When two or more individuals are in a heated argument and you need to intervene, begin by gaining their attention. Anything short of physical force may be used. A shrill whistle, a loud clap, a loud voice, a silly request (e.g., "I need a glass of water"), or other attention-getting devices may be used for this purpose.
- Ask those in conflict to sit down. If they do not sit, you should also remain standing.
- Separate the disputants as necessary without compromising your own safety. Bring them back together only after they have quieted down and gained self-control.
- If possible, always intervene in a crisis situation with a parter.
- Do not physically intervene if those in conflict are threatening each other with weapons or if they are engaged in a high level of physical violence.

Agency Procedure and the Potentially Violent Client

- The agency should keep waiting rooms and offices clean and create a pleasant and inviting physical environment. Dirty, unpleasant, unfriendly, impersonal, or unkempt locations convey disrespect to clients and tend to generate hostility.
- The agency should provide services in a timely manner, avoid waiting lists whenever possible, and reduce waiting periods for eligibility determination or services.
- The agency should develop policy and protocols on how staff members are to assess danger and respond to dangerous situations, such as bomb threats or hostage taking. These procedures should be reviewed regularly.
- The agency should provide training on personal safety and related agency procedures to staff and students and repeat or update this training on a regular basis, allowing for rehearsal, drills, and incorporation of new information.
- The agency should develop a protocol about when and how to use police assistance, including a written agreement with local law enforcement officials.
- The agency should post a statement in waiting rooms and in other prominent places explaining that alcohol, drugs, and weapons are not allowed in the building and that threats and violence or the possession of a weapon will prompt an immediate call to the police and potential legal action.
- The agency should make sure that the exterior of the agency's building and parking lot are well lighted.
- The agency should designate a specific office or room for meetings with potentially violent clients. This room should be one that is easily observed by others nearby.
- The agency's record-keeping system should use color codes or other markings that identify individuals or households with a history of violence.

- The agency should use coded language and designated staff responders when social workers are threatened and need to call for help.
- The agency should institute security measures within the building. This might include the installation of a call-for-help button in each office space and establishment of telephone code words that are requests for police assistance.
- The agency administration should strongly encourage the staff to report threats or attempts at violence in light of research showing that many incidents go unreported.
- The agency should maintain a log of all threats of violence so staff can identify those individuals and situations that present a special risk.
- The agency should review any actual incidents to determine the effectiveness of agency threat protocol and make revisions as necessary to protect social workers.
- The agency should file criminal charges against those who harm or threaten physical injury to either the worker or the worker's family.
- When a worker is harmed, the agency should respond with appropriate counseling, support, time off, and emotional support to lessen the effects on the worker and the worker's family.
- The agency should provide critical incident debriefing support for all staff, even those not involved in an incident.

Policy Practice

Practice Behavior Example: Social workers analyze, formulate, and advocate for policies that advance social well-being.

Critical Thinking Question: What are the local and state laws and organizations from which you can learn about the legal ramifications of violent client behavior?

Reducing the Risk of Harm: A Workbook Activity

1. What training does your university offer students in violence prevention?

   _____

   _____

2. What training is provided in your agency to help social workers prevent and deal with threatening or violent clients or situations?

   _____

   _____

3. What kinds of high-risk clients or situations are you likely to encounter in your practicum? How will you prepare yourself to deal with them?

   _____

   _____

4. What agency policies and procedures are in place to ensure personal safety and reduce risk to agency employees and clients?

   _____

   _____

5. Have any employees in your practicum agency been threatened or harmed by clients or consumers? If yes, describe the circumstances that gave rise to the incident.

_____

_____

6. Is it possible that policies or agency environment could contribute to client frustration? If so, what changes do you recommend?

_____

_____

7. Does your agency have a formal, written agreement with law enforcement authorities detailing when they are to be called for assistance?

_____

_____

8. Are there any clients or situations that frighten you? If so, how can you deal with your concerns and fears?

_____

_____

9. Does your agency have an incident reporting system for documenting threats and violence toward workers?

_____

_____

10. What services does your agency provide to workers who are threatened, injured, or traumatized by threats or violence (e.g., counseling, critical incident stress debriefing, or support groups)?

_____

_____

Suggested Learning Activities

- Invite a local police officer to offer guidance on how to reduce risk in and around your agency.
- Interview experienced social workers and ask for their advice on reducing personal risk.
- Role-play situations that illustrate each of the stages of potentially violent situations described in this chapter.
- Educate yourself on the specific safety issues faced by your agency (e.g., methamphetamine abuse, use of restraining orders).
- Attend training offered by your agency on safety.
- Determine what services (i.e., counseling or legal services) would be offered to you or others in your agency should you experience a threat or actual incident of violence.
- In Sheafor and Horejsi (2012), read the sections titled "Increasing Personal Safety in Dangerous Situations" (158–161).

References

Birkenmaier, Julie, and Marla Berg-Weger. *The Practicum Companion for Social Work: Integrating Class and Field Work*. 3rd ed. Boston: Allyn and Bacon, 2011.
Newhill, Christina E. *Client Violence in Social Work Practice*: Prevention, Intervention, and Research. New York: Guilford Press, 2004.
Sheafor, Bradford, and Charles Horejsi. *Techniques and Guidelines for Social Work Practice*. 9th ed. Boston: Allyn and Bacon, 2012.
Weinger, Susan. *Security Risk: Preventing Client Violence against Social Workers*. Washington, DC: NASW Press, 2001.

CHAPTER 6 REVIEW

PRACTICE TEST

The following questions will test your knowledge of the content found within this chapter.

1. The main purpose of clear agency protocol in regard to social worker safety is
   a. to protect clients
   b. to protect social workers
   c. to avoid lawsuits
   d. to measure effectiveness of services

2. Social workers who do not follow agency protocol about safety
   a. may not be protected legally if they are injured
   b. will be sanctioned by their agency
   c. have violated the NASW *Code of Ethics*
   d. are covered legally if they have their own liability insurance

3. Which is true in regard to agency agreements with law enforcement agencies?
   a. Agreements should be developed on an ad hoc basis.
   b. Agreements should be formalized in advance of a threat to workers.
   c. Agreements should be informal.
   d. Agreements should be made between individual officers and social workers.

4. Premature use of physical containment of threatening clients may
   a. deescalate the situation
   b. destroy trust between the social worker and client
   c. escalate the situation
   d. undermine the effectiveness of interventions

5. The best predictor of client violence toward social workers is
   a. a mental disorder
   b. threats of violence
   c. social worker skill and ability
   d. previous history of behavior problems

6. Agencies that provide personal safety training to their social workers
   a. will be immune from prosecution if injuries occur
   b. will be able to demonstrate reasonable efforts to protect workers
   c. are required to provide training to each social worker once
   d. do not need to carry professional malpractice insurance

7. Describe the ways in which the approach to deescalating potential violence changes in response to client changes.

7

©Yuri Arcurs/Fotolia

Communication

Competencies Applied with Practice Behavior Examples—in This Chapter				
X Professional Identity	X Ethical Practice	X Critical Thinking	X Diversity in Practice	Human Rights & Justice
Research-Based Practice	X Human Behavior	Policy Practice	X Practice Contexts	X Engage, Assess, Intervene, Evaluate

CHAPTER PREVIEW

This chapter focuses on the importance of effective oral and written communication to social work practice as well as the impact of effective and ineffective communication. Information is provided on the purposes and uses of organizational and written communication at all levels of practice, including communication with clients and colleagues. Guidelines for all forms of agency-based communication are provided.

Communication is at the heart of social work practice. A social worker must be able to communicate verbally with clients or consumers, other social workers, members of other professions (e.g., physicians, teachers, lawyers, and judges), agency supervisors and administrators, leaders and decision makers (e.g., elected officials), and with a cross section of the people who make up the community. The social worker must be able to communicate in a one-on-one situation, within the context of a small group, and sometimes before a large audience. The worker must also be able to use several modes of communication effectively, including the **written word**, the **spoken word**, the **electronic word**, and **nonverbal communication**. A social worker must also understand communication within an organization, and how effective organizational communication can enhance the quality of services.

Students are often surprised at how much time social workers must devote to reading and writing. Because written documentation required of social workers is time-consuming, effective writing skills will help to reduce unnecessary time spent documenting your written work. Written communication may take the form of a letter, a memo, a case record, the minutes of a committee meeting, a lengthy formal report, or a grant proposal. The extensive use of written and electronic communication in social work requires that the worker be able to write well and read rapidly.

Effective and skilled communication is central to success in any social work setting. A variety of problems can result from insufficient, inaccurate, or somehow distorted and misunderstood communication. In order to ensure that communication at all levels and between all parties is effective, a sound understanding of the purposes of various types of communication is needed. In addition, communication skills must be developed, and the ethical and legal aspects of communication must be understood. This chapter is designed to assist students in developing essential communication skills for use in the practicum agency.

BACKGROUND AND CONTEXT

Communication can be defined as the process by which a person, group, or organization transmits information back and forth between individuals, groups, or organizations. Both the sender and the receiver of information, whether on the personal or organizational level, must be skilled in both sending and receiving in order for communication to be successful.

Interpersonal communication refers to communication that involves talking, listening, and responding in ways that place an emphasis on the personal dimensions of those involved. It usually takes place in a face-to-face exchange but may occur on the telephone, in highly personalized correspondence, through text messages, or by e-mail. Providing direct services to clients requires frequent and fairly intense interpersonal communication.

The term ***organizational communication*** refers to the somewhat impersonal exchange of messages and information between the various levels, departments, and divisions of an organization, and also between the organization and various individuals and groups outside the organization. Compared to other types of communication, communication within an organization tends to be more formal and more often in written form. Moreover, the nature and flow of information within an organization is strongly influenced by lines of authority and the chain of command.

Downward communication consists of messages, directions, and instructions from those higher in the chain of command to those working at lower levels in the organization. The term ***upward communication*** refers to communication to those higher in the chain of command, such as when a supervisor sends a message to the agency's executive director. As a general rule, upward communication occurs less often than downward communication. This can be a source of problems within an organization because those persons lower on the chain of command often feel that they are not heard and that their communication is not valued. ***Horizontal communication*** refers to the exchange of messages among persons or units at the same level within the organization.

A wide variety of ***communication networks*** exists within social service agencies. Mainly, they differ in the degree to which they are centralized. In a highly centralized network, all messages must flow through some central office or person who can then control what information moves up or down. A decentralized network is characterized by an exchange of information between people and organizational levels without first passing through a particular channel or central point. As a general rule, ***centralized communication networks*** are faster and more accurate if the information has to do with relatively simple tasks. ***Decentralized communication networks*** are faster and more accurate if the communication is about complex tasks and unique activities. This type of communication network may also be more informal and feel more personal to those within an organization. Both centralized and decentralized communication networks have advantages and disadvantages, and should be used judiciously depending on the situation.

Practice Contexts

Practice Behavior Example: Social workers continuously discover, appraise, and attend to changing locales, populations, scientific and technological developments, and emerging societal trends to provide relevant services.

Critical Thinking Question: Is the communication network in your agency centralized or decentralized? Does this meet the needs of your organization?

A common problem within organizations is ***information overload***. This refers to frustration and miscommunication caused by an overwhelming volume of messages, instructions, and reports. Centralized communication networks and highly bureaucratic organizations are especially vulnerable to information overload because so many messages must pass through all levels as they move up and down the organization. This overload can also result in lost or delayed messages and subsequent miscommunication.

Although modern communication technology has solved some problems caused by slow communication, it has created others. It has probably added to the problem of information overload because it is now very easy to send a message and copies of it to many more people. E-mail encourages the use of written communication over face-to-face communication, thus eliminating the opportunity to observe nonverbal communication in order to accurately interpret a message.

Professions and organizations develop and communicate by the use of a specialized language, or ***jargon***, as a way to simplify communication. However, this has the effect of making many of their messages unintelligible to outsiders, including students and clients. You will need to learn agency-specific terminology, acronyms, and jargon quickly in order to understand what is said and written on a daily basis.

Social workers often refer to **communication styles**, which refer to very individualized ways they have learned to communicate with clients and colleagues. These styles build on individual skills such as rapport building, genuineness in communicating, and gaining of clients' trust. Although communication styles may differ greatly, the goals of communication are essentially the same—to engage clients in a helping relationship or to build a working relationship with a colleague. Over time you will develop your own professional style of communication that will allow you to effectively engage with clients.

Cross-cultural communication is one of the most challenging forms of communication, and includes communication differences based on ethnicity, gender, level of education, age, and many other factors. It is difficult for social workers to know if they accurately understand people different from them well enough to make their communication effective. In addition, our communication is influenced by such factors as one's own cross-cultural life experiences and familiarity with the language being used. The symbols we use in language do not have universal meanings—they are influenced by our background, experiences, and the cultural content of the exchanges between sender and receiver. (See Chapter 12, "Diversity and Cultural Competency," for additional information on cross-cultural communication.)

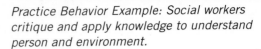

Human Behavior

Practice Behavior Example: Social workers critique and apply knowledge to understand person and environment.

Critical Thinking Question: How can an understanding of human behavior help you develop positive interpersonal communication skills and avoid barriers to good communication?

Engage, Assess, Intervene, Evaluate

Practice Behavior Example: Social workers critically analyze, monitor, and evaluate interventions.

Critical Thinking Question: How might cultural differences in communication impact the quality of interventions?

GUIDANCE AND DIRECTION

Good communication skills, verbal and written, are of central importance in social work practice. Do your best to learn communication skills now because you will need them throughout your career. You will continually be challenged to develop these skills and identify methods to monitor the effectiveness of your communication. Effective communication serves to build professional and client relationships. Table 7.1 illustrates the major positive communication skills you need to develop, as well as the impact of the use of these skills on others.

In nearly every organization you will have the opportunity to observe effective and ineffective, functional and dysfunctional, communication. Take note of which styles and methods work and which do not. Consider why communication may be especially difficult and flawed at times. Knowing some of the following pitfalls of communication may keep you from making these same mistakes. Table 7.2 describes various ineffective communication skills and illustrates the impact of these negative techniques on professional communication outcomes.

Table 7.1   **Effective Interpersonal Communication**

Effective Communication Skills	Impact on Professional Communication
Active listening	• Enhances accurate understanding • Communicates intent to understand
Building rapport	• Establishes effective working relationship • Sets stage for ongoing professional communication
Taking turns	• Demonstrates interest in two-way communication • Results in improved sending and receiving of messages
Clarity of expression	• Increases probability of mutual understanding • Reduces amount of time spent trying to understand
Nonjudgmental responses	• Promotes trust and openness • Communicates good faith
Genuineness	• Demonstrates real intent to communicate • Promotes trust and openness
Use of nonverbal communication	• Enhances verbal communication • Promotes understanding
Listening to underlying messages	• Suggests intent to understand what is not communicated • Deepens level of understanding
Use of open-ended questions	• Promotes listener-directed responses • Deepens sharing
Paraphrasing	• Demonstrates understanding • Communicates motivation to understand
Nondefensive attitude	• Reduces misunderstandings • Increases level of sharing
Looking for common ground	• Encourages further communication • Reduces defensiveness and divisiveness
Respect	• Promotes respectful response • Fosters ability to understand diverse viewpoints
Fostering dialogue	• Communicates desire to understand • Promotes desire of listener to respond genuinely
Seeking mutual understanding	• Promotes additional responses • Demonstrates willingness to listen
Checking for accuracy	• Demonstrates desire to understand • Promotes precision for sender and receiver
Self-awareness	• Reduces chance of misinterpretation • Promotes conscious use of self to promote communication
Allowing adequate time	• Reduces chances of misunderstanding • Demonstrates motivation to understand
Structuring physical environment	• Reduces environmental barriers to communication • Increases opportunity for effective communication

Table 7.1   **Continued**

Effective Communication Skills	Impact on Professional Communication
Matching language	• Reduces misunderstanding due to language barrier • Enhances understanding by tailoring terminology
Managing emotional content	• Lowers interference because of emotions • Demonstrates value of communication over personal issues
Summarizing	• Consolidates communication for sender and receiver • Allows for effective end of communication session

Table 7.2   **Ineffective Interpersonal Communication**

Ineffective Communication Skills	Impact on Professional Communication
Dominating conversation	• Discourages mutual communication • Demonstrates lack of interest in understanding
Rushing rapport building	• Assuming trust without establishing relationship • Suggests a hidden agenda
Interrupting	• Demonstrates lack of respect for speaker • Lowers chance for mutual understanding
Sending unclear messages	• Reduces clarity of content • Reduces chances of accuracy in receiving
Responding judgmentally	• Shows lack of acceptance • Reduces sender's expectation of being understood
Sending mixed or confusing messages	• Reduces accuracy of understanding by listener • Lowers chances that mutual goals will be reached
Missing cues	• Suggests lack of interest in message • Reduces level of understanding
Using poor nonverbal communication	• Misses opportunity to understand verbal message received • Detracts from effectiveness of verbal message sent
Missing underlying messages	• Results in surface-level understanding • Demonstrates lack of interest in what is not said
Using closed-ended questions	• Reduces opportunities for deepened responses • Results in factual and limited responses
Not allowing adequate time	• Communicates disinterest in allowing adequate time • Reduces level of mutual understanding
Failing to check for accuracy	• Bases understanding on assumptions • Suggests disinterest in message sent
Assuming	• Closes off genuine inquiry • Results in limited and distorted understanding
Displaying defensive attitude	• Reduces sender's motivation to communicate • Reduces receiver's ability to hear message
Trying to prove a point or win	• Suggests that communication is one-sided contest • Reduces commitment of listener to communicate

(*continued*)

Table 7.2   **Continued**

Ineffective Communication Skills	Impact on Professional Communication
Failing to show respect	• Shuts down open communication • Results in similar response
Setting up environmental barriers	• Provides limitations and barriers to communication • Demonstrates lack of commitment to communication
Asking excessive why questions	• Builds listener defensiveness • Increases respondent justification
Failing to match language	• Increasing chance that misunderstanding will occur • Demonstrates inability to connect with listener
Lacking genuineness	• Limits honest communication by listener • Demonstrates lack of interest in understanding
Experiencing information overload	• Interferes with communication task • Reduces ability to send and receive messages
Lacking observation skills	• Misses opportunity for enhanced understanding • Reduces level of mutual communication
Misinterpreting	• Distorts understanding • Results in diminished effectiveness of shared work goals
Stacking questions	• Confuses listener • Results in inadequate responses
Asking leading questions	• Intimidates listener • Pushes respondent toward a certain response

Diversity in Practice

Practice Behavior Example: Social workers recognize the extent to which a culture's structures and values may oppress, marginalize, alienate, or create or enhance privilege and power.

Critical Thinking Question: In what phases of the helping process are effective communication skills most vital?

Depending on your practicum assignments, you will probably be surprised at the amount of written documentation required in agency practice. You will learn to write memos, letters, case notes, assessments, treatment plans, reports, and perhaps public relations material and grant proposals. At various times your writing will be used to document important events or actions, provide information to the general public, persuade someone to take action, provide a base for legal action, or report to a funding source.

Remember that all forms of written communication, whether client case records or documents about an organization, have a *specific purpose* and must meet a *professional standard*. For example, written records are used to document services offered, make decisions based on social workers' recommendations, record progress or lack of it, provide rationale for a proposal, confirm verbal agreements, record decisions, demonstrate the use of best practices, serve to address legal requirements, and are required by licensing or accreditation organizations. With this in mind, follow these guidelines in your written communication:

• Understand who your audience is, what they need to know, and how they want the information presented so it is readable for the purposes of the document.
• Use the documentation format required by your agency.

- Organize your material before starting to write, and recognize that you may need to make several revisions.
- Use professional language, but do not overuse jargon.
- Avoid slang and language that could be judgmental, derogatory, biased, disorganized, speculative, or ambiguous and that could be interpreted in more than one way.
- Use direct, clear language rather than vague, tentative, insipid words.
- Check for accuracy of all statements made, using factual and objective wording.
- Choose words carefully, making sure you understand their meaning.
- Complete all required documentation in a timely manner to ensure accuracy and promptness, as it may be needed quickly.
- Abide by agency policies about how much personal information about clients is to be included.
- Understand agency policies about making corrections to client records, and avoid any action that could be viewed in retrospect as falsification of records.
- Assume that all records might be subpoenaed and write accordingly.
- Make sure that overall records are comprehensive and include all required elements.
- Remember that records may be read by someone in your absence or after your practicum is completed, and you will have no opportunity to explain or clarify what you wrote.
- Seek and incorporate feedback from your supervisor into your revised drafts.
- Make copies of all written communication that is sent out of the office, including correspondence, reports, and grant proposals.

Agencies differ somewhat in their standards and expectations for written communication. Ask your field instructor for specific directions on how to prepare required written materials. Also, ask your field instructor for feedback regarding the quality of your writing. Doing so will demonstrate your openness to learning and willingness to receive constructive criticism. It will also help you to better understand your strengths and limitations and help you avoid patterns of ineffective communication. Be appreciative of constructive feedback on your writing, because improved writing skills improve your chances of securing grants, developing linkages with other agencies, and representing the views of clients as shown in treatment plans and case notes that will greatly impact their lives. Your credibility as a professional social worker often rests on the quality of your writing skills.

You may wonder how much detail is required. A good guideline to follow regarding documentation about clients is to include enough detail to bring the client or issue to life for anyone reading it, but not to overwhelm the reader with unnecessary and extraneous information. Every written word should help to convey meaning, and each one counts toward that purpose. This means that you need to include enough information to be clear and communicate what needs to be documented, but concise enough that extraneous information is not included.

When writing about programs or client systems, remember to be clear, convincing, and attuned to the needs, requirements, or motives of those who may be the readers. In contrast, there are many subtle components to written communication, so it is necessary not to leave written statements open to misinterpretation. There is much at stake for clients whose lives and experiences are being written about, and social workers' assessments and recommendations can have major positive or negative impacts on their clients' lives. There is also much at stake for agencies in regard to their record keeping, report writing, accreditation documents, grant proposals, and annual reports. Keep the potential outcomes in mind when learning to write during your practicum.

There are a number of legal guidelines for written communication, and you need to learn and abide by them. Because electronic record-keeping systems are used to store a wide variety of very personal information about clients, be very aware of ***confidentiality of client records*** and learn to anticipate potential breaches in confidentiality that could occur when sharing information between agencies. Learn what can be shared and what cannot. Learn when and how to use release of information documents which demonstrate clients' permission and approval to share information with other professionals or agencies which need this information. Remember that even though clients waive some of their rights to confidentiality in order to be eligible for third-party payments for services, this does not mean that they understand the degree to which their confidentiality may be compromised.

Clients have the ***right to see and obtain copies*** of any documentation about them. They are partners with the agency in the services they are offered, including when they are involuntary clients. Because of this, it is important to consider what to enter into the formal record and to use factual, nonjudgmental language. ***Informed consent*** means that clients understand the impact of what they are signing or agreeing to, and it is often the social worker's responsibility to advocate for clients, making sure they truly do understand and agree. Be cautious with the use of ***electronic forms of communication*** such as computerized client database information, faxes, voice mail, and e-mail, so that client confidentiality is always guarded and is electronically locked so that only those who are involved have access to the information. Abide by all agency policies as well as state and federal regulations about the sharing and protection of client information. Remember that each form of communication can be very helpful to social workers and other entities which serve clients, but also potentially very harmful to clients if confidentiality is compromised.

There are also important ***ethical components of professional communication,*** including the obligation to protect client rights to privacy and confidentiality. Communication should also ensure that clients are treated with dignity and respect, and that interventions are based on the effective and ethical use of documentation.

Developing Communication Skills: A Workbook Activity

Organizational Communication (Written and Oral)

1. What are the major forms of written communication expected of social workers in your agency (e.g., assessments, treatment plans, reports, case notes, minutes, press releases, memos, letters, grant proposals)?

_____

_____

_____

2. What specific policies does your agency have regarding written communication (e.g., deadlines for completion, suggested or required formats, and supervisory review of documentation) that are relevant to your work?

_____

_____

_____

3. What might be the effects of communication problems on agency clients and operations?

_____

_____

_____

4. What types of communication styles, patterns, strengths, and problems have you observed in the following situations?

Case conferences including social workers and other professionals involved with clients

_____

_____

Meetings between social workers and clients

_____

_____

Meetings with agency administrators

_____

_____

Meetings with board members or funding sources

_____

_____

5. How do your agency's chain of command and organizational chart affect communication patterns and the flow of information? Is communication between management and staff centralized or decentralized?

_____

_____

_____

Interpersonal Communication with Clients

6. What effective communication styles and skills have you observed between social workers and clients? How can you learn these skills?

_____

_____

_____

7. What ineffective communication styles and skills have you observed between social workers and clients? How can you avoid these pitfalls?

_____

_____

_____

8. How might forms of diversity such as culture, life experience, gender, and special training enhance or limit your ability to communicate with agency clients?

_____

_____

_____

9. Review Tables 7.1 and 7.2, which list both effective and ineffective interpersonal communication skills and their impact on others. List the ones you see as most important to the situations in which you are involved and make a plan to acquire them.

_____

_____

_____

Suggested Learning Activities

- Ask your field instructor to show you examples of both well-written and poorly written letters, memos, reports, and case records. Examine these materials and observe how writing style, organization, and choice of words affect their quality. Compare your written work to these examples.
- Rewrite a report you have written (three to five pages in length), reducing its length by half. Unnecessary words. Shorten your sentences. Eliminate all repetition of content.
- Seek opportunities to make a presentation to your agency or a community group.
- Ask your field instructor to help you develop your own communication style, including what skills you have and what you need to do to become a more effective communicator.
- In Sheafor and Horejsi (2012), read the section titled "Written Reports and Correspondence" (128–130).

References

Baird, Brian. *The Internship, Practicum, and Field Placement Handbook: A Guide for the Helping Professions*. 5th ed. Upper Saddle River, NJ: Prentice Hall, 2011.

Falender, Carol, and Edward Shafranske. *Casebook for Clinical Supervision: A Competency-Based Approach*. Washington, DC: American Psychological Association, 2008.

Knapp, Mark. *The Sage Handbook of Interpersonal Communication*. 4th ed. Thousand Oaks, CA: Sage Publications, 2011.

Neuliep, James. *Intercultural Communication: A Contextual Approach*. Thousand Oaks, CA: Sage Publications, 2011.

Sheafor, Bradford, and Charles Horejsi. *Techniques and Guidelines for Social Work Practice*. 9th ed. Boston: Allyn and Bacon, 2012.

Sidell, Nancy, and Denise Smiley. *Professional Communication Skills in Social Work*. Boston: Allyn and Bacon, 2008.

Sidell, Nancy. *Social Work Documentation: A Guide to Strengthening Your Case Recording*. Washington, DC: NASW Press, 2011.

Thomas, Janet. *The Ethics of Supervision and Consultation: Practical Guidance for Mental Health Professionals*. Washington, DC: American Psychological Association, 2010.

Thompson, Neil. *Effective Communication: A Guide for the People Professions*. Basingstoke: Palgrave MacMillan, 2011.

CHAPTER 7 REVIEW

PRACTICE TEST

The following questions will test your knowledge of the content found within this chapter.

1. Social workers who do not document their interventions in writing and need to testify in court about their assessments or client outcomes
   a. may not be able to prove what they actually did
   b. can substitute verbal testimony that will be legally acceptable
   b. are in violation of HIPAA requirements
   d. can provide written documentation after the fact

2. if clients request to see written documentation about them and their case, agencies
   a. must comply with their request
   b. must have a written request from the client
   c. must provide copies of documentation within 24 hours
   d. do not have to comply with their request

3. Effective interpersonal communication
   a. is legally mandated for minority clients
   b. is irrelevant to the quality of the helping relationship
   c. can be taught through written materials
   d. positively impacts the helping relationship

4. Clients may have to waive their rights to confidentiality
   a. to third-party payers
   b. when they have violated agency policies
   c. when they request to see their own records
   d. when they cannot pay for services

5. Public funding sources
   a. allow agencies to design their own reporting systems
   b. use agency documentation as a way to influence social policy
   c. often require agency staff members to sign confidentiality agreements
   d. require standardized documentation of services and outcomes

6. Social workers' responsibility to understand clients' concerns
   a. is a legal responsibility
   b. is a documentation responsibility
   c. is an ethical responsibility
   d. is an agency responsibility

7. What social work values and ethics provide a foundation for agencies in developing policies related to case records, releases of information, and electronic forms of communication?

8

The Agency Context of Practice

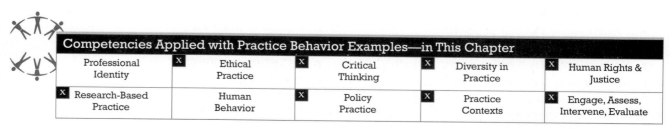

Competencies Applied with Practice Behavior Examples—in This Chapter									
	Professional Identity	X	Ethical Practice	X	Critical Thinking	X	Diversity in Practice	X	Human Rights & Justice
X	Research-Based Practice		Human Behavior	X	Policy Practice	X	Practice Contexts	X	Engage, Assess, Intervene, Evaluate

CHAPTER PREVIEW

This chapter focuses on the agency context of practice, and it provides information on types of agencies, practice hypotheses upon which agencies build their programs, and the structure and culture of social agencies. It also lists the contextual factors surrounding agency operation and the organizational tasks necessary for agency effectiveness, relevance, and sustainability. Also featured is the potential positive or negative impact of organizations on clients.

The daily activities and decisions of a social worker are heavily influenced by the nature and purpose of the organization that employs him or her. Throughout its history, social work has been an agency-based profession. A majority of social workers are employed by agencies, and they provide their services within an organizational context. Given this reality, you must examine and understand your practicum agency mission, goals, structure, funding sources, and level of effectiveness.

BACKGROUND AND CONTEXT

The word *agency* refers to an organization that is authorized or sanctioned to act in the place of or on behalf of others in one area of social functioning, or in response to a particular social problem. Acting on behalf of others can mean supporting clients in their social functioning, advocating for individuals and groups who cannot act on their own behalf, providing substitutive services that clients are unable to provide for themselves or their families, planning and developing programs, developing and implementing social policy, and conducting research that informs social work practice. Agencies are often created in response to state or federal legislation with the intent to implement social policies designed to address identified social problems. It is important to understand much about your agency in order to work effectively within it.

Most social workers are employed by human services agencies that fall into two broad categories: private nonprofit agencies and public agencies. *Public agencies* are created by a legislative body made up of elected officials (e.g., a state legislature, the U.S. Congress, or county commissioners) and funded by tax dollars. The goals of public agencies are described in legal codes and government regulations. Elected officials are ultimately responsible for the operation of public agencies and staff members of public agencies are considered government employees.

Private nonprofit agencies (also called *voluntary agencies*) are created by a legal process known as incorporation, which has the effect of creating a legal entity known as a *nonprofit corporation*. These corporations are given nonprofit status under section 501(c)3 of the Internal Revenue Service guidelines for charitable and nonprofit organizations. This type of agency is governed by a board of directors whose basic responsibilities are to establish the agency's mission and direction, set policies for its operation, approve budgets, ensure adequate funds for the agency, maintain a communication link with the wider community, and hire and regularly evaluate the executive director. The basic responsibilities of an agency's *executive director* are to implement the policies set by the governing board, hire staff and regularly evaluate their performance, make programmatic decisions, and direct and monitor day-to-day operations.

A subcategory of private nonprofit agencies is the **sectarian** or **faith-based agency**, which means an agency affiliated with or operated by a religious organization (e.g., Jewish Community Services or Catholic Social Services). The term **membership agency** is used to describe an agency (e.g., YWCA) that derives some of its budget from membership fees and in which members are involved in setting policy.

In contrast to a public agency or a private nonprofit agency, a **for-profit agency** is a business corporation that sells a set of services and is designed and operated to yield a profit for investors and stockholders. Increasingly, nonprofit hospitals, treatment centers, and nursing homes are being purchased by large corporations and operated as for-profit organizations.

Many social workers are employed in **host settings** in which the organization's primary mission or purpose is something other than the delivery of social services. Examples include schools and hospitals where the primary missions are the provision of educational and medical services. In these host settings, the social worker must work with many other professionals (e.g., doctors, nurses, physical therapists, teachers, or school psychologists) and may be under the supervision of someone who has only a limited understanding of social work and possibly holds professional values somewhat different from those of a social worker.

Private nonprofit agencies are funded by private contributions, by grants and contracts, and sometimes by fees charged for the services they provide. Some conduct their own fund-raising activities and some receive funds from the local united giving organization. Private agencies may receive tax dollars indirectly through contracts with public agencies. Both public and private agencies may establish **advisory boards** that provide advice and guidance to the executive director or to the formal **board of directors**. As suggested by its name, an advisory board does not have the authority to make final decisions or set policy. It simply serves in an advisory capacity. An advisory board often has members who are agency clients and therefore is intended to solicit client input and perspective on agency policies and services.

Research-Based Practice

Practice Behavior Example: Social workers use research evidence to inform practice.

Critical Thinking Question: What empirical evidence is there to support the theoretical approach of your agency?

A typical social agency is designed and structured to provide one or more **social programs**. A social program is an organized and planned activity designed to accomplish one of the following:

- **Prevention of a social problem** (i.e., prevent a problem from developing, such as programs working to reduce child abuse or racism)
- **Enhancement of social functioning** (i.e., improve functioning when no significant problem exists, such as programs which provide parent training or respite care)
- **Remediation of an existing problem** (i.e., address an existing problem such as child abuse, unemployment, or delinquency)

Social agencies operate on an integration of beliefs, data, objectives, approaches and anticipated outcomes. They actually have **practice hypotheses** about how their services and programs will address social problems and what sort of outcomes they expect. They also identify expected **outcomes,** which can be short-term results, longer-term changes, and even accumulated outcomes at the community level. Such hypotheses can be at all levels of practice, such as the examples given in Table 8.1.

Table 8.1   Practice Hypotheses at Micro, Mezzo, and Macro Levels

Level of Practice	Sample Hypotheses
Micro Level Practice	
• Practice with individuals	• Child neglect can be reduced by targeting and serving teen parents.
• Practice with families	• Elder abuse can be prevented through caregiver support, respite, empowerment of older adults, and family therapy.
Mezzo Level Practice	
• Practice with groups	• Mutual aid groups can help members deal effectively with addictions by providing peer support and understanding.
• Practice with organizations	• Program improvement is the result of environmental scanning, use of best practices, and evaluation of services.
Macro level Practice	
• Practice with communities	• Community organization must be driven by the perspectives and motivations of citizens involved in the social issue being addressed.
• Practice with social policy	• Social policy development is impacted through collaborative efforts between advocacy groups and those most impacted by such policies.

Social agencies also fall into several categories based on the nature of their mission, purpose, and strategy. They tend to use one or more broad ***strategies*** to achieve their purposes:

- ***Socialization:*** assisting and encouraging people to understand, learn, and abide by the norms of society
- ***Social integration:*** encouraging and helping people to interact more effectively with other individuals and with the social systems or resources they need in order to function effectively and cope with special problems
- ***Social control:*** monitoring and restricting those who exhibit self-destructive or dangerous behavior
- ***Social change:*** expanding the number and types of life-enhancing opportunities available to people, taking actions that will improve the environment in which people must function, and taking actions necessary to reduce or eliminate negative and destructive forces in their social environment

An agency's ***budget*** describes anticipated income and expenses for a given period of time, usually one or two years. Agency budgets are influenced by many

Policy Practice

Practice Behavior Example: Social workers analyze, formulate, and advocate for policies that advance social well-being.

Critical Thinking Question: What legislation and social policies shape or dictate the work of your agency?

factors, including public attitudes, political changes, and shifts in funding priorities. It is important to understand that the donations, grants, and legislative allocations received by an agency typically have many "strings attached." In other words, the money is given or allocated to the agency for a specified purpose and cannot be spent for other purposes. In addition, the agency's acceptance of money from a certain source (e.g., United Way or a federal agency) may require that it adhere to certain rules, regulations, accounting, and auditing procedures that add administrative costs. When much of an agency's money is earmarked for very specific purposes, the agency has limited capacity to modify its programs and little flexibility in responding to emergencies or unanticipated expenses.

Many human services agencies are quite **bureaucratic,** especially public agencies. Bureaucracies are characterized by the following:

- A clear **chain of command** in communication and assigned authority
- An **organizational structure** consisting of a vertical hierarchy with numerous units, each of which has a designated leader responsible for that unit's operation and who has authority over those working in the unit
- A set of **written rules, policies, and guidelines** that outline procedures to be followed in performing work
- Clear **eligibility guidelines** that regulate the provision of services
- **Standardized policies and programs** geared toward equal treatment among clients
- **Division of labor** which gives, each employee a specific job to perform with an accompanying job description
- **Centralization** of power and communication channels
- **Supervision** of each employee's work
- An emphasis on **formal communication**, written documentation, and recordkeeping
- A higher level of **job security** than that which exists in a business or in nonprofit organizations

Some agencies have developed less bureaucratic structures in an effort to be more responsive to clients and to their ever-changing environments. They often use feminist, partnership, and empowerment principles; seek to involve their clients in the work of the agency; promote shared power and decision making at all levels; develop flexible guidelines and approaches; and strive to individualize and customize their interventions and services. As a general rule, these agencies are more flexible and provide a less stressful environment for the social workers working for them. Agencies that operate on these principles often are private, smaller organizations that do not need the structure of bureaucracy in order to be efficient or to provide equal services to all clients.

Be alert to the fact that all organizations have both a formal and an informal structure. The **formal** or **official structure** of an agency is described by organizational charts, policy and procedure manuals, and documents that explain the structure and function of various organizational units and the official chain of command. The term **informal structure**, sometimes referred to as the **shadow structure,** refers to various networks of employees and unofficial channels of communication that operate through unwritten but universally understood rules. This informal structure is sometimes cynically described by staff as "the way the agency really works." It becomes apparent only after working in the agency for an extended period of time.

An agency's informal structure is that framework or set of guidelines that allow for some flexibility and individualization of services for clients and that recognize the need to adapt services for diverse clients. This informal structure allows for staff members to give input through informal channels when needed and adapts decision-making procedures as needed. It includes frank behind-the-scenes discussions among staff members that are not shared with the public. Informal structure may also be used to describe the influence of key staff members who may not possess official power, but are listened to and looked to for guidance and wisdom.

Organizational climate and ***organizational culture*** are other terms used to describe the way that organizations function. Organizational climate refers to the "tone" of the agency, and includes relationships, level of teamwork, morale, communication, and the level of mutual support among employees. Organizational culture refers to the values of the agency that impact the programs and are the underpinnings of the services provided.

GUIDANCE AND DIRECTION

Your practicum agency will be a learning laboratory in which you will develop professional social work skills, observe other social workers providing services, and learn how agencies are organized and structured to address social needs and problems. You will begin to understand how organizations are administered and managed, learn about the common problems of organizations, and see how to work effectively with others within an organizational context.

Learn about your agency's history, why and when it began, and how it has evolved over time. Inquire about how your agency may have modified its original mission, changed its structure, and adapted to a shifting community and political context. This will help you understand how agencies survive within an ever-evolving environment and continually adjust and adapt their efforts to address the changing social problems and needs on which they focus.

Ask your field instructor about external forces that shape or limit your agency, such as funding priorities and sources, community attitudes, client feedback, regulatory bodies, political pressure, and research findings. Ask how much influence internal forces such as staff suggestions, changes in personnel, and staff morale have on the agency and its programs.

Agencies are always changing. Notice how shifts, increases, or cuts in funding cause changes in the services that can be provided. Observe how public attitudes and political forces shape the ways in which your agency functions. Your agency may go through some significant changes during your practicum. It may even experience a crisis in funding, be negatively evaluated, or be required to change significant portions of its program because of financial or political forces. You may even observe the birth of a new agency, or perhaps the dismantling of one that has lost its support or outlived its usefulness. You will learn about the dynamic nature of human services organizations if you closely observe the functioning of your own agency and that of others in the community.

Your agency will use one or more specific ***perspectives, practice theories, models,*** or **approaches** in the design and provision of its services

Human Rights and Justice

Practice Behavior Example: Social workers advocate for human rights and social and economic justice.

Critical Thinking Question: What human rights does your agency commit to, and what social justice issues does it address?

Diversity in Practice

Practice Behavior Example: Social workers recognize and communicate their understanding of the importance of difference in shaping life experiences.

Critical Thinking Question: What groups of clients might feel positively or negatively about your agency and why?

and programs. Determine what they are and why they were chosen. For example, does your agency use the strengths, ecological, or diversity perspective? Does it operate on social systems theory? Does your agency use a family systems or family preservation approach to intervention? Does your agency invest its resources in prevention, early intervention, or rehabilitation? Is the approach therapeutic or correctional? Does your agency hire generalist social workers or those with specializations in certain fields of practice? Does your agency see itself as working toward social change and social justice? Does your agency provide holistic services or does it specialize? Review courses you have taken and books you have read to help you understand why a particular approach was chosen by your agency to address the problem or concern identified. Consider what other theoretical approaches might also be used.

Become familiar with your ***agency's methods of evaluating its programs and services.*** Find out how your agency assesses its effectiveness, determines whether it is reaching its goals, measures client or community satisfaction, and decides whether it is making a difference. Your agency may use formal or informal methods of evaluation, process or outcome measures, and collect quantitative or qualitative data. Ask your field instructor whether he or she thinks these approaches or evaluation tools are valid and adequate. Ask what methods he or she would ideally recommend using to evaluate services provided enough time and money were available.

Agencies regularly reexamine their effectiveness, review their mission and goals, adjust their objectives, and engage in ***strategic planning*** for the future. This is done to maintain focus on the mission and vision of the organization, shift priorities in light of changing political climates or financial resources, and continuously search for better ways to serve those to whom they are committed. If you have the opportunity to become involved in such efforts, count yourself lucky to participate in an agency's work to redefine itself or improve its services.

Agencies may do this work through staff retreats where they review history and mission, and identify new ways to meet their goals. They engage in strategic planning, identify strengths and weaknesses, as well as clarify opportunities and threats. Agencies that are most effective are those that stay current, adjust priorities as needed, build on past success, measure their effectiveness, and look to the future. Watch for these qualities in your organization.

It is vital to understand how your agency is perceived by its clients, including their view of your agency's openness, effectiveness, and ability to address their needs. Observe the ways in which your agency works to maintain links to clients, opens itself to client feedback, and works in partnership with client groups, especially diverse populations. In the end, clients are best served by ***learning organizations*** that continue to value their input and continually work to improve services. Consider the portrayal of the potential positive and negative impact of organizations on clients in Table 8.2.

Table 8.2   **Impact of Organization on Clients and Client Systems**

Dimension of Organization	Potential Positive Impact	Potential Negative Impact
Mission Fidelity	Fidelity to mission enhances commitment to clients.	Diverging from mission reduces commitment to clients.
Value Base	Values promote self-determination, dignity, and self-worth of clients.	Values undermine self-determination, dignity, and self-worth of clients.
Staffing	Adequate, trained staff members ensure quality services.	Understaffing and lack of training reduce quality of services.
Funding	Adequate funding supports ongoing quality and stability of services.	Inadequate funding undermines quality and continuity of services.
Nonprofit or Profit Status	Nonprofit status focuses on service provision.	Profit status focuses on service provision and profit.
Sponsorship	Public or private auspices direct or guide programs.	Public or private auspices limit or prohibit services.
Quality of Services	Effective evidence-based services support clients and result in positive outcomes.	Ineffective services may hurt clients or result in negative outcomes.
Flexibility	Flexibility allows for individualization of services.	Flexibility can reduce standardization and equality of services.
Equality	Equal treatment promotes equal protection and access to services.	Equal treatment discourages individualization and professional discretion.
Eligibility Criteria	Reasonable and clear criteria promote fair access.	Restrictive and unclear criteria promote unfair access.
Level of Bureaucracy	Controlled bureaucracy insures standardization and efficiency.	Excess bureaucracy reduces flexibility and humanistic approach.
Evaluation of Programs and Services	Commitment to effective evaluation promotes evaluation and improvement in services.	Lack of commitment to evaluation lowers quality of services and improvement in programs.
Cultural Competence	Sensitivity and competence increases effectiveness with diverse clients.	Insensitivity and incompetence reduces effectiveness with diverse clients.
Leadership	Skilled and creative leaders promote growing organization to address changing needs.	Ineffective and stagnant leaders reduce effectiveness in addressing changing needs.

Agencies which grow, thrive, sustain themselves, and provide measurably effective programs and services must work hard to achieve these outcomes. Effective organizations, their leaders, and their staff members must continually work in coordination with entities outside the agency boundaries, accurately assess the multiple contexts of agency practice, and see themselves as part of a much larger social system made up of interacting parts. This is often referred to as *environmental scanning* and includes being knowledgeable about and able to incorporate an understanding of the following *contextual factors* into their work on behalf of those they serve. Consider the immense challenges that all agencies face in understanding all of these contextual factors and integrating them into their mission and operation of everyday activities.

- Current and projected *client needs*
- Current and projected *social problems*
- *Expectations* of clients, communities, funding sources, and other agencies
- *Values* of clients, communities, funding sources, and other agencies
- *Political economy* which impacts funding, program focus, and client need
- Social, cultural, and political *forces for change*
- Social, cultural, and political *forces for the status quo*
- Environmental *barriers* to service delivery
- Current and emerging *social policies*
- Current and emerging social work *research* on agency-related social problems
- Current and emerging *practice models*, including evidence-based practice
- Emerging *best practices* in agency's field of practice
- *Cultural changes* in the social environment
- Professional *standards* for practice
- External issues regarding *regulations*, *licensing, and accreditation*
- *Continuum of services* addressing social issues in the community

In order for agencies to be considered effective, growing, and in touch with social needs and the most appropriate ways to address those needs, they must become what are called *learning organizations.* A learning organization is one that adapts, continuously works to improve its approach and outcomes, customizes its work to client needs, and regularly redesigns itself as necessary. Again, this is no easy task, but necessary for organizations to remain relevant, stable, and sustainable. To that end, learning organizations must engage themselves in the following organizational tasks:

- *Scanning* of other learning organizations to learn from their successes
- Periodic *review of mission*, vision, goals, and objectives and revision as needed
- Commitment to remaining on the cutting edge of *emergent and evidence-based best practices*
- Development of *agency-specific best practices* based on program evaluation
- Development of *practice wisdom* that is integrated into policies and programs
- *Theory-building*, *innovation*, and creative approach to practice
- Identification and building upon *agency strengths*
- Identification and addressing of *agency gaps* in services
- Future orientation and *planning*

- Commitment to employee ***continuing education***, knowledge building, and skill development
- Adjusting ***staffing patterns*** and redesigning position requirements and duties
- Diversification of ***staff and administration***
- Periodic review of ***agency policies and procedures*** and revision as needed
- Inclusion of ***client input*** into program planning and evaluation
- ***Team building*** and empowering of employees to engage in program planning
- Engaging in ***sustainability activities*** to maintain and support agency
- Ongoing ***supervision and leadership*** development
- Commitment to continuous ***program quality improvement***

Finally, commit yourself to understanding your agency, work to integrate yourself into the organization in a productive way, observe and participate in as many agency activities as possible, learn about its inner workings, and imagine yourself as a supervisor or administrator. This process may help to consider the vital role of a social agency and all that is involved in keeping it effective and responsive to client needs at all levels of practice.

Agency Analysis: A Workbook Activity

1. Review the information presented in this chapter on types of social agencies. Which of the following types of agencies describe your practicum site?

   _____ Private Agency _____ Public Agency

   _____ Nonprofit Agency _____ For-profit Agency

   _____ Sectarian/Faith-Based Agency

   _____ Agency that works to prevent a social problem

   _____ Agency that works to enhance social functioning

   _____ Agency that works to remediate an existing problem

2. What practice theories and models are used in your agency? (See Chapter 16, Social Work as Planned Change).

   _____

   _____

3. What social problem(s) does your agency address?

   _____

   _____

4. What practice hypotheses does your agency use to design its programs?

   _____

   _____

5. How does your agency include client input into its programs and services?

_____

_____

6. What statistics are recorded on a regular basis by agency personnel (e.g., number of clients served each month, number of cases opened and closed, or characteristics of clients)? Are they included in a database for analysis and program development?

_____

_____

7. How does the agency determine if it is effective (e.g., in terms of recidivism rates, client completion of treatment plans, number of clients served, client satisfaction, goal attainment, pre- and post-tests, quality assurance, objectives achieved, or social change)?

_____

_____

8. What are the sources of funding for the agency? Has the level of funding increased or decreased in recent funding cycles? Is the funding adequate? How does the level of funding impact services and agency clients?

_____

_____

9. What political forces impact your agency, its operation, and its ability to meet its mission?

_____

_____

10. Is the agency meeting its mission? What evidence can be used to determine that? What suggestions do you have for improvement?

_____

_____

11. Ask your field instructor if your agency has faced any recent or historical crises, major changes, or threats to its existence.

_____

_____

12. If you were to start a social agency to address a social issue or problem about which you care deeply, what would it be and how would it address that issue or problem?

_____

_____

Suggested Learning Activities

- Attend meetings of the agency's board of directors or advisory board and consider how the topics discussed relate to the agency's mission, goals, programs, and funding.
- Find out how ordinary citizens or the general public view your agency. Speak with friends and acquaintances who know little about social work and ask what they know or have heard about your agency.
- Attend public meetings sponsored by United Way or other social welfare planning groups in order to better understand how your agency fits into the overall social welfare system.
- Accompany a client applying for services at another agency and identify attitudes reflected in how agency staff members treat clients and handle client requests.
- Visit other agencies that provide similar services to those of your agency and compare approaches and programs.
- In Sheafor and Horejsi (2012), read the sections titled "Preparing a Budget" (303–305), "The Process of Agency Planning" (245–247), and "Assessing Agency Structure" (220–221).

References

Austin, Michael J., Ralph P. Brody, and Thomas Packard. *Managing the Challenges in Human Services Organizations.* Thousand Oaks, CA: Sage Publishing, 2008.

Calley, Nancy. *Program Development in the 21st Century: An Evidence-Based Approach to Design, Implementation, and Evaluation.* Los Angeles: Sage Publications, 2011.

Cooperider, David, and Suresh Srivasta. *Appreciative Management and Leadership.* San Francisco: Jossey-Bass, 1999.

Coulshed, Veronica, Audrey Mullender, David N. Jones, and Neil Thompson. *Management in Social Work.* 3rd ed. New York: Palgrave Macmillan, 2006.

Dudley, James R. *Social Work Evaluation: Enhancing What We Do.* Chicago: Lyceum Books, 2009.

Hasenfeld, Yeheskil. *Human Services as Complex Organizations.* 2nd ed. Los Angeles: Sage Publications, 2010.

Kettner, Peter, Robert Moroney, and Lawrence Martin. *Designing and Managing Programs: An Effectiveness-Based Approach.* Los Angeles: Sage Publications, 2008.

Kirst-Ashman, Karen, and Grafton Hall. *Brooks/Cole Empowerment Series: Generalist Practice with Organizations and Communities.* 5th ed. Boston: Brooks/Cole, 2012.

Morales, Armando, Bradford Sheafor, and Malcolm Scott. *Social Work: A Profession of Many Faces.* 12th ed. Boston: Allyn and Bacon, 2010.

Moxley, David. *Beyond Oversight: Developing Grassroots Nonprofit Boards for Community and Institutional Change.* Washington, DC: NASW Press, 2011.

O'Connor, Mary Catherine, and F. Ellen Netting. *Organization Practice: A Guide to Understanding Human Services Organizations.* 2nd ed. Hoboken, NJ: John Wiley and Sons, 2009.

Rae, Ann, and Wanda Nicholas-Wolosuk. *Changing Agency Policy: An Incremental Approach.* Boston: Allyn and Bacon, 2003.

Sheafor, Bradford, and Charles Horejsi. *Techniques and Guidelines for Social Work Practice.* 9th ed. Boston: Allyn and Bacon, 2012.

Weinbach, Robert. *The Social Worker as Manager: A Practical Guide to Success.* 5th ed. Boston: Allyn and Bacon, 2008.

PRACTICE TEST

The following questions will test your knowledge of the content found within this chapter.

1. The nonprofit status of agencies known as 501(c)3 is a
   a. designation given by states
   b. designation given by the U.S. Internal Revenue Service
   c. designation given by United Way
   d. designation given by local city ordinances

2. An agency dealing with exploitation of elders is working toward what end?
   a. prevention of a social problem
   b. enhancement of social functioning
   c. social integration
   d. remediation of a social problem

3. The main advantage of a bureaucratic structure for an agency client is that
   a. services are standardized and equally provided
   b. there is a clear chain of command
   c. this structure reduces staff turnover
   d. each employee is well supervised by a superior

4. When there is a conflict between agency policy and state law,
   a. agency policy is binding
   b. state law is primary
   c. agency directors and state employees can negotiate an outcome
   d. the particular situation will dictate which is primary

5. A public agency is
   a. funded with grant money
   b. mandated or directed by state or federal legislation
   c. either nonprofit or for profit
   d. accountable to legislators

6. Public social agencies are required to be accountable to the taxpayers through
   a. client comments at public hearings
   b. statistical recordkeeping
   c. website postings
   d. evaluation of outcomes against mission, goals, and objectives

7. What practice hypotheses are used by your agency to design and implement its programs and services?

9

The Community Context of Practice

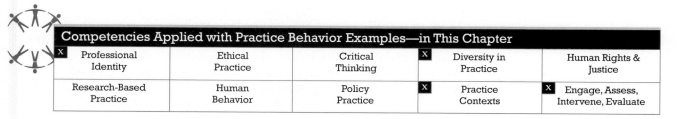

Competencies Applied with Practice Behavior Examples—in This Chapter				
X Professional Identity	Ethical Practice	Critical Thinking	X Diversity in Practice	Human Rights & Justice
Research-Based Practice	Human Behavior	Policy Practice	X Practice Contexts	X Engage, Assess, Intervene, Evaluate

CHAPTER PREVIEW

This chapter examines the role of the community context in enhancing or reducing the level of social functioning of individuals, families, and groups. It describes types of communities, includes the functions of a community, and discusses the use of power and influence within communities. Further, it describes the range of goals of community social work practice and their accompanying social work roles. Orienting/explanatory theories that inform community-level practice and practice theories/models used in community-level practice are shown as interrelated conceptual frameworks that can be used by practicum agencies.

The community is one of the most important contexts of social work practice as well as one of the most common targets of social work practice. It is in communities that relationships are forged, ***social functioning*** is enhanced, ***social capital*** is built, ***social assets*** are developed, attitudes are shaped, and ***socialization*** takes place. Community resources, assets, problems, and programs can either support or undermine the social functioning of its residents. Communities are dynamic systems that interact with the individuals, families, groups, and organizations within them as well as with the larger social systems which impact them, such as social policies, societal attitudes, and social movements. Because of the immense impact of communities on both clients and social agencies, it is vital to understand how communities work in order to strengthen them and help them develop the assets needed to meet the needs of residents through ***community development*** and ***community organization***.

BACKGROUND AND CONTEXT

Practicum agencies exist in and are influenced by the communities of which they are a part. Because of this, it is important to study the community in which your practicum agency is located. It is obvious that agencies do not exist in a vacuum. In fact, an agency mission, programs, and operation are often a reflection of the community's characteristics, such as its values, politics, history, and special problems. Most of your clients live and work in this community, so it is not possible to understand your clients without understanding their wider social environment and both the positive and negative conditions and forces within that environment. If you work within a direct services agency, the client assessments and intervention plans you develop must take into consideration your client's interactions with the community, as well as the resources available in it.

Practice Contexts

Practice Behavior Example: Social workers continuously discover, appraise, and attend to changing locales, populations, scientific and technological developments, and emerging societal trends to provide relevant services.

Critical Thinking Question: In what ways is your agency impacted by community factors and characteristics?

Your informal study of the community will allow you to begin to identify unmet human needs as well as the gaps in the service network that should be addressed in order to better serve the people of the community. By gathering information about community values, history, power structure, economic base, demographics, and decision-making processes, you will be able to identify those groups or individuals who have the power and influence to either facilitate needed social change or block harmful social change within the community.

The term ***community*** refers to a group of people brought together by physical proximity or by a common identity based on shared experiences, interests, or culture. There are two major types of communities: communities of interest and identification and communities of place or location. A ***community of interest and identification*** can be described as a group of individuals who share a sense of identity and belonging because they share a characteristic, interest, or life experience such as ethnicity, language, religion, sexual orientation, or occupation. The social work community, the business community, the gay community, the African American community, the Islamic community, the Catholic community, and the university community are examples of a community of interest and identification.

The second type of community, a ***community of place or location***, is defined mostly by geography and specified boundaries. Such communities include neighborhoods, suburbs, towns, and cities. The boundaries of a community of place might be a legal definition, a river, or a street. They may have formal or informal names such as Woodlawn, the South Bronx, Orange County, the Blackfeet Indian Reservation, the university area, the west side, and the warehouse district. People living in these areas or places may share some level of identification, but typically they are more diverse in terms of values, beliefs, and other characteristics than the people of a community of interest and identification. Also, it is common for the people within this type of community to be in conflict over a variety of issues. Living in proximity to others, in and of itself, does not create a social bond and a sense of belonging. In fact, for many of your clients, the community in which they live does not provide a sense of belonging and may even negatively impact their quality of life. Within a given community of place, there may be many different communities of interest and identification.

Learning about a community takes time and effort. However, you will find this to be an invaluable and interesting experience. You will become fascinated as you begin to observe and understand the interplay between the functioning of individuals and families and their neighborhood and community. If your practicum agency is concerned mostly with micro level practice, you will soon see how your clients' lives are either enriched or harmed by community factors. If your practicum is in an organization heavily involved in macro level practice, you will come to understand that every community has its own personality and profile, and that in order to deal effectively with social problems and bring about needed social change, you must understand and appreciate that uniqueness.

Social workers and social agencies must be knowledgeable about how power and influence are used in the community. ***Power*** is the ability to make others do what you want them to do, whereas ***influence*** is the capacity to increase the chances that others will do what you want. Successful efforts to develop a new agency program, pass a law, modify social policy, and bring about social change all depend on the skilled use of power and influence. By themselves, social workers may possess little power or influence. Thus, in order to promote social change, they must have access to and relationships with those individuals and organizations that have power and influence and are willing to use it on behalf of the social agency or its clients.

There are various forms of power and influence within the community context. It is important to remember that the movers and shakers of a community (i.e., those with real power and influence) are not

Critical Thinking

Practice Behavior Example: Social workers analyze models of assessment, prevention, intervention, and evaluation.

Critical Thinking Question: What have you learned in your academic career about communities that will help you in your role in community-level practice?

always the visible leaders. Many key decision makers work behind the scenes and hold no formal positions, but are capable of contributing greatly to social change. Those are the individuals with whom you will develop relationships in order to call attention to the issues you care about and to help you work toward social change. The following individuals are the influential people that social workers involved in community practice must engage with while undertaking effective and long-lasting community development and organization efforts: elected officials; those who control credit and loans; those who control the media and information; executive directors or corporations and owners of businesses; respected religious and moral leaders; recognized experts in their field; long-time, respected residents; natural leaders without formal power; leaders or advocacy organizations; and clients or citizens that are skilled in self-advocacy.

GUIDANCE AND DIRECTION

Understanding the community context of practice will help you see that people are all shaped in both positive and negative ways by their life experiences. They are supported or undermined, protected or put at risk, guided or controlled, served or stressed, and encouraged or discouraged by their interactions with the individuals, groups, and organizations that make up the communities in which they live. These interactions have a profound effect on social functioning and quality of life.

Be conscious of the fact that the clients or consumers served by a social agency are members of a particular community of place and probably members of several communities of interest and identification. You need to understand the meaning of these groups for clients and the ways in which they impact clients both positively and negatively. It is entirely possible that your clients may not perceive the community in which they live as supportive, accepting, and willing to include or support them. It is not uncommon for people experiencing stresses of life to view the community as uncaring, unresponsive, or culturally insensitive to them, even though the residents and social agencies in the community are desirous of helping.

If you have not been exposed to the negative aspects of community life as your clients may have been, acknowledge that your privileged position may make it difficult to understand your clients' views of the community. They may not have the option to live in a neighborhood of their choice or they may lack the social skills to engage productively with others to give and gain social support. Your clients may have had significant life experiences that have shaped their attitudes toward the community, as well as toward your practicum agency.

When working directly with clients, identify their social roles (e.g., spouse, parent, or employee) and then consider how specific community characteristics may make it easier or more difficult for them to fulfill those roles. As you examine the influence of a community on the social functioning of individuals and families, consider whether your client has the benefits and opportunities listed below which support social functioning or whether he or she lacks these benefits or perceives them as not available.

- Adequate **employment opportunities** to support himself or herself and a family
- Adequate, safe, and affordable **housing**
- **Safety** when at home and in the community and protected by law enforcement and environmental safety policies

- *Support and empowerment* by interactions with others in the community
- *Acceptance and equitable treatment* by others in the community
- Access to public *transportation, education and training*, and *affordable health care*
- *Political power* to influence conditions and policies which impact him or her

As social work students gain experience and carefully observe and participate in a given community, they often become aware of factors that are common to many communities. For example, be alert to the following community dynamics:

- All communities and neighborhoods have *social support networks and informal helpers*. However, special effort may be required to identify and access these resources for clients or social workers.
- There may be a degree of *overlap and duplication* in the functions and programs of various agencies in the community. Sometimes this duplication is unnecessary and wasteful, but in many cases the duplication is beneficial to clients and healthy for the total system of services.
- There may be "*turf" issues and conflicts* between agencies within a community, brought on in part by their competition for funding, the differences in how they define and explain problems, and what they consider to be their territory.
- An agency with the *support of powerful and influential individuals* can secure funding and gain recognition, even when its mission may be less important and worthy than that of other agencies in the community.
- *Negative community attitudes* toward a certain client group or a certain type of agency can be a major obstacle to developing and providing needed services to a particular group.
- Certain *groups are better organized* and better able to act as advocates for themselves than are others.
- Communities under *economic stress* are sometimes ripe for the development of social problems and may not be able to support their citizens in positive ways.

Research-Based Practice

Practice Behavior Example: Social workers use practice experience to inform scientific inquiry?

Critical Thinking Question: How can you use your practicum experience to formulate research and program evaluation questions?

Social workers involved in mezzo- and macrolevel practice need to understand the community because the focus of their work may be the community itself rather than individual clients. This level of practice sees the community itself as the client, the target, or the focus of action and service. When social workers engage in this level of practice, they must use their knowledge of community, their communication skills, their commitment to creating healthy communities, and their ability to partner with others to this important work. Innovative combinations of these skills will help to enhance social functioning of clients and client systems, which is truly the overall goal and purpose of social work.

The goals of community-level practice are many, and all are based on a belief that communities are central agents in positive and negative human development,

Professional Identity

Practice Behavior Example: Social workers use supervision and consultation.

Critical Thinking Question: How can you identify mentors in the community who will help you understand the role of community developers and organizers?

Table 9.1   **Goals of Community Social Work Practice**

Building Goals (ones that strengthen community assets)	Blocking Goals (ones that address community problems)
Support social functioning of individuals and families	Address problems that undermine or reduce social functioning of individuals and families
Identify and enhance community assets	Identify and address community problems and gaps
Build social capital	Address barriers to building social capital
Empower individuals and groups to identify, own, and reach goals	Address barriers to citizen and impacted group participation
Create community conditions that increase overall and specific community development	Address community problems that impede overall and specific community development
Engage in community organization efforts directed toward specific community problems	Address overall conditions responsible for community problems
Build coalitions, networks, and partnerships to effect community change	Reduce conflict, strain, and power differentials between groups
Create social change desired by community	Address barriers to social change efforts

and that their assets can enhance social functioning while their problems can negatively impact social functioning. **Building approaches** to community practice are those which identify and strengthen community assets based on the belief that building strong communities will result in the enhancement of social functioning. **Blocking approaches** to community practice are those which identify and address community problems and gaps based on the belief that reducing such community problems will also result in the enhancement of social functioning. The two approaches are not mutually exclusive and in fact are often used simultaneously by community practitioners. Goals of community social work practice are given in Table 9.1. A number of conceptual frameworks provide the underpinnings of community-based social work, including **orienting/explanatory theories** which attempt to explain and describe both the positive and negative development and functioning of individuals, families, groups, organizations, communities, and societies. They serve to orient social workers to what can be expected in terms of development, how clients and their social environments interact, how social problems emerge, and what influences development at all levels. Commonly used orienting/explanatory theories used to explain social phenomenon at the community level of practice include conflict theory, multicausal theory, political economy theory, social exchange theory, social learning theory, social movements theory, social systems theory, strain theory, structural theory, and subculture theory. Review each of these theories to determine their utility in understanding your community and its development.

Practice theories/models at the community level of practice are those which build on orienting/explanatory theories, are matched to client resources and needs, and fit with client values and perspectives. These theories are built into intervention plans, guide the implementation of the plan, and provide opportunities to evaluate effectiveness of interventions. Commonly used community practice theories/models include community development model, community organization model, community resilience model, harm reduction

Table 9.2 **Orienting Theories, Practice Theories/Models, and Social Work Roles for Community Practice**

Orienting Theories	Practice Theories/Models	Social Work Roles
• Conflict	• Community development	• Advocate
• Multicausal	• Community organization	• Broker
• Political economy	• Community resilience	• Community developer
• Social exchange	• Harm reduction	• Community organizer
• Social learning	• Social change	• Facilitator
• Social movements	• Social development	• Mediator
• Social systems	• Social justice	• Networker
• Strain	• Social planning	• Policy analyst/developer
• Structural	• Social policy	• Researcher
• Subculture	• Structural	• Social planner

model, social change model, social development model, social justice model, social planning model, social policy development model, and structural model.

Social work roles played at the community level are both similar to and distinct from those social work roles played at the micro level of practice, and are listed in the third column of Table 9.2. Review each of these orienting/ explanatory theories, practice theories/models, and social work roles, making sure that you understand the meaning of each, how they can be combined to effectively bring about community change, and what skills and practice behaviors are needed to actually implement interventions.

Watch for opportunities to engage in community practice. You may have the chance to participate in such efforts as grant writing, community development, self-advocacy efforts by community groups, and interagency collaborations. Reread the portions of your textbooks that refer to the roots of the social work profession, and you will be reminded of the historical focus on community development as a way to enhance social functioning and the interplay between individual well-being and the health of communities.

Developing Community Practice Skills: A Workbook Activity

The following questions and reflection activities are designed to help you understand your community and its effects on your agency and its clients.

1. What geographical area is served by your agency?

_____

_____

2. What are the names of the communities, neighborhoods, or areas served by your agency?

_____

_____

3. Describe the demographic characteristics of the community in terms of:

Population

_____

Population density

_____

_____

Percentage of population by age groups

_____

Children _____ Adolescents _____ Older adults _____

Education level of groups by age, income, ethnic group

_____

_____

Median income of groups by age, gender, ethnic group

_____

_____

Percentage of population living under the poverty line

_____

_____

Percentage of population on public assistance

_____

_____

Cost of housing, utilities, transportation, child care

_____

_____

_____

Percentage of ethnic groups

_____

_____

4. What is considered a living wage in your community for an individual and family?

_____

_____

5. How do these data on income compare with state and national averages?

_____

_____

6. What problems (e.g., crime, pollution, lack of affordable housing, poverty, corruption, violence, poor roads, high taxes) does the community have?

_____

_____

7. Of what is the community especially proud (e.g., physical beauty, history, climate, schools, sports teams, community spirit)?

_____

_____

8. Does your community have a United Way or another combined fund-raising program that raises money for numerous human service agencies? By what process does this fund-raising organization decide which agencies it will support? Does your agency receive such funding?

_____

_____

9. What significant gaps exist in the array of human services and programs within the community? Why do they exist?

_____

_____

_____

10. Do "turf" conflicts and competitions exist between human services agencies within the community? If so, how do they affect your clients?

_____

_____

11. In what ways is (or could) your agency engage in community development or community organization?

_____

_____

12. What goals and purposes of community-based practice illustrated in Table 9.1 does your agency have?

_____

13. What theories of orientation/explanation illustrated in Table 9.2 does your agency use to understand the social issues and problems faced by your client base?

_____

14. What practice theories/models discussed in Table 9.2 does your agency use to guide its interventions at the community level of practice?

_____

15. What social work roles illustrated in Table 9.2 do social workers in your agency play as they engage in the community level of practice?

___

16. In the opinion of experienced human services professionals and experts of the community, such as your field instructor, how adequate are the following community elements?

Housing	Good_____	Adequate_____	Inadequate_____
Schools	Good_____	Adequate_____	Inadequate_____
Police and fire protection	Good_____	Adequate_____	Inadequate_____
Recreational programs	Good_____	Adequate_____	Inadequate_____
Public transportation	Good_____	Adequate_____	Inadequate_____
Health care and hospitals	Good_____	Adequate_____	Inadequate_____
Mental health services	Good_____	Adequate_____	Inadequate_____
Day-care centers for children	Good_____	Adequate_____	Inadequate_____
Family support programs	Good_____	Adequate_____	Inadequate_____
Programs for troubled youth	Good_____	Adequate_____	Inadequate_____
Addiction treatment	Good_____	Adequate_____	Inadequate_____
Programs for persons with disabilities	Good_____	Adequate_____	Inadequate_____
Programs for the elderly	Good_____	Adequate_____	Inadequate_____

Suggested Learning Activities

- Participate in interagency committees or task groups that are made up of representatives of various community organizations.
- Read grant proposals and reports written by your agency to see how it claims to meet community needs.
- Locate and study community resource directories and historical materials to help deepen your understanding of a particular social problem addressed by your agency.
- Use the Internet to examine census data related to the area served by your agency. The home page for the U.S. Census Bureau is www.census.gov. Once there, click on Access Tools, then on American FactFinder.
- Attend meetings of support groups whose goals are related to the problems addressed by your agency.
- In Sheafor and Horejsi (2012), read the sections titled "Learning about Your Community" (168–170) and "Community Decision-Making Analysis" (222–224).

References

DiNitto, Diane, and Aaron McNeece. *Social Work Issues and Opportunities in a Challenging Profession.* 3rd ed. Chicago: Lyceum Books, 2008.

Hardcastle, David, Stanley Wenocur, and Patricia Powers. *Community Practice: Theories and Skills for Social Workers.* 3rd ed. New York: Oxford University Press, 2011.

Hardina, Donna. *Analytical Skills for Community Organization and Practice.* New York: Columbia University Press, 2002.

Homan, Mark. *Promoting Community Change.* 5th ed. Pacific Grove, CA: Brooks/Cole, 2011.

Lohmann, Nancy. *Rural Social Work Practice.* New York: Columbia University Press, 2005.

Netting, F. Ellen. *Social Work Macro Practice.* 5th ed. Boston: Allyn and Bacon, 2012.

Rothman, Jack, and John Ehrlich, eds. *Strategies of Community Interventions.* 7th ed. Peosta, IA: Eddie Bowers Publishing, 2008.

Rubin, Herbert J., and Irene S. Rubin. *Community Organizing and Development.* 4th ed. Boston: Allyn and Bacon, 2008.

Sheafor, Bradford, and Charles Horejsi. *Techniques and Guidelines in Social Work Practice.* 7th ed. Boston: Allyn and Bacon, 2006.

Sheafor, Bradford, and Charles Horejsi. *Techniques and Guidelines for Social Work Practice.* 9th ed. Boston: Allyn and Bacon, 2012.

Twelvetrees, Alan. *Community Work.* 4th ed. New York: Palgrave MacMillan, 2008.

Weil, Maria. *The Handbook of Community Practice.* 2nd ed. Thousand Oaks, CA: Sage Publications, 2012.

CHAPTER 9 REVIEW

PRACTICE TEST

The following questions will test your knowledge of the content found within this chapter.

1. A community of place or location refers to
   a. a geographic community
   b. the community in which a social agency is located
   c. a community of identification
   d. a neighborhood

2. A community of interest or identification refers to
   a. a voluntary group with shared interests or common characteristics
   b. a geographic community
   c. a kinship system
   d. the focus of an intervention

3. If a community is not able to support the social functioning of its citizens,
   a. it would qualify for federal funding
   b. social workers need to utilize family supports instead
   c. agencies are likely to be underfunded
   d. the community itself could be the target of intervention

4. The difference between formal power and social influence in a community
   a. is minimal and unlikely to impact decisions
   b. is important because those who can support social change may not be those who have formal power
   c. is a legal one that divides power among leaders
   d. is irrelevant

5. Social capital is based on relationships and interactions in a community, and
   a. is the same as informal networks
   b. works to organize communities
   c. consists of the collaboration and trust within a community upon which an intervention can be built
   d. refers to mutual aid groups

6. Community asset mapping
   a. refers to the grids of transportation systems in a community
   b. is required by United Way
   c. refers to community focus groups
   d. is often done in conjunction with community needs assessments

7. What practice theories/models are used by social workers at the community level of practice? What practice roles are required to implement these models?

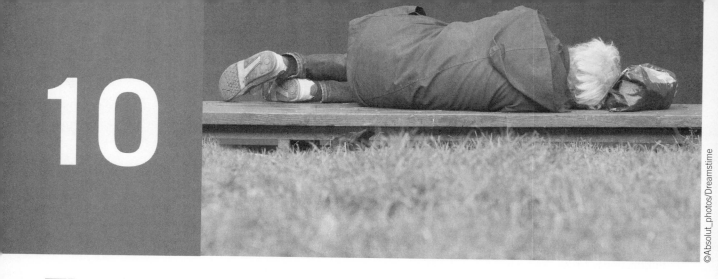

10

The Social Problem Context of Practice

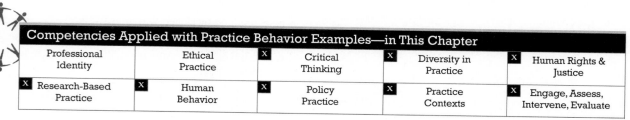

Competencies Applied with Practice Behavior Examples—in This Chapter									
	Professional Identity		Ethical Practice	X	Critical Thinking	X	Diversity in Practice	X	Human Rights & Justice
X	Research-Based Practice	X	Human Behavior	X	Policy Practice	X	Practice Contexts	X	Engage, Assess, Intervene, Evaluate

CHAPTER PREVIEW

This chapter defines the terms social condition, social stressor, social problem, social policy, social problem clusters, and social well-being clusters. Information is provided on the varied perspectives on and approaches to social problems as well as the relationship between social conditions, social stressors, and social problems. It also proposes a variety of social work roles in dealing with social problems. Guidelines for understanding social problems and their impact on social functioning are provided.

Most of the agencies and organizations that employ social workers were created in response to specific social problems or needs as perceived and understood by elected officials (in the case of public agencies), by powerful and committed community leaders (in the case of private nonprofit agencies), or by investors (in the case of for-profit organizations). In order for you to understand your agency's purpose, policies, and operation, it is important to carefully examine the social problems or conditions on which it focuses its attention and resources.

BACKGROUND AND CONTEXT

The definition and conceptualization of a **social problem** is a complex process that is shaped by historical, political, and cultural forces as well as by existing scientific knowledge. There can be intense disagreement over whether a particular condition is to be defined as a problem. Even when there is agreement that a problem exists, there can be much debate over its cause, its severity, and what can and should be done about it. There can also be great disagreement over whether those experiencing a social problem are to be blamed or held accountable for their situation or are to be supported by others as they attempt to cope with or change their situation.

For example, one segment of society may view the situation of child abuse as the failure of an individual parent to treat his or her child well and not consider the impact of a history of child abuse, family stress, and financial insecurity as contributors to inadequate parenting. Homelessness may be viewed as the responsibility of the individual by some, whereas others may see this problem as related to low wages, high cost of living, lack of health insurance, and an inadequate safety net during financially stressful times.

Ethical Practice

Practice Behavior Example: Social workers tolerate ambiguity in resolving ethical conflicts.

Critical Thinking Question: Will you be able to tolerate differences in ethical views of the work your agency does?

How a problem is defined and the predominant beliefs about its causation have a profound effect on the formulation of social policies and the design of social programs that are intended to address the problem. Moreover, as an understanding of the problem changes, agencies must modify their guiding principles and adapt their services and interventions to these new interpretations.

A **social condition** is a factual reality that can be observed and measured. Examples include the fact that many marriages in the United States end in divorce, a large percentage of the homeless population is families, in some communities a majority of students do not graduate, and that a growing number of college graduates are not able to secure a job after completing their education.

These are facts, but are they actually social problems? If yes, why? Who decides that a particular condition is a problem? When does a social problem require action by the community or government? Whose values, norms, and beliefs are to be used in forming a judgment?

A ***social stressor*** is an event, series of events, or crisis experienced by a vulnerable individual, family, group, or community that moves the social condition to the status of a social problem. Given enough social stressors without sufficient resources, assets, or resiliency factors, the individual, family, group, or community finds itself dealing with all of the impacts of a true social problem, and may be in need of informal and formal services.

A ***social problem*** can be defined as a social condition that negatively impacts individuals or communities, and as a situation in which the welfare, values, and well-being of at least a portion of society may be threatened. A social problem is considered as such because many people believe that its existence is wrong, harmful, or immoral. Others may define a social problem as a violation of human rights or a social or economic injustice. Some people may view a given condition as a problem that violates the values they hold dear and demands collective action and an investment of resources. Others presume that it is simply an acceptable part of life that requires no special response. A condition becomes a problem when it threatens the values, the sense of morality, the security, or safety of those in a community or a society who have the power and influence to bring forth collective action and, eventually, the new policies, programs, and agencies that will address this problem. Such action may be at the community or governmental level.

Human Rights and Justice

Practice Behavior Example: Social workers understand the forms and mechanisms of oppression and discrimination.

Critical Thinking Question: What are the social injustices addressed by your agency?

Figure 10.1 illustrates the way in which social stressors impact a family at risk because of surrounding social conditions, moving them to the status of a family experiencing a social problem.

Social problem clusters often develop, which means that social problems tend to be associated with each other in complex ways, sometimes in terms of causation or increased vulnerability. The stressed social environment in which these social problems are experienced at the micro, mezzo, and macro levels attempts to shift and address these problems, sometimes successfully and sometimes not. In contrast, ***social well-being clusters*** may emerge when the social environment has the ability to learn, cope, and adjust to the social problems experienced. Table 10.1 illustrates both ***social problem clusters*** and ***social well-being clusters*** in response to the social problem of poverty and homelessness at the micro, mezzo, and macro levels of practice. The table demonstrates how social problems cluster negatively together at all levels of practice, resulting in compromised functioning. It also demonstrates how social well-being factors cluster together positively at all levels of practice, resulting in enhanced functioning. Social problem clusters can be targeted for reduction or elimination, and social well-being clusters can be targeted for enhancement.

When powerful and influential individuals and groups come to view a social phenomenon or condition as a problem and a threat to what they value, they must decide what social policies and actions are needed to solve this problem or lessen its negative impact. There may be several competing theories of causation, each of which purports to explain why the problem exists and what can and should be done about it. Many different solutions or actions may be proposed. Each will rest on a particular set of assumptions, values, and

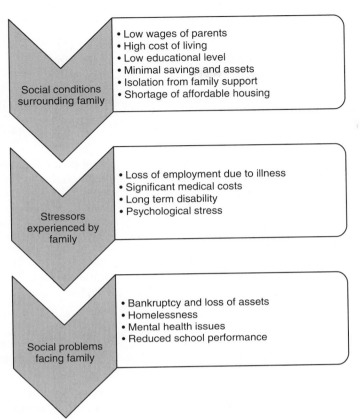

Figure 10.1
Relationship of Social Conditions, Social Stressors, and Social Problems

---

Table 10.1 | **Clustering of Social Problems and Social Well-Being: Examples at Micro, Mezzo, and Macro Levels**

Social Problem Clusters	*Micro Level (Family)*	*Mezzo Level (Organization)*	*Macro Level (Social policy)*
Experience of one social problem increases vulnerability to others ↓	Poverty results in homelessness ↓	Increase in homelessness raises demand for agency services ↓	Increase in homelessness creates competition for funding ↓
Problems overwhelm resources, resiliency, and assets ↓	Stressors lead distressed family to dysfunction and instability ↓	Increased demand overwhelms agency resources ↓	Social policy and programs unable to meet demand ↓
Lowering of hope, self-efficacy, and coping skills ↓	Individuals and families lose hope in themselves and social systems ↓	Agency lowers expectations for addressing problems and meeting mission ↓	Administrators and policy makers lower expectations for social policy ↓

(*continued*)

Table 10.1　　**Continued**

Social Problem Clusters	Micro Level (Family)	Mezzo Level (Organization)	Macro Level (Social policy)
Increase in number and severity of social problems ↓	Deeper poverty, health and mental health problems, unemployability ↓	Compromised services impact quality of outcomes and effectiveness ↓	Inability of social policy to address problems increases other problems ↓
Experience of social problem prepares social system to deal with more problems ↓	Poverty leads to pursuit of education, realignment of priorities ↓	Strategic planning and future planning prepare agency to respond to need ↓	Social policy designed for adaptation to increased need ↓
Resources, resiliency, and assets sufficient to address additional social problems ↓	Stressors lead distressed family to use and develop resources ↓	Agency stability and contingency plans help agency succeed ↓	Social planning and budgeting allow for additional resource allocation ↓
Maintenance of hope, self-efficacy, and coping skills ↓	Small successes result in maintenance and strengthening of personal skills ↓	Agency learns from challenge and adjusts according to need ↓	Policy makers use experience to plan for future social problems and needs ↓
Maintenance of social well-being in face of social problems	Individuals and family remain intact and use experience to stabilize well-being	Agency remains viable and responsive	Policy effectiveness leads to continued support

beliefs about the cause of the problem and what interventions are necessary, feasible, and effective. There are likely to be various views of what is a viable and desirable solution, as well as how to measure outcomes and success. There will be critiques of historical and contemporary approaches based on the reluctance to raise taxes to fund additional programs, a view of social programs and policies as approaches that create dependency, a belief that root causes rather than symptoms need to be addressed, and that solutions are the responsibility of individuals and families rather than the community or society.

Those in ***decision-making positions*** may sponsor research into the causes of the problem and seek the advice of experts, but in the final analysis, the decisions about the nature and cause of the problem will be heavily political and will reflect the views and preferences of those who have power and influence. That is why social workers must become competent in the political and social policy arena if they are to effect change in the social policies that impact their clients. This, of course, requires that social workers can also understand the complex etiology of social problems, articulate this understanding to decision and policy makers, persuade those with power and influence to collaborate in addressing the social problem, and assume leadership in influencing program development and social policy formation to effectively address the social problems.

The decisions made concerning which actions should be taken to address a social problem eventually give rise to specific ***social policies***. Social policies, described in detail in Chapter 11 (The Social Policy Context of Practice), are the federal, state, and local laws; statutes; and ordinances enacted to address social problems. Social policies can mandate services to be provided, enable organizations to provide services, fund programs, create unfunded mandates, set priorities for social programs, or set standards for types and quality of services to be provided. Many of the social agencies that serve as social work practicum settings have the responsibility of carrying out these social policies and designing specific programs and interventions to solve the problem. The specific actions by agency employees can be viewed as their **practices**.

GUIDANCE AND DIRECTION

In any community or society, there is great variety in the perspectives of its members as they try to understand and explain the social problems they observe and experience. These different viewpoints will be based on personal experiences, attitudes, values, information, misinformation, and even stereotypes. You may think that some of these perspectives are uninformed or biased, but it is important to realize that the beliefs make sense and seem valid to those who hold them. Not everyone agrees that a social condition is a social problem, and not everyone agrees on the causes of social problems. Further, there is much disagreement on what social policies should be put in place to address social policies.

Although this can be confusing and may make it hard to know how to begin addressing social problems, it may be helpful to ask yourself the following questions in order to gain a broad perspective on a social problem that concerns you and that your agency addresses:

- What is the actual **social condition** that you are concerned about?
- How is it **described** by those who observe it? What **definitions** are used by those individuals or groups?
- Who considers it to be a **social problem** and who does not?
- How do groups with **different viewpoints** frame their perspectives?
- What is the **scope and scale** of the condition? Is it worsening? How does it compare to the same condition in other geographic areas?
- What **societal values** about human existence are potentially threatened by the social condition?
- What are some of the **proposed theories of causation** of this social condition?
- How do these **theories of causation** impact the development of social policies to address this condition?

Research-Based Practice

Practice Behavior Example: Social workers use research evidence to inform practice.

Critical Thinking Question: What empirical evidence is there to support the ways in which your agency approaches social problems?

The contrasting viewpoints and the political debate that arises from them will sometimes result in social policy that you support and, at other times, in social policy that you see as ineffective or harmful. Remember that the democratic political process is influenced by public attitudes, values, information, and power. In order to influence the process, you will need to venture into the process of politics and use your skills to advocate for social policies that benefit those you serve. This will rarely be easy because of the strongly held beliefs of everyone involved in the issue and because those negatively impacted by existing social problems or policies may not have access to power.

As our society becomes more **diverse and pluralistic**, there will be even more diversity in how people think about social conditions and social problems. Strive to understand perspectives that are different from your own and think about how these perspectives lead to definitions and potentially different solutions. Expect increasing numbers of lively discussions, heated debates, conflicts, and sometimes stalemates between groups with very different views about what constitutes social problems and what ought to be done about them. If you wish to address social problems at the community or societal level, you will need to contribute reason, reliable data, and political influence to this debate.

To a large extent, your understanding of social conditions and social problems will be rooted in your **liberal arts background**, including course work in sociology, psychology, economics, political science, anthropology, and history. You may also have had personal experiences that deepen your understanding of certain problems, or perhaps these experiences serve to bias your viewpoint, particularly if the associated pain and conflict have not been satisfactorily resolved at an emotional level. Work to understand what you truly believe about social problems and why.

Diversity in Practice

Practice Behavior Example: Social workers gain sufficient self-awareness to eliminate the influence of personal biases and values in working with diverse groups.

Critical Thinking Question: What might get in the way of truly listening to and learning from others whose opinions about social problems may differ from yours?

It is important to remember that clients who are experiencing problems firsthand may view them very differently from the way you do. A situation that you or other professionals define as a problem may not seem like a problem to your client or vice versa. If you have never been poor or homeless, were not raised in an unsafe home or neighborhood, or have not been affected by racism, you may not fully appreciate the profound effects these experiences can have on people. Listen sensitively to accounts of your clients' life experiences so that you can better understand their importance and the impact on their lives.

Continually deepen your knowledge about how social problems such as poverty, crime, or racism develop not only to help clients improve their social functioning but also to work to prevent these social problems. As you have learned, most social problems are a result of a complex **interplay between individual, family, community,** and **societal forces.** Because of this interaction, attempts to address large-scale social problems such as poverty or racism need to be multifaceted and geared toward societal changes as well as support for individuals experiencing poverty or racism directly. If you are familiar with the multitude of interrelated individual, family, community, and economic factors associated with various social problems, you will be better equipped to devise effective strategies of intervention and prevention.

Draw on your understanding of the **ecosystems perspective** and **social systems theory** to examine how social problems develop and change over time. Identify the many factors, conditions, and circumstances that interact to create a social problem. As you gain experience, you will see more clearly how one social problem can lead to or exacerbate others, or how several problems clustered together can overwhelm clients or communities and have devastating consequences. You will also see that social change at the macro level must often take place in order to enhance the social functioning of individual clients and families.

Think hard about the ***concept of prevention*** and the ways in which you could become involved in preventing the social problems you are attempting to address. What changes at the community and societal level are needed in order to prevent adverse conditions and social problems from developing in the first place? Do existing prevention programs appear to be effective? Do we have the knowledge, the resources, and the political will to launch effective programs of prevention? What would various solutions cost and from where would this money come? As you ponder various strategies, consider the advantages, disadvantages, feasibility, and probable effectiveness of various prevention efforts at the micro, mezzo, and macro levels. What groups might oppose prevention programs and why? Can something that did not happen even be measured?

During your practicum, you will most likely meet clients who are truly remarkable, positive human beings despite the fact that they grew up in very challenging or destructive social environments. For reasons that we are just beginning to understand, some individuals are resilient and able to resist the negative influences of a corrosive environment. There may have been social supports available at a variety of levels to these individuals that enhanced individual strengths and coping skills, allowing them to function well in spite of their experiences.

Seek to understand why individuals respond differently to the positive and negative aspects of their social environment. Learn from your clients about the strengths and ***resiliency factors*** that have made it possible for them to overcome adversity. However, refrain from believing that your work is only to empower individuals, although that is crucial. Remember that it is also crucial to be involved in macrolevel practice that prevents negative environments from developing in the first place.

Consider and reflect upon the following potential roles for social workers in addressing social problems in the areas of ***increasing awareness of social problems, designing and implementing interventions and programs, engaging in research,*** and ***influencing social policy.*** Table 10.2 illustrates the ways in which social workers can address social problems through effective ***social policy practice***.

Table 10.2	**Social Work Roles in Social Policy Practice**
Identification of social problem	Social workers engage in the planned change process in order to address social problems, including the identification, naming, and highlighting of social problems so that they and others can respond. They shine a light on the existence, scope, and depth of the problem; show the negative impacts on all levels of society; explain the complex causation of social problems; standardize definitions of social problems; give voice to impacted populations; and illustrate the relevance of diversity on social problems.
Intervention to address social problem	Social workers, in collaboration with stakeholders, set goals and objectives and design programs to address social problems. They destigmatize the problem, work to shape attitudes, appeal to commonalities, clarify societal values, incorporate diverse stakeholders into intervention, and anticipate forces for change and opposition to intervention. They incorporate best practices and innovations into plans. They include impacted social systems in efforts and evaluation of outcomes and effectiveness of interventions and programs.

(continued)

Table 10.2   **Continued**

Research on social problem	Social workers research evidence-based practices to apply to social problems, and engage in program evaluation to determine effectiveness of interventions and programs. They utilize varied research approaches, including process, outcome, quantitative, qualitative, and action research. They include client groups in evaluation. They use research results to understand causes and contributors to social problems, and disseminate this information to practitioners, social planners, policy makers, and educators.
Social policy practice	Social workers utilize program evaluation data to inform clients, stakeholders, and policy makers. They make recommendations for new policy initiatives and for policy amendments based on findings. They use an ecosystems perspective and social systems theory to impact social policy development in a holistic manner.

Social Problems and Social Work Responses: A Workbook Activity

1. What specific social conditions, needs, or problems does your practicum agency address? What criteria or measures are used to document the seriousness of the problem or condition?

   _____

   _____

2. In recent years, have they worsened, stayed the same, or improved? How do they compare with the severity of these problems at the state or national level?

   _____

   _____

3. How will the community be harmed if these conditions or problems grow larger and more serious?

   _____

   _____

   _____

4. Have any groups and organizations in your community argued that the concerns or conditions addressed by your agency should not be viewed as real or significant problems and that the programs and services provided by your agency are unnecessary, misdirected, or of low priority? In other words, does anyone not believe in and support what your agency is trying to do?

   _____

   _____

   _____

5. Are there different opinions and perspectives about the seriousness of the problem? If so, are these differences based on different definitions of the problem, different statistics, or differences in attitudes toward the problem?

_____

_____

_____

6. In what ways, if any, are new research findings, best practices, and evidence-based practice changing the way your agency conceptualizes and explains the problems, conditions, and needs that it attempts to address?

_____

_____

_____

7. How are the problems and concerns addressed by your agency related to other broad social problems such as poverty, crime, racism, violence, high rates of divorce, substance abuse, lack of affordable health care, lack of jobs, or changes in societal values and attitudes?

_____

_____

_____

8. What specific steps and actions would be needed to prevent these problems or conditions? What would it take to eliminate these problems altogether?

_____

_____

_____

9. What research or demonstration projects would you recommend to be undertaken in order to build knowledge about the social problems your agency addresses (e.g., impact of welfare reform on poverty rates, genetic influences on chemical dependency, principles of violence prevention, long-term costs associated with lack of health care)?

_____

_____

_____

10. How do you plan to remain optimistic that social problems can be addressed, reduced, or eliminated?

_____

_____

_____

11. How would you respond to the following statements regarding social problems, often made by people in the general public, and sometimes by those working in the social services arena?

"Social problems will never be solved."

_____

_____

"It doesn't impact me."

_____

_____

"It's not my problem or my responsibility."

_____

_____

"One person can't do anything about such overwhelming problems, so I'd rather work one-to-one with clients."

_____

_____

"It's all politics."

_____

_____

"Someone should do something."

_____

_____

Suggested Learning Activities

- Conduct interviews with experienced professionals in your agency to better understand the theories of causation that shape the agency's programs and interactions with the agency's clients and consumers.
- Attend public meetings (e.g., city council meetings) and read the letters to the editor of the local newspaper in order to better understand the various ways in which people explain the existence of social problems and the variety of solutions that may make sense and seem logical to them.
- Attend the meetings of a group or organization that defines the problem addressed by your agency much differently than does your agency. Try to understand the basis for their views.
- Identify a self-help group that addresses the social problem your agency addresses. Attend a meeting to determine if it explains the social problem and its solution differently from your agency.
- Examine the *Encyclopedia of Social Work* for chapters that offer summaries of basic information related to the various problems addressed by social workers and social agencies.
- Examine the most recent edition of the *Social Work Almanac* or a similar reference book that presents national statistics on the social problem addressed by your agency and compare them with those of your area.
- Read print and electronic media descriptions of social problems. Pay attention to whether the media takes a strengths or deficit perspective on these social problems.

References

Eitzen, D. Stanley, Maxine Baca Zinn, and Kelly E. Eitzen Smith. *Social Problems: Census Update.* 10th ed. Boston: Allyn and Bacon, 2012.

Hardcastle, David A., Patricia R. Powers, and Stanley Wenocur. *Community Practice: Theories and Skills for Social Workers.* 3rd ed. New York: Oxford University Press, 2012.

Hoefer, Richard. *Advocacy Practice for Social Justice.* 2nd ed. Chicago: Lyceum Books, 2012.

Jansson, Bruce. *Becoming an Effective Policy Advocate: From Policy Practice to Social Justice.* 6th ed. Belmont, CA: Brooks/Cole, 2011.

Kettner, Peter M., Robert M. Moroney, and Lawrence L. Martin. *Designing and Managing Programs: An Effectiveness-Based Approach.* 4th ed. Thousand Oaks, CA: Sage, 2012.

Kinsterbusch, Kurt. *Taking Sides: Clashing Views on Social Issues.* Columbus, OH: McGraw Hill, 2012.

Leon-Guerrero, Anna. *Social Problems: Community, Policy, and Social Action.* 3rd ed. Thousand Oaks, CA: Pine Forge Press, 2010.

Lieberman, Alice. *The Social Workout Book: Strength-Building Exercises for the Pre-Professional.* 2nd ed. Thousand Oaks, CA: Pine Forge Press, 2010.

Mizrahi, Terry, and Larry Davis. *The Encyclopedia of Social Work.* 20th ed. Washington, DC: NASW Press and Oxford University Press, 2010.

Sullivan, Thomas. *Social Problems.* 9th ed. Boston: Allyn and Bacon, 2012.

Unrau, Yvonne A., Peter A. Gabor, and Richard M. Grinnell. *Evaluation in Social Work: The Art and Science of Practice.* 4th ed. New York: Oxford University Press, 2007.

CHAPTER 10 REVIEW

PRACTICE TEST

The following questions will test your knowledge of the content found within this chapter.

1. Not all stakeholders agree on whether a social problem exists because
   a. of a lack of information
   b. of differing values and views of what social conditions are acceptable and unacceptable
   c. there is no clear definition of a social problem
   d. social workers have not succeeded in public relations

2. Social problems
   a. fit federal criteria for disaster relief
   b. cannot be adequately addressed through social policies
   c. often get in the way of agency work
   d. violate human rights and social work ethics

3. Public social programs are often established to address particular social issues. Which is true about these programs?
   a. They are mandated to address identified social problems.
   b. They do not have to address social problems.
   c. They receive funding based on how well they address social problems.
   d. They are focused primarily on prevention of social problems.

4. Looking at social problems as the result of a number of interrelated causes is
   a. critical social work theory
   b. an example of the strengths perspective
   c. structural family theory
   d. taking an ecosystems perspective

5. The prevention of social problems is best achieved through

   a. recognition of the multifaceted etiology of social problems

   b. school-based primary prevention programs

   c. reliance on evidence-based practice

   d. increased state funding

6. Social programs need to be based on a good assessment of social problems

   a. because money is limited

   b. because funding sources require this

   c. because interventions are more effective if based on a good assessment

   d. because outcomes must be measured against assessment data

7. From an ecosystems perspective, discuss the dynamics of the clustering together of both social problems and social well-being factors.

©Sylumagraphica/Dreamstime

11

The Social Policy Context of Practice

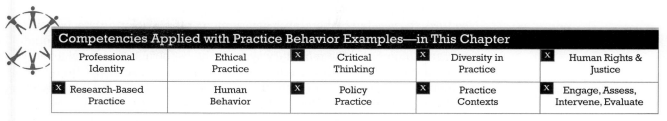

Competencies Applied with Practice Behavior Examples—in This Chapter									
	Professional Identity		Ethical Practice	X	Critical Thinking	X	Diversity in Practice	X	Human Rights & Justice
X	Research-Based Practice		Human Behavior	X	Policy Practice	X	Practice Contexts	X	Engage, Assess, Intervene, Evaluate

CHAPTER PREVIEW

This chapter provides a summary of social policy practice, including definitions of social policy and related terms. It presents a typology of social policies and describes the ideal and actual trajectories often seen in social policy formation and implementation. Also offered is a social policy analysis framework recommended to understand the effectiveness and efficiency of policies in addressing social problems. It also presents a rationale and values base for involvement in social policy practice, as well as direction in comprehending the ways in which social policies can be implemented or adapted.

Previous chapters focused on the agency context, the community context, and the social problem context of social work practice. This chapter examines a fourth context, the social policy context. The clients served by your practicum agency, the other social workers and staff within this agency, and even your practicum experiences are affected by social policy. This chapter attempts to clarify the nature of social policy by defining and distinguishing between various terms and explaining the impact of social policy on a social agency and those that it serves. Specific suggestions are offered on how you can identify and locate information concerning the social policies most relevant to your practicum setting.

The study of social policy can be an exciting activity because it involves an examination of what we as a society believe about people and the problems experienced by people, and what can and should be done about these problems. It forces us to carefully examine our own assumptions, beliefs, and values, and in the process we are sometimes surprised by what we discover about ourselves and our views. Although stimulating, the study of social policy is also a complex undertaking. For example, the analysis of a particular social policy requires students to be able to locate relevant governmental documents and legal codes; understand the legislative process; and acquire a basic understanding of the many historic, political, cultural, and economic forces that shaped the development of a particular policy.

BACKGROUND AND CONTEXT

For purposes of this chapter, ***social policy*** is defined as a decision made by public or governmental authorities regarding the assignment and allocation of resources, rights, and responsibilities and expressed in laws and governmental regulations. In this definition, ***resources*** refer to various social and economic benefits and opportunities, both tangible and intangible. The terms ***assignment*** and ***allocation*** imply that a policy may either offer or curtail these resources for all people or for certain individuals. ***Responsibilities*** refer to the expectations of those providing services and those receiving services. ***Rights*** refer to the protection of guaranteed freedoms or entitlements.

Needless to say, lawmakers and government officials formulate policies on a wide variety of topics. Thus, there are public policies on international relations, economics and the monetary system, the tax structure, interstate and international commerce, military and defense, highways, use of public lands, environmental safety, education, and the like. For the most part, social policies address matters or issues related to the social well-being of people and the relationships between various groups within society. Thus, social policies focus on such concerns as marriage, divorce, adoption, domestic abuse, the needs of the elderly, juvenile delinquency, mental health, discrimination against minority groups, training and job opportunities for the disadvantaged, economic assistance to the poor, availability of affordable housing, immigration, and other similar concerns. The term **social welfare policy** is often applied to those social policies that focus primarily on the distribution of economic benefits to those in need (e.g., public assistance, subsidized housing, Medicaid, or subsidized child care). These approaches account for the ways in which many federal and state laws and social policies have been enacted, some of which result in effective social policy, and some of which do not.

Social policies are directly related to social problems and are intended to address them in a way that will hopefully prevent or reduce the extent of the problem. Thus, once a social problem is identified, various groups, all with different values, belief systems, and political affiliations, begin the process of addressing these social problems in the form of a law that may actually change the social structures that contribute to or add to the social problems. Social policies often direct agencies to do what is required, perform to a certain standard, and accomplish within a given budget. Further, they provide the tools that are to be used to measure effectiveness and show accountability in the use of public money.

Social policies are in a constant state of evaluation and are impacted by the dimensions of social policy development, illustrated in Table 11.1 as the

Policy Practice

Practice Behavior Example: Social workers analyze, formulate, and advocate for policies that advance social well-being.

Critical Thinking Question: How is policy practice similar to and different from planned change at the micro level?

Table 11.1   **Ideal and Actual Social Policy Trajectories**

Dimension of Social Policy	Ideal Trajectory	Actual Trajectory
Value base	Idealistic	Political compromise
Knowledge base	Comprehensive understanding of social problem and its etiology	Partial understanding of social problem and its etiology
Scope	Comprehensive and universal	Limited and partial
Time orientation	Timely and future oriented	Slow and crisis oriented
Stakeholder base	All stakeholders including client base	Stakeholders with political power and influence
Empirical base	Based on facts and sound research	Based on interpretation of facts and emotion
Relationship to existing and future policy	Built upon effective policy and allows for future growth	Detached from effective policy future orientation
Rationality	Purposeful and planned	Reactive and pendulum swing

ideal and actual trajectories which often characterize social policy formation, implementation, and revision. In an ideal world, each of the dimensions of social policy would be fully developed to form an ideal trajectory of social policy development. However, social policy development rarely follows an ideal trajectory, which means that social policies are not always comprehensive, inclusive, and effective. As you learn about social policy development, consider the process using these terms.

A social policy is created when a legislative body enacts a law, usually at the federal or state level but in some cases, at the county or city level. Once the law is enacted, high-level governmental officials and various governmental legal departments will usually prepare a set of rules and regulations that clarify the provisions of the law and describe in detail how the law is to be implemented. These directives are often called ***administrative rules and regulations.*** Subsequently, key provisions of the law and many of the rules and regulations are written into a public agency's manual of policy and procedure that guides its day-to-day operation and the decisions and actions of agency staff. Statements of social policy are found in legal codes, in executive orders issued by the president and state governors, in administrative rules and regulations issued by governmental officials, and sometimes in statements and speeches made by high-ranking public officials. In some instances, legal decisions handed down by courts have the effect of creating social policy.

Although an ***agency policy*** is not a social policy, social policies do filter down to the level of a local or community agency and find their way into the agency's policy manual. At the local level, social policies have a significant impact on an agency's services and programs and on what a social worker actually does or does not do in his or her work with clients. The impact of social policy on agency policy is most evident in the operation of a public agency in which one will find that many of the statements found in the manual are direct responses to specific legal codes and various governmental rules and regulations.

Human Rights and Justice

Practice Behavior Example: Social workers understand the forms and mechanisms of oppression and discrimination.

Critical Thinking Question: What social policies protect your clients from oppression and discrimination?

Social policies are a reflection of values and what is believed to be right and wrong, desirable and undesirable. They are shaped mostly by those who have power and influence. The formulation of social policy is basically a political process and politics are primarily about power. The art of gaining, exercising, and retaining power in order to influence and enact social policies is the goal of policy practice. Hopefully the effectiveness of social policy implementation is monitored, measured, and evaluated, and results are shared with policy makers so that social policies can be continually improved in order to address social problems more effectively.

If social policies are ill conceived because the decision makers either do not understand the problem or have erroneous beliefs about its causes, the resulting social programs will also be flawed. Those who understand the concerns being addressed and the inadequacies of existing policies and programs have both an obligation and an opportunity to provide accurate information to the decision makers so they can develop appropriate and effective social policies. In the absence of such information, policy makers will assume that social policies are addressing the needs they were intended to address. Social workers can thus be extremely influential in not only providing needed information but also lobbying for just, equitable, and effective social policy changes.

GUIDANCE AND DIRECTION

You may be surprised at the degree to which your work is impacted by social policy. You need to learn about social policy so that you can take part in its formulation. Hopefully you are excited at the prospect of working at the macro level to design social policies and social programs that could improve the lives of many people. Social change and social policy development are the most efficient and exciting ways to help large numbers of people and promote social justice. As mentioned earlier, this level of practice is referred to as ***social policy practice.***

Perhaps you see yourself primarily as a direct services provider and you may prefer to help clients and families one by one and in a very personal way. The idea of becoming involved in political action and social change efforts may not be the focus of your emerging practice. However, it is still imperative for you to understand social policy and how it affects your clients, positively or negatively. In order to be an informed advocate for your clients and a skilled provider of direct services, you must understand specific social policies, their strengths and limitations, and why they exist in their current forms. Depending on your practicum setting, you will need to become familiar with a cluster of social policy issues and concerns. You must acquire a basic or working understanding of the social policies that most directly influence the operation of your agency, its own agency policies, your role, and its clients or consumers. Below is a list of social policy domains that are of interest to many social workers and many social agencies.

Abortion	Health care and rehabilitation
Adolescent pregnancy	Homelessness
Adult protection	Housing
Caregiving	Immigration and refugee issues
Child care	Intimate partner violence
Child protection	Job creation and unemployment
Child support	Juvenile delinquency and adult crime
Community development	Long-term care
Custody	Marriage and divorce
Discrimination and racism	Mental health and mental illness
Economic development	Parenting
Education	Physical and mental disabilities
End of life	Public assistance/welfare
Family planning	Public health and safety
Foster care and adoption	Substance abuse

Social policy is constantly evolving as a result of changing societal needs, shifting social values, increases or decreases in financial resources available to implement policy, and, of course, political forces. You will need to keep abreast of proposed legislative changes and find ways to have input into the political process. During your practicum, make a special effort to involve yourself in activities that prepare you for social work practice. Look for the opportunity to participate in task forces or serve on committees working to pass a law or

Human Behavior

Practice Behavior Example: Social workers critique and apply knowledge to understand person and environment.

Critical Thinking Question: What social policies impact your clients' interaction with their social environment?

assist grassroots or advocacy groups seeking to change social policy. You may be able to observe and give testimony at public meetings or legislative hearings that solicit public input before social policy decisions are made.

Be aware that when social workers do not engage in the politics of forming social welfare policy and allocating funding for social welfare programs, many client needs and concerns are overlooked by the decision makers, and the insights and values of the social work profession are omitted from the development of social policy. Your knowledge and skills are needed in the ongoing work of social policy development, so you must develop competence in policy practice.

You will need to develop and utilize a ***social policy analysis model*** or conceptual framework to guide your examination and analysis of the social policies that impact the operation of your agency and either support or undermine the social functioning of your clients. The questions listed in the workbook activity in this chapter are the ones often addressed in the various models and conceptual frameworks used in policy analysis. Learn to view such models as tools to help you understand and assess the effectiveness of social policies with which you work. Recognize that these frameworks will not only guide your evaluation of social policy but can also provide you with the insights needed to improve social policy.

Sources of information regarding a social policy include the original code or statute, administrative rules and regulations, and other governmental documents that describe and explain the policy. Various professional and advocacy organizations (e.g., Child Welfare League of America, National Association of Social Workers, American Association of Retired Persons, Children's Defense Fund, American Public Welfare Association, American Hospital Association, Urban League, Southern Poverty Law Center) distribute reports of their analysis of social policies relevant to their particular concerns. In addition, the observations of social workers and of clients will give you insight into how a given policy affects the lives of individuals and families. The social workers in your agency will have opinions about how social policy could be improved, how it benefits or harms clients, and how it complements or conflicts with other social policies. Clients may also have insights based on their experiences with effective or ineffective social policies, so seek opportunities to learn from them.

During your analysis, consider the following categories of social policies, each of which reflects a philosophy, a set of values, and a belief system about how society should deal with social problems:

- ***Policies of social and financial support*** are those intended to help or encourage people to carry out their roles and responsibilities and meet their basic needs for food, shelter, and so on. Examples include policies related to financial assistance, medical care for the poor, and subsidized housing for low-income elders.
- ***Policies of protection*** are those that seek to protect people from harm and exploitation, especially those who are most vulnerable. Examples are policies related to child abuse and neglect, domestic violence, the frail elderly, and to groups often subjected to discrimination and oppression.
- ***Policies of rehabilitation and remediation*** are those intended to correct or minimize the impact of certain disabling conditions such as serious mental illness, restorative justice, and chronic illness.

- ***Policies of prevention*** are those that attempt to prevent certain social and health problems from developing or increasing. Examples are social policies that encourage economic development, immunizations, parent education, family planning, proper nutrition, and curfews for youth.
- ***Policies of punishment and correction*** are those that seek to punish and control persons who violate laws and societal norms. Examples are policies related to crime and delinquency, probation and parole, and the monitoring of convicted sex offenders.

The social policy you are analyzing will probably be one of these types, and thinking about it this way will help you understand the overall intent of the policy, the values that drive it, and how it may reflect public attitudes and political ideology. You will soon be able to understand, describe, and analyze the social policy in terms of the following:

- Its ***authority and auspices*** (federal, state, or local law)
- Its ***history*** and the reasons for its development
- Its stated ***purpose and goals***
- The ***assumptions, values, and beliefs*** upon which it is based
- Its ***key principles*** and ***main provisions***
- Its ***impact on your agency's operation***
- Its ***impact on your clients***
- Its advantages and ***positive effects***
- Its disadvantages and ***negative effects***
- Its ***relationship to other social policies***
- Its ***gaps*** and need for revision and improvement

After you have become familiar with a specific social policy and its effects, consider how it could be improved and what steps or actions would be necessary to achieve those improvements, such as changes in existing legislation, changes in administrative rules, or the creation of incentives to adhere to the policy.

Finally, follow these values-based guidelines for the rationale of achieving social justice through social policy practice. Over time, even as social conditions change and policies evolve, these principles will serve you well as a social worker.

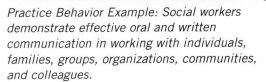

Critical Thinking

Practice Behavior Example: Social workers demonstrate effective oral and written communication in working with individuals, families, groups, organizations, communities, and colleagues.

Critical Thinking Question: How can you observe and learn from the testimony of professionals about the social policies being considered in your state?

- Social policy practice is a vital arena for social workers because social policy strongly impacts the social functioning of individuals, families, groups, organizations, and society.
- Human rights are universal and should be protected through social policy.
- Social policies are social contracts based on societal values and commonalities.
- Social policy should be based on the values of equity, access, dignity, worth of the individual, opportunity, and fairness.
- Social policy should proactively promote social functioning through empowerment, client involvement, and prevention of social problems.
- Social policies should address social problems from all levels of practice.

- Social policies should be based on both historical and future orientations.
- Social policies should be based on empirical evidence about the causes of social problems.
- Social policy should responsively address, reduce, and eliminate social problems.
- Clients, constituents, and stakeholders must be involved in social policy.
- Social policies should be measured and evaluated for effectiveness and efficiency.

Social Policy Analysis: A Workbook Activity

As a way of learning about social policy, identify a social problem (e.g., homelessness) that your agency addresses. Next, identify a specific social policy related to that problem (e.g., public assistance laws, unemployment compensation laws, health-care policies, minimum-wage laws). Using the questions found in the workbook activity below, analyze this social policy and determine if it is adequate, effective, and positive in its effects. The questions below will guide your analysis.

1. What is the official name and legal citation of the social policy being studied?

_____

_____

2. When was the social policy enacted or established and when, if ever, was it significantly modified?

_____

_____

_____

3. What historical factors, values, and assumptions underlie this policy? Are these values compatible with the ethics and values of the social work profession?

_____

_____

_____

5. What conditions, problems, or needs does this social policy address (e.g., violence, poverty, homelessness, addictions, unemployment)?

_____

_____

_____

6. Which of the types of social policies listed on page 119 best describes the social policy you are studying?

_____

_____

_____

_____

7. Based on your observations and experience in your practicum site, is this social policy doing what it is supposed to do? If not, why?

_____

_____

_____

8. How could this social policy better address the needs of those it is designed to assist (e.g., fill gaps in services, coordinate with related programs, increase funding, and change eligibility criteria)?

_____

_____

_____

_____

9. What would it take to actually change this policy (e.g., legislation, amendments, coalition building, or lobbying)?

_____

_____

_____

10. Does one political party support this policy more than another? If yes, why?

_____

_____

_____

Social Policy Reflections: A Workbook Activity

1. What social work values are most central to you? How should they be incorporated into social policies?

_____

_____

2. Social workers engaged in social policy practice may experience defeats and partial successes in their work. How do you plan to deal with these sorts of experiences throughout your social work career?

_____

_____

3. What barriers to client involvement in social policy formation do you foresee? How would you address these barriers?

_____

_____

4. In an ideal world, what social policy would you like to see? What would it take to make progress toward that goal?

_____

_____

5. Individuals in the general public often make statements about social policy such as the following. How would you respond to them?

"The fewer laws, the better."

_____

_____

_____

"We need to get government out of people's lives."

_____

_____

_____

"Government has a great responsibility to its people's welfare."

_____

_____

_____

"You can't legislate change."

_____

_____

_____

"I'm not political."

_____

_____

_____

_____

Suggested Learning Activities

- Interview a social worker in your agency about a social policy that most directly affects his or her clients and obtain his or her recommendations for improving the social policy.
- Review the NASW *Code of Ethics* (1999) guidelines regarding the social worker's responsibility in the area of social policy (www.socialworkers.org).

- Read *Social Work Speaks,* which describes NASW's position on a wide variety of social issues.
- Attend legislative or public hearings that gather public input before a social policy is enacted or modified.
- Identify your personal position regarding a controversial area of social policy, such as abortion. Attend meetings of an organization that takes an opposing position to try to understand that perspective, including the values, beliefs, knowledge, and assumptions on which it is based.
- Invite a state legislator to discuss his or her experiences with proposing, formulating, and passing legislation.
- Use the Internet to monitor the progress of a bill before the U.S. Congress or your state legislature. For information on federal legislation relevant to social work, explore the legislative section of the website of the National Association of Social Workers.
- Explore the websites of organizations that monitor social policy, such as the Electronic Policy Network, Center for Law and Social Policy, U.S. Department of Health and Human Services, and World Wide Web Resources for Social Workers.

References

Almgren, Gunnar, and Taryn Lindhorst. *The Safety Net Health Care System: Health Care at the Margins.* New York: Springer Publishing Company, 2011.

Barusch, Amanda S. *Foundations of Social Policy: Social Justice in Human Perspective.* 3rd ed. Florence, KY: Brooks/Cole, 2009.

Blau, Joel, and Mimi Abramovitz. *The Dynamics of Social Welfare.* 3rd ed. New York: Oxford University Press, 2010.

Bochel, Hugh, Catherine Bochel, Robert Page, and Robert Sykes. *Social Policy: Themes, Issues and Debates.* 2nd ed. Boston: Longman, 2009.

Chambers, Donald, and Kenneth Wedel. *Social Policy and Social Programs: A Method for the Practical Public Policy Analysis.* 5th ed. Boston: Allyn and Bacon, 2009.

DiNitto, Diana, and Linda Cummins. *Social Welfare: Politics and Public Policy.* 6th ed. Boston: Allyn and Bacon, 2007.

Dolgoff, Ralph, and Donald Feldstein. *Understanding Social Welfare: A Search for Social Justice.* 8th ed. Boston: Allyn and Bacon, 2009.

Ferguson, Migeul, Heather Neuroth-Gatlin, and Stacy Borasky. *Caught in the Storm: Navigating Policy and Practice in the Welfare Reform Era.* Chicago: Lyceum Books, 2010.

Fitzpatrick, Tony, Huck-ju Kwon, Nick Manning, James Midgely, and Gillian Pascall. *International Encyclopedia of Social Policy.* Clifton, NJ: Routledge, 2010.

Gilbert, Neil, and Paul Terrell. *Dimensions of Social Welfare Policy.* 7th ed. Boston: Allyn and Bacon, 2010.

Jansson, Bruce. *Becoming an Effective Policy Advocate.* 5th ed. Pacific Grove, CA: Brooks/Cole, 2008.

Karger, Howard, James Midgely, and Peter Kind. *Controversial Issues in Social Policy.* 3rd ed. Boston: Pearson Education, 2007.

Libby, Pat, and Associates. *The Lobbying Strategy Handbook: 10 Steps to Advancing Any Cause Effectively.* Thousand Oaks, CA: Sage Publications, 2011.

Long, Dennis D., Carolyn J. Tice, and John D. Morrison. *Macro Social Work Practice: A Strengths Perspective.* Belmont, CA: Thomson Brooks/Cole, 2006.

Midgely, James. *The Handbook of Social Policy.* 2nd ed. Thousand Oaks, CA: Sage Publishing, 2009.

Mkandawire, Thandika. *Social Policy in a Developmental Context.* New York: Palgrave Macmillan, 2004.

National Association of Social Workers. *Social Work Speaks: NASW Policy Statements 2006–2009.* 7th ed. Washington, DC: NASW Press, 2006.

Perez-Koenig, Rosa, and Barry Rock, eds. *Social Work in the Era of Devolution: Toward a Just Practice.* New York: Fordham University, 2001.

Popple, Philip R., and Leslie Leighninger. *The Policy-Based Profession: An Introduction to Social Welfare Policy Analysis for Social Workers.* 4th ed. Boston: Allyn and Bacon, 2008.

Rocha, Cynthia. *Essentials of Social Policy Practice.* Thousand Oaks, CA: Sage Publications, 2007.

Segal, Elizabeth. *Social Welfare Policy and Social Programs: A Values Perspective.* 2nd ed. Florence, KY: Brooks Cole, 2010.

van Wormer, Katherine. *Confronting Oppression, Restoring Justice: From Policy Analysis to Social Action.* Alexandria, VA: CSWE Press, 2004.

CHAPTER 11 REVIEW

PRACTICE TEST

The following questions will test your knowledge of the content found within this chapter.

1. Agency policies and social policies are in constant interaction. What is the difference between them?

   a. Agency policies and social policies are essentially the same.

   b. Agency policies provide guidelines for programs while social policies are based in laws.

   c. Agency policies refer to human resource rules and social policies define eligibility.

   d. Agency policies are dependent upon social policies.

2. The term which refers to the assignment of federal economic resources in a social policy is

   a. allocation

   b. guidelines for oversight

   c. rights and responsibilities

   d. entitlements

3. Federal policy rules and responsibilities

   a. are the standards of a social policy

   b. clarify the provisions of the social policy and implementation guidelines

   c. set job descriptions for agency employees

   d. specify budget amounts and categories

4. Social work practice that focuses on social change and policy formation is

   a. advocacy

   b. mezzo level practice

   c. evidence-based practice

   d. policy practice

5. Social policies which support mental health services are what type of social policy?

   a. policies of financial support

   b. policies of rehabilitation or remediation

   c. policies of punishment or correction

   d. policies of protection

6. The United Nations Declaration of Human Rights

   a. forms the basis for the NASW *Code of Ethics*

   b. is binding on all nations

   c. is incorporated into federal law based on treaties between nations

   d. is the foundation for many nations' social policies and programs

7. What are the greatest challenges to achieving social change based on the principles of social justice?

©Filograph/Dreamstime

Diversity and Cultural Competency

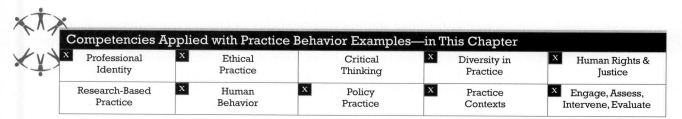

Competencies Applied with Practice Behavior Examples—in This Chapter				
x Professional Identity	x Ethical Practice	Critical Thinking	x Diversity in Practice	x Human Rights & Justice
Research-Based Practice	x Human Behavior	x Policy Practice	x Practice Contexts	x Engage, Assess, Intervene, Evaluate

CHAPTER PREVIEW

This chapter focuses on the importance of cultural competence in social work practice, including a description of cultural competence, related concepts, and a discussion of the levels of cultural competence of both individual social workers and organizations. Emphasis is given to both client and social worker experiences, identities, and belief systems, including their impact on cross-cultural interventions. The domains of social worker–client relationships which are impacted by diversity are discussed, as well as the common misinterpretations of difference. Finally, the challenge of engaging in lifelong efforts to achieve cultural competence is presented.

Members of the social work profession believe that all people have worth simply because they are human beings. All persons are entitled to fundamental human rights, and all have basic responsibilities, including the responsibility to treat others with respect, dignity, and fairness. These beliefs are prerequisites to peaceful relations among people, to social justice, and to the effective and proper operation of human services organizations.

Social workers and social services agencies are being challenged to find ways to balance the value of diversity with the value of universal human development. They must be capable of recognizing, respecting, and accommodating differences while treating all clients with fairness and equality under the law. Agencies must be thoughtful and fair in decisions about who is eligible for the services they offer and how best to allocate limited resources. They must avoid discrimination based on all forms of diversity.

BACKGROUND AND CONTEXT

Culture refers to the learned patterns of thought and behavior that are passed from generation to generation. Culture consists of the unspoken and unquestioned assumptions and ideas about the nature of reality, the human condition, and how life should be lived. Everything we do is influenced by the ways of thinking, values, beliefs, expectations, and customs that make up our culture. Professional knowledge, practice, social policies, and agency policies and procedures are shaped by culture. Broadly defined, culture includes not only references to ethnicity or background but also such variables as age, religion, level of physical ability, and gender and sexual orientation. Each form of diversity shapes clients' thoughts, behavior, and worldview.

That, of course, means that every time clients and social workers engage with each other, differences related to those diverse experiences will come into play. It is vital to understand that cultural differences may emerge as the most important factors in the professional relationship, even more vital than other components of that relationship such as client motivation, social worker genuineness, client ability, and social worker skills. Knowing this, we must rely on our professional ability to acknowledge and bridge cultural differences.

We are all limited by *ethnocentrism*, which is the tendency to assume that one's own culture is normal and even superior, and that it is an appropriate standard for judging the beliefs and behaviors of others. We cannot avoid being ethnocentric to some degree because our own beliefs, values, and patterns feel natural and normal and seem rooted in common sense and our daily lives. These are so integral to us that it is difficult to realize there are other ways of thinking and living. We must strive to become aware of how our culture influences our thoughts, decisions, and actions in order to avoid misunderstanding our clients and failing to recognize and respect their unique culture.

Ethnocentrism leads to the possibility that we do not actually recognize the importance of cultural differences; that we view differences as having lesser value; and that we risk developing irrelevant, ineffective, or even harmful interventions for diverse clients. Further, it is even possible for social workers to blame clients for the failure of interventions on clients when it is actually the lack of cultural understanding and competence on the part of the social worker that explains the outcome.

Diversity in Practice

Practice Behavior Example: Social workers gain sufficient self-awareness to eliminate the influence of personal biases and values in working with diverse groups.

Critical Thinking Question: In light of the dynamics of ethnocentrism, is it possible for an agency to assess its own level of cultural competency?

Prejudice can breed **discrimination**, which refers to decisions, behaviors, or actions that deprive an individual or a whole group of certain rights and opportunities. Discrimination can be either intentional or unintentional, depending on whether it was motivated by prejudice and the intent to harm and depending on the person's understanding of or denial of the potential to be discriminatory. However, either can be harmful to clients. Discrimination can also be personal or institutional. In **personal discrimination**, an individual behaves in ways that cause harm to the members of a group. In **institutional discrimination**, beliefs and practices that are embedded in law, in social and economic systems, and in governmental or organizational policy cause harm to members of certain groups.

Examples often given of institutional racism include policies requiring English as a primary language, those restricting refugees' or illegal immigrants' access to basic services, and those that disallow insurance and governmental benefits to same-sex partners. It is possible for social workers to engage in **unintentional discrimination**, which is usually understood as behavior rooted in denial of one's own racism or stereotypical thinking. In this case, denial of our own biases gets in the way of an honest self-assessment and may keep us from seeing our own limitations.

Clients' membership in a minority group may have a more significant influence on their interaction with a social worker or agency than does their membership in a specific cultural group. Minority status is not simply a function of numbers. In a given society, a particular group may be in the majority in terms of percentage of the overall population, but still have minority status because they are discriminated against. For example, even though females are slightly more numerous than males, women are often considered a minority group because they have less power and control over their lives than do men, and because they experience prejudice and discrimination based on gender. Minority status may also be tied to age, sexual orientation, physical or mental disability, socioeconomic status, educational background, or religion.

If clients perceive themselves as different from others or as less powerful and more vulnerable, these perceptions have an impact on their help-seeking behavior, on how they expect to be treated, on their level of trust in a social worker or agency, and on what they consider to be a useful and relevant service or program. It is also important to note that clients' membership in a minority group does not automatically mean that they are an expert on their culture, that they are able to engage with social workers from different backgrounds, or that they have cultural competence themselves because of their minority status.

Table 12.1	**Client Factors Which Impact Cross-cultural Interventions**

- Cultural history
- Personal experiences with stereotyping, discrimination, and oppression
- Level of cultural identity
- Disparities in access, income, health
- Cumulative disadvantage
- Cumulative cultural trauma
- Self-awareness
- Level of ability to move between cultures
- Previous experience with social workers
- Beliefs about help-seeking
- Multiple forms of diversity and their impact

Human Rights and Justice

Practice Behavior Example: Social workers understand the forms and mechanisms of oppression and discrimination

Critical Thinking Question: How can a diversity perspective and a strengths perspective be used together?

Table 12.1 highlights a number of client factors which impact cross cultural interventions. Consider these as you learn how to work with people different from you in terms of age, ethnicity, gender, sexual orientation, or other characteristics.

Many of the issues related to diversity that the social work profession deals with are at their core human rights issues with national and international contexts. The work you will be doing in the practicum may be very personal and individual for one client or family, but may also be tied to much larger human rights organizations and their declarations, which include the following:

- United Nations Universal Declaration of Human Rights
- International Covenant on Economic, Social, and Cultural Relations
- International Federation of Social Workers
- Declaration of Human Responsibilities of the InterAction Council
- United Nations Convention on the Elimination of All Forms of Discrimination against Women
- United National Convention on the Rights of the Child
- Geneva Convention

GUIDANCE AND DIRECTION

In an effort to see your agency from the perspective of diverse clients, examine its physical environment, written materials, internal policies, and staffing patterns. Assess whether your agency is accessible to persons with disabilities. Look to see if reading material, posters, and artwork would appeal to diverse groups of people, including language adaptations and visual representations of people from a variety of backgrounds. Read agency written materials to determine if they are free of bias and whether they use inclusive language. Finally, learn if the agency staff is diverse and represents people of various ages, cultures, sexual orientations, and other backgrounds. Take advantage of any training in working with diverse populations that might be available to you as a student.

No doubt you will work hard to be culturally sensitive and respectful of differences among people. However, you, like other people, may not always recognize your own biases, prejudices, or ignorance regarding diverse groups. The practicum offers you an important opportunity for self-examination and self-correction in terms of such personal limitations. Seek opportunities for professional growth in cross-cultural work while you are a student, knowing that you will need to continue this learning throughout your career.

You may believe that people are more alike than different and that treating all clients alike is fair and reasonable. However, these beliefs do not recognize the importance of diversity, and may cause you to overlook unique aspects of a client's background and the powerful impact of minority status. Although it is true that people have much in common, it is also true that there are differences and these can greatly affect social work practice.

Recognize the positive experiences resulting from minority group status, such as ethnic pride, bilingual abilities, community solidarity, extended family cohesion, and a strong sense of history. These experiences are strengths on which a professional relationship and a possible intervention can be built. Do not assume that membership in a minority group has only negative implications.

Work to understand any negative experiences your clients may have had because of their minority status, such as discrimination in school, housing, or employment; inappropriate placement in foster homes; or threats and violence in the form of hate crimes. Remember that many personal problems such as depression, poverty, dropping out of school, substance abuse, suicide, and even physical illness may have some roots in the stress and inner turmoil a person feels when subjected to discrimination or oppression.

If you are a member of a minority group, you may be better able to understand the effects of prejudice and discrimination, as well as the unique benefits that are a result of such membership. It is also important for you to have satisfactorily resolved any related personal issues, anger, and resentment in order to be objective and to perceive the uniqueness of every situation and individual. However, such negative experiences of personal discrimination or marginalization can provide motivation and passion for the work you may do with others who are experiencing oppression. If you have experienced discrimination because of your minority status, do not assume your minority clients will have the same experiences or conclusions about them as you do.

Social work with diverse clients is complex and demanding. Stereotypical adaptations of usual approaches or slight changes in the agency's standard operating procedures are not likely to be effective. Rather, you will need to develop distinct methods that are acceptable, relevant to, and appropriate for the specific group with which you are working, and this necessitates involving them in any such steps.

Be alert to the fact that misunderstandings and misinterpretations in cross-cultural interactions can occur in many areas and situations including:

Research-Based Practice

Practice Behavior Example: Social workers use research evidence to inform practice

Critical Thinking Question: What evidence exists to support the effectiveness of culturally sensitive interventions with diverse clients and groups?

- **Spoken and written language** including misunderstanding words, accents, and nuances
- **Nonverbal communication** such as misunderstanding gestures, facial expressions, touch, and eye contact
- **Verbal communication** including tone of voice, word choice, turn-taking

- **Interpersonal differences** such as appropriate level of directness, assertiveness, and self-disclosure
- **Gender relations and beliefs** about appropriate touching and expressions of attraction for another person
- Judgments concerning **appearance,** appropriate dress, body decorations, and level of modesty
- **Views of time**, including punctuality, use of time, and planning ahead
- Use of **physical space** and judgment as to appropriate distance between people
- Ways of **learning and teaching** and giving and taking direction
- Ways of **negotiating and handling conflict**
- Ways of **expressing emotion**
- Help-seeking beliefs and use of professional or culturally valued helpers
- Differences in **definition of family** and the involvement of family in social work interventions

Recognize that different groups may hold very different beliefs about the nature and cause of personal problems. For example, some ethnic groups may view depression or physical illness as primarily a problem of spirituality (e.g., a consequence of eating a taboo food, having broken one's relationship with God, or of a lack of balance between one's spirit and body).

Seek to understand your clients' beliefs about the appropriateness of asking for help and receiving help from professionals and agencies. Some ethnic groups may believe that personal and family problems should not be discussed with anyone outside the family. Some may feel great shame if they must seek help from a stranger. Others may prefer to seek help from religious leaders, and some may view social workers with mistrust for historical reasons such as discriminatory agency or social policies.

Different groups have different ideas about what is an appropriate method of helping and who has the capacity and authority to help with or treat certain types of problems. Some people may choose to use informal helpers and spiritual leaders, prayer, purification ceremonies, and religious rituals rather than the services of a professional helper. You will need to learn how to work cooperatively with spiritual leaders, healers, and clergy. Expect to learn from them about approaches to helping that are valued by your clients.

Remember that clients from a minority group may have had or may expect to have negative experiences when they must have contact with social workers or social agencies, based on their group's history with the dominant culture. Clients may also be fearful of interacting with social workers because they fear legal recrimination for themselves (e.g., illegal immigrants or homosexual clients living in states that have laws prohibiting homosexual activity). Their fears may be a barrier to their development of trust and their willingness to invest themselves in a professional helping relationship. Be careful not to interpret such mistrust, fear, or anger as client resistance.

Do not automatically interpret client quietness, reticence, or anxiety as pathology or dysfunction. Silence may mean respect or it may signal that the client does not feel understood or valued. When appropriate, acknowledge to your client that you recognize the differences that separate you, and show your appreciation for their struggles by validating their experiences and perspectives. Remember that your level of cultural competence may be more important in your work with diverse clients than your overall knowledge and skill in social work. Since *we use ourselves as the tool to help others*, if we are not culturally

Table 12.2   **Belief Barriers to Culturally Competent Practice**

Social Work Belief	Negative Outcome
"All people are alike."	Devaluing difference
"People are more like than they are different."	Devaluing difference
"It is best to be color blind."	Ignoring/dismissing difference
"As long as I care about my client, I don't need to adapt."	Naivete about need for cultural competence
"Clients need to be bicultural."	Judgment and unwillingness to adapt intervention
"All.........act the same."	Stereotyping and overgeneralizing
"Minority groups should forget about the past."	Dismissing individual and cultural history/oppression
"Agency policy requires us to treat everyone the same."	Devaluing difference
"I have no biases."	Lack of self-awareness
"How can I be expected to understand all cultures?"	Defensiveness regarding cultural competency
"There is too much emphasis on being politically correct."	Dismissing meaning and importance of language
"If a client doesn't tell me something, how should I know?"	Dismissing communication differences
"These people are so amazing."	Romanticizing of diverse groups
"..............are so resistant and unmotivated."	Inability to recognize meaning of behavior
"The reason this person is doing this is because of their culture."	Attributing too much to cultural difference
"This is how we deal with............"	Stereotyping and use of inappropriate intervention
"Don't be disappointed if they don't do well."	Low expectations for diverse groups, blaming client for ineffective intervention, and not recognizing client definition of success

competent, the use of self is greatly compromised. Table 12.2 lists a number of that might be beliefs held by social workers engaged in cross-cultural practice. The beliefs underlying these statements can be significant barriers to effective professional relationships and the outcome of interventions. Consider how these beliefs might be considered inappropriate, limited in cultural sensitivity, or offensive in working with diverse clients. Think about the list of negative impacts these beliefs might have and reflect on any of your own beliefs which might lead to similar negative outcomes.

Each of the beliefs in Table 12.2 which are held by social workers have the potential to undermine and limit the effectiveness of the professional relationship with diverse clients, illustrating a lack of understanding and even misinterpretation of what is said and done by clients. This lack of understanding can easily lead to inappropriate interventions and false cooperation by clients who believe they must go along with a treatment plan even if it does not fit them. Remember that there can be a big difference between what is said and meant and what is heard, due to communication differences on both sides. There may be questions that should not be asked because of cultural differences, and others that need to be asked in order to more fully understand clients' situations.

Developing competence in working with diverse people and acquiring the knowledge about diverse client groups required for culturally competent practice will be a long-term, even lifelong process. Relish the possibilities available to you as you venture into work with clients and communities who are very different from you and remain aware of the limitations of your ability to understand others' experiences and interpretations of them. Even skilled and experienced social workers cannot know the intricacies of every culture or minority group, so try to learn about the world of others in an authentic way.

The reasons for ongoing growth in cultural competence are listed below. Reflect on them to understand why cultural competence will need to be enhanced over a career, and how these reasons, both psychological and social, go to the core beliefs, experiences, and assumptions of social workers.

Ethical Practice

Practice Behavior Example: Social workers make ethical decisions by applying standards of the National Association of Social Workers Code of Ethics

Critical Thinking Question: Upon which NASW ethical principles is cultural competence based?

- We operate on **assumptions** about people and the world that we may not be aware of until they are challenged in some way.
- We **process information** about people based on these assumptions.
- Our **values** shape the way we view others.
- The way we are **socialized** to view difference may negatively impact our ability to relate to people who are different from us.
- Our **social systems and peers** tend to support our assumptions and beliefs, not challenging our views of diverse peoples' experiences.
- Our **cultural identity** is central to all aspects of our relationships and interactions.
- Our **integration of cultural identity** is so strong within us that encounters with diverse people may cause discomfort, fear, or judgment.
- Our **social reality** is very different from that of our clients.
- Our **rhetoric** about being culturally competent may not be consistent with the actual **reality** of our professional behavior.

Develop what is called a **dual perspective**, which is the ability to focus simultaneously on the attitudes, values, and customs of the larger society and the attitudes, values, and customs of the individual client or family. Doing this while being aware of the impact of your own values, attitudes, and customs will help you effectively relate to diverse clients, understand how they are impacted by the larger society, and at least partially view your clients' experiences from their point of view and not just your own.

Agencies sometimes intentionally or unintentionally adopt attitudes, engage in behavior, and enact agency policies that reinforce stereotypes, widen the gap between social workers and clients, and eventually result in clients choosing to separate themselves from these agencies. Watch for agency attitudes, behaviors, and policies that might be uninformed, stereotypical, or culturally inappropriate.

Work to develop the ability to move between your culture and that of your clients, recognizing that this can be done only partially in spite of your best efforts because of ethnocentrism. Expand your knowledge of diverse people, increasing your awareness of the impact of your own cultural identity on your work and recognizing that communication with your clients and their communication with you are both seen through personal and cultural filters. This will reduce the chances of misinterpretation and inappropriate interventions, while increasing the chances that an effective professional relationship will set the stage for a culturally appropriate and effective intervention. Remember that your own position in relation to your clients may be one of privilege. If so, try to understand how clients might view you, look for commonalities while respecting difference, challenge oppression, learn from your clients, work to identify any biases, and equalize power when you can.

Table 12.3 illustrates a number of major practice guidelines for culturally competent practice which should be followed by both individual social workers and organizations. Study yourself, other social workers, and your agency to assess their

Table 12.3 Guidelines for Culturally Competent Practice

Social Work Guidelines	Organizational Guidelines
Learn history of diverse groups served	Learn history of diverse groups served
Seek training in cultural competence	Conduct outreach activities
Utilize supervision for professional growth	Design inviting physical environment
Adapt communication styles	Prepare inclusive written materials
Adapt all phases of planned change efforts	Develop comprehensive referral network
Recognize limits of cultural competence	Train staff in cultural competence
Resist tendency to overgeneralize	Diversify workforce
Resist tendency to become defensive	Develop culturally sensitive agency policies
Resist tendency to confirm stereotypes	Develop culturally sensitive interventions
Recognize client view of social work	Include diverse groups in client feedback loop
Learn from diverse clients	Utilize strengths perspective on diverse groups
Utilize strengths perspective on clients	Be willing to engage in social justice efforts
Utilize culturally appropriate tools	Recognize limits of charity orientation
Remember impossibility of cultural neutrality	Remember impossibility of cultural neutrality
Understand client views of help-seeking	Acquire best practices in cross-cultural work
Understand client view of success	Include commitment to diversity in mission

level of cultural competence. Is your agency working to serve diverse clients well and appropriately? Does it engage in the practices listed in the table to enhance its ability to work with diverse clients? What else might it do to increase its organizational competence, given the fact that true cultural competence is probably never fully achieved by either individual social workers or social agencies?

In order to understand specifically how cultural competency positively impacts the success of interventions and how cultural incompetency negatively impacts the success of interventions, refer to Table 12.4. Consider

Table 12.4   Impact of Cultural Competency and Incompetency on Social Work Practice

Cultural Competencies	Impact of Culturally Competent Social Work	Impact of Culturally Incompetent Social Work
Knowledge Understands meaning of culture and is aware of history of diverse groups and intergroup relations, knowledgeable about social policy impact on diverse groups, and insightful about impact of diversity on social development and functioning	**Understanding** Results in multilevel interventions which consider history and context, incorporates history and diversity, and influences social policies	**Misunderstanding and lack of information** Results in less effective multilevel interventions not based on history and context, ignores history and diversity, and does not challenge social policies
Self-awareness Aware of how personal history and experience influence practice; understands impact of privilege and oppression experiences; works to reduce own biases, stereotypes, and ethnocentricity	**Knowledge of self** Increases accuracy of assessment of clients based on personal experience, aware of own privilege or oppression, and works to address biases and stereotypes	**Unaware of self** Prone to inaccurate assessment of clients based on personal experience, lacks awareness of own privilege or oppression, and unaware of need to address biases and stereotypes which negatively impact clients
Values Focuses on social work values such as social justice and appreciation of diversity, works for equality and empowerment, works to alleviate oppression and promote human rights	**Incorporates social work values** Bases multilevel interventions on social justice and human rights, includes cultural differences in intervention, empowers clients to reduce oppression	**Unaware of relevance of social work values** Does not recognize how social justice and human rights provide foundation for practice, unaware of impact of inequality and lack of power on client functioning and intervention success
Multilevel Skills (individuals and families) Incorporates culturally competent communication skills in assessment, planning, implementation, and evaluation at micro, mezzo, and macro levels of practice	**Uses culturally competent approaches at micro level** Designs and implements culturally appropriate interventions, uses culturally appropriate evaluation techniques and standards, and is more likely to be effective	**Uses culturally inappropriate approaches at micro level** Designs and implements culturally inappropriate interventions, uses culturally inappropriate evaluation techniques and standards, and is less likely to be effective

"Six Levels of Cultural Competency and Cultural Sensitivity Among Human Services Agencies (list) adapted from *Services to Minority Populations: Cultural Competence Continuum*" by T. L. Cross, from FOCAL POINT, Edition 3(1), 1988. Copyright © 1988 by Research & Training, Regional Research Institute, Portland State University, Portland, OR. Reprinted with permission.

how successful or unsuccessful the interventions you and clients who are very different from you might be in these particular ways depending upon how culturally competent you are.

Developing Cultural Competence: A Workbook Activity

1. How might your own cultural identity (including ethnicity, gender, age, religion, political orientation, sexual orientation, ability) affect your work with clients who are different from you?

_____

_____

_____

2. Think of a time when you experienced one of the following:

Inaccurate assumptions about you by others _____

Misunderstanding of core aspects of your identity _____

Stereotyping _____

Categorizing _____

Discriminating _____

Demeaning treatment based on your diversity _____

Oppression _____

Consider how these personal experiences might also be those of your clients, maybe in interaction with you. Think about how you can avoid doing this with a client.

_____

_____

_____

3. What biases and stereotypes, if any, have you identified within yourself as you work with clients who are different from you? What can you do to ensure that these do not color your work negatively?

_____

_____

_____

4. What steps can you take to improve your skills in working with diverse clients?

_____

_____

_____

5. What should you do if you make a mistake based on a lack of cultural knowledge?

_____

_____

_____

6. How can you find a trusted person to teach you about their culture and how social workers can engage effectively with people who identify with this culture, broadly defined?

_____

_____

_____

Cultural Competence in Your Agency: A Workbook Activity

1. What specific actions has your agency taken to make sure it is in compliance with the federal law that prohibits discrimination on the basis of race, color, sex, national origin, age, religion, creed, physical or mental disability, and familial status?

_____

_____

_____

2. In what ways does your agency make accommodations for clients or consumers who have a physical or mental disability or limitation or who are not fluent in or comfortable with the English language?

_____

_____

_____

3. What special efforts, if any, has your practicum agency made to reach out to and provide relevant services or programs to members of minority groups?

_____

_____

_____

4. What culturally sensitive assessment instruments or practice techniques, if any, does your agency use with clients who are members of minority groups?

_____

_____

_____

5. Is there anything about your agency that might discourage minorities from using its services (e.g., the racial, ethnic, or gender makeup of staff; location; office hours and days of operation; reputation in community; costs; perceived attitude toward minorities)?

_____

_____

_____

6. What recourse and grievance procedures are available to clients or consumers if they believe they have experienced discrimination by the agency or its staff?

_____

_____

_____

7. Does your agency or organization have an affirmative action program that is applied when hiring new staff? If yes, does the program achieve its purpose?

_____

_____

_____

Diversity in Client Behavior: A Workbook Activity

Many factors influence the behavior and decisions of clients. One important set of factors, but certainly not the only one, is the client's cultural and ethnic background. Below is a list of situations that a social worker might encounter. Read each one carefully and answer each of the following questions the situations.

    A. What **diverse beliefs, values, minority status, or customs** are operating in this situation that might explain or clarify the client's behavior or choices?

    B. How might these **situations be misunderstood** if you are not familiar with the beliefs and customs of the client?

    C. What else would you **need to know** in order to be competent in this situation?

    D. What individual, family, or **cultural strengths** might be identified in these situations?

1. A low-income couple with six children lives in a small and crowded house and has great difficulty financially. They choose to have additional children, which will strain the family even more financially.

    A. _Religious beliefs related to birth control?_

    B. _Think of family as not planning or being responsible_

    C. _Ask about their beliefs + what they think the solution is._

    D. _Strong focus on family life_

2. A man who needs his job and wants to keep it did not report to work today. Instead, he drove 200 miles to be with a relative who had phoned him last night and requested his assistance.

    A. _Strong emphasis on dedication to family_

    B. _He doesn't want the job._

    C. _What are the cultural values at play and how can he fulfill both roles?_

    D. _Loyalty, respect, cares, community_

3. Parents of two children refuse to allow them to participate in their school's sex education programs.

   A. _____

   B. _____

   C. _____

   D. _____

4. The family of a hospital patient moves into the hospital room and begins using cultural healing practices unknown to the medical staff.

   A. _____

   B. _____

   C. _____

   D. _____

5. A family with a child who is deaf refuses to let him learn sign language.

   A. _____

   B. _____

   C. _____

   D. _____

6. A family with conservative religious views will only accept services from faith-based organizations.

   A. _____

   B. _____

   C. _____

   D. _____

7. A family chooses to home school their children and refuses to cooperate with governmental guidelines regarding the education of their children.

   A. _____

   B. _____

   C. _____

   D. _____

8. During the first meeting with a social worker, a client asks the worker many personal questions about the worker's parents, children, marriage, religion, and family history.

   A. _Low power difference – relationships_

   B. _Noisy_

   C. _What's their background + how is it shaping their values_

   D. _They are engaging with me and building report._

9. A woman whose husband restricts her movement, and verbally and physically abuses her, returns to live with her husband after seeking shelter for herself and her children in a domestic violence shelter.

    A. _____

    B. _____

    C. _____

    D. _____

10. An immigrant family who was robbed of several valuable possessions refuses to report the crime to the police.

    A. *Past trauma with police, corruption, questioning authority*

    B. *Not assertive*

    C. *Why?*

    D. *They still have lots of strengths and have told me about what*

11. An enrolled member of an American Indian tribe is in need of social services, but is reluctant to accept them from an agency that provides these services to individuals and families from many different backgrounds.

    A. _____

    B. _____

    C. _____

    D. _____

12. A family eligible for needed social services available on proof of citizenship chooses not to use these services.

    A. _____

    B. _____

    C. _____

    D. _____

13. An elderly woman who could benefit from mental health services declines them.

    A. _____

    B. _____

    C. _____

    D. _____

14. A person involved in a same-sex relationship is experiencing intimate violence at the hands of his or her partner, but declines to seek legal protection.

    A. _____

    B. _____

    C. _____

    D. _____

15. A student with a severe learning disability refuses university-provided accommodations, and is in danger of being placed on academic probation because her grade-point average is below the university requirement for good academic standing.

A. _____

B. _____

C. _____

D. _____

Suggested Learning Activities

- Attend cultural and religious celebrations and activities that are meaningful to many of the clients or consumers served by your agency (e.g., powwows, religious ceremonies, and gay pride events).
- Invite respected members of various ethnic and religious groups to explain how cultural and religious factors might influence clients' perceptions of the agency's programs and services and whether they would be inclined to use those services.
- Listen to music and read books and poetry by members of cultural or minority groups served by your agency.
- Visit agencies that specifically serve members of minority groups (e.g., refugee programs, women's centers, gay and lesbian community centers, and advocacy groups for persons with disabilities). Ask how their programs differ from yours.
- Seek special training designed to help human services personnel respond more effectively to diverse clients.
- Examine assessment tools used in your agency to determine if they are culture-bound or culturally inappropriate.
- In Sheafor and Horejsi (2012), read the section titled "Applying Cultural Competence to Helping" (123–127).
- Seek opportunities for cultural immersion experiences.

References

Anderson, Joseph, and Robin Wiggins Carter, eds. *Diversity Perspectives for Social Work Practice.* Boston: Allyn and Bacon, 2003.

Appleby, George A., Edgar Colon, and Julia Hamilton. *Diversity, Oppression, and Social Functioning: Person-in-Environment Assessment and Intervention.* 2nd ed. Boston: Allyn and Bacon, 2007.

Child Welfare League of America. *Cultural Competence Self-Assessment Instrument.* Washington, DC: Child Welfare League of America, 2002.

Coggins, Kip, and Bonnie Hatchett. *Skill Building from a Multicultural Perspective.* 2nd ed. Peosta, IA: Eddie Bowers Publishing, 2009.

Dhooper, Sirjit Singh, and Sharon S. Moore. *Social Work Practice with Culturally Diverse People.* Thousand Oaks, CA: Sage Publications, 2001.

Dominelli, Lena. *Anti-Racist Social Work.* 3rd ed. New York: Palgrave MacMillan, 2008.

Gerstein, Lawrence, P. Paul Heppner, Stefania Aegisdottir, Ming A. Leung, and Kathryn Norsworthy. *Essentials of Cross-Cultural Counseling.* Thousand Oaks, CA: Sage Publications, 2011.

Hunt, Matthew. *Race, Racial Attitudes and Stratification Beliefs.* Thousand Oaks, CA: Sage Publications, 2011.

Lum, Doman. *Culturally Competent Practice: A Framework for Understanding Diverse Groups and Justice Issues.* 3rd ed. Florence, KY: Brooks/Cole, 2007.

National Association of Social Workers. *NASW Standards for Cultural Competence in Social Work Practice.* Washington, DC: NASW Press, 2007.

Rothman, Juliet. *Cultural Competence in Process and Practice: Building Bridges.* Boston: Allyn and Bacon, 2008.

Shaefer, Richard. *Racial and Ethnic Groups.* 10th ed. Upper Saddle River, NJ: Prentice-Hall, 2006.

Sheafor, Bradford, and Charles Horejsi. *Techniques and Guidelines for Social Work Practice.* 8th ed. Boston: Allyn and Bacon, 2012.

Sisneros, Jose, Catherine Stakeman, Mildred C. Joyner, and Catheryne L. Schmitz. *Critical Multicultural Social Work.* Chicago: Lyceum, 2008.

Sue, Donald, and David Sue. *Counseling the Culturally Diverse: Theory and Practice.* 5th ed. New York: John Wiley and Sons, Inc., 2008.

Weaver, Hilary. *Explorations in Cultural Competence: Journeys to the Four Directions.* Florence, KY: Brooks/Cole, 2005.

Wronka, James. *Human Rights and Social Justice: Social Action and Service for the Helping and Health Professions.* Thousand Oaks, CA: Sage Publications, 2007.

CHAPTER 12 REVIEW

PRACTICE TEST

The following questions will test your knowledge of the content found within this chapter.

1. The learned patterns of thought and behavior which are passed from generation to generation and which include values, beliefs, and customs are referred to as
   a. family of origin issues
   b. diversity
   c. ethnicity
   d. culture

2. Evaluating a person negatively based on a group or category to which he or she belongs is
   a. ethnocentrism
   b. prejudice
   c. affirmative action
   d. privilege

3. Ethnocentrism is
   a. the belief that all cultures are central
   b. the belief that equality is impossible to achieve
   c. the belief, probably unconscious, that one's culture is superior to other cultures
   d. discrimination based on stereotypes

4. The NASW cultural competency standards for social workers
   a. set a firm standard in each potential intervention
   b. provide specific guidelines for individual interventions
   c. require a lifelong commitment to increasing competency
   d. are in conflict with the NASW *Code of Ethics*

5. The NASW cultural competency standards
   a. suggest client assessment tools that are standardized
   b. include mandatory cultural sensitivity training
   c. suggest evaluations that can be universalized
   d. focus on service delivery and a diverse workplace

6. The concept of human rights is
   a. separate from the NASW *Code of Ethics* in concept and values
   b. in line with the NASW *Code of Ethics* in concept and values
   c. restricted to global issues
   d. the basis of U.S. laws

7. Describe and provide a rationale for two major organizational practices for ensuring culturally competent social work for diverse clients.

©Monkey Business Images/Dreamstime

13

Professional Social Work

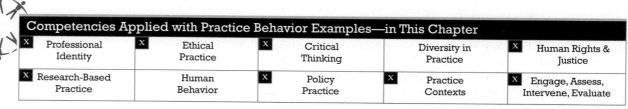

Competencies Applied with Practice Behavior Examples—in This Chapter				
X Professional Identity	X Ethical Practice	X Critical Thinking	Diversity in Practice	X Human Rights & Justice
X Research-Based Practice	Human Behavior	X Policy Practice	X Practice Contexts	X Engage, Assess, Intervene, Evaluate

CHAPTER PREVIEW

This chapter focuses on the profession of social work, including the unique scope and domains of social work practice. It offers information on professional social work behavior, moving from the role of practicum student to the role of professional social worker, and skill expectations for the generalist social worker at the micro, mezzo, and macro levels. It discusses the variety of social work roles required and offers insight into the balance of the art and science of social work practice.

Social workers see themselves as professionals and they describe their occupation as a profession. As a social work student you are expected to behave in a professional manner during your practicum, but what exactly is a profession and what does professional behavior look like? How does one decide whether clients are treated in a truly professional manner and always receive professional services? Does the presence of professionally trained social workers in an agency have an observable and positive effect on the nature and quality of the services received by clients?

Social work is one of many helping professions. Social workers often work closely with other helpers such as physicians, nurses, speech therapists, psychologists, substance abuse counselors, school counselors, and others. What do social workers do that is not done by the members of other helping professions? Is there anything unique or special about what social workers know or do? How is social work different? What exactly does a practicum student need to do to develop into a professional social worker?

BACKGROUND AND CONTEXT

All professions are expected to be unique and all professionals are expected to have special and unique knowledge and skills. They understand certain phenomena better than those who do not have this special training. Because they adhere to a code of ethical conduct, their clients and the public at large can expect ethical conduct and behavior from them. They are accountable for their decisions and actions. Professionals also lay claim to a certain domain of activities, which is the basis for professional licensing and certification. From a legal perspective, professionals are responsible for providing their clients with a certain standard of care, and if they fail to do so, they may be sued for malpractice or professional negligence. Broadly speaking, a **profession** is an occupation that possesses certain characteristics:

- Unique **body of knowledge and theories** from which special skills and techniques are derived
- **Unique set of skills and abilities** to perform professional tasks that other professionals or persons cannot perform
- **Professional, accredited education** for those entering the profession
- **Recognition by society** that the members of the profession possess a special expertise
- **Sanction by the community or state** to perform certain activities
- Practitioners who share a distinct **culture, specialized language** or terminology, **sense of purpose, identity, history, and set of values**
- Set of **professional values and a written code of ethics** that guide practice activities

- *Professional organizations* whose members are bound together by a common purpose
- *Capacity and authority*, usually by law, *to regulate practice*, admitting new members and ensuring quality of services to clients
- A *sense of "calling"* to the profession by those entering it by virtue of their values, interests, or natural abilities

The social work profession uniquely assumes responsibility for promoting the social functioning of individuals, families, and communities at the *micro, mezzo,* and *macro levels*. This means that social workers not only provide services to individuals, families, groups, organizations, and communities, but just as importantly work to implement social policies and promote societal conditions that will also support social functioning. The term *social functioning* refers to the social well-being of people and especially their capacity and opportunity to meet their basic needs such as food, shelter, safety, and self-worth, and to satisfactorily perform their social roles such as spouse, parent, student, employee, and citizen. It is the promotion of social functioning that is the unique focus and domain of the profession.

Professional Identity

Practice Behavior Example: Social workers engage in lifelong learning.

Critical Thinking Question: In what circumstances might a social worker be expected to simultaneously intervene at the micro and macro levels?

Social work professionals focus primarily on the interactions or transactions between the individual and his or her social environment. That environment is composed of a multitude of units and systems such as family; support networks; neighborhood and community groups and organizations; workplace; and various legal, educational, health, and human services systems. This is often referred to as the *person-in-environment focus* of the social work profession. Social workers focus on how well the social environment supports individuals and families, and what clients can do to enhance the social systems of which they are a part. A social worker will perform tasks and activities aimed at achieving these broad goals:

- Enhance the *problem-solving and coping capacities* of people
- Restore and maintain the *social functioning* of people
- *Prevent the occurrence* of serious personal and social problems
- Link people with those *systems and resources* that can provide needed support, services, and opportunities
- *Protect the community* from persons who consistently behave in ways that harm others
- Promote *humane and effective social policy and social services programs*
- *Plan, develop, and administer* social agencies and social programs
- Protect the most *vulnerable members of society* from destructive social influences
- Conduct *research* and develop and disseminate knowledge relevant to the practice of social work

A profession can be viewed as an organized effort to actualize its core values. Social work is often described as a *values-driven profession* because so much of what a social worker does is guided by a particular set of core values. However, all professions are rooted in a particular set of values. The social work profession has a foundation of values which include service, equality, promotion of human rights, and working toward social justice. These social work values are at play in all of the interactions social workers have with clients, and form the basis for their work. You will find it interesting to think about, observe, and participate in interventions that are intentionally based on social work values.

The social work profession holds high standards for its members, including the demonstration of professional behavior. This is vital for you as a new social worker to understand, because adhering to these standards will help to ensure that clients receive the highest quality of services. Engaging in nonprofessional behavior puts clients at risk, reduces the quality of services, undermines the public image of the profession, and may violate the profession's ethical principles. Although social work is a profession, social workers may or may not behave in a professional manner. Nonprofessional behavior leads to diminished quality of services and may also violate the National Association of Social Workers (NASW) *Code of Ethics*.

Most social workers are employed by some type of social agency or social welfare organization and often experience a push and pull between loyalty to their organization and loyalty to the values and principles of the social work profession. They believe in the core values and mission of the **organization**, but find the core values of the **social work profession** to be more important to them if they are ever in conflict. Much of what a social worker does is shaped—and sometimes driven—by agency policy. For this reason, social workers must be attentive to the nature and purpose of their agency's policies and how they impact clients. From the perspective of professional social work, an agency policy should have the following characteristics:

- It promotes the **well-being of clients** and the community as a whole.
- It is **respectful and fair** to those most directly affected.
- It serves to **empower clients**, recognizing and building on their strengths.
- It promotes **social and economic justice**, directly or indirectly.
- It is consistent with the values and principles of the **NASW Code of Ethics**.
- It is consistent with **evidence-based practice**.
- It holds social workers and other agency employees **accountable** for the work they perform and the services they provide.
- It is **clearly written, realistic and in compliance** with relevant legal codes and regulations.

GUIDANCE AND DIRECTION

A big challenge you will face in your practicum, but hopefully one you will take on enthusiastically, is making the transition from the status of student to the role and expectations of a professional social worker. As a student in the classroom, you were allowed to listen without responding, or to learn about theory without having to apply it. In the practicum, all that changes. Consider how the roles of student and social worker differ, as shown in Table 13.1.

Engage, Assess, Intervene, Evaluate

Practice Behavior Example: Social workers select appropriate intervention strategies.

Critical Thinking Question: What learning experiences can you design for yourself that will help you make the transition from student to professional?

Table 13.1   Student versus Social Worker Role

Student Role	Social Worker Role
Learns passively	Learns actively and applies learning
Engages in theoretical discussions and hypothetical decisions	Applies theory to real clients
Has occasional absences from class or practicum without consequence to self or client	Needs to be fully present to ensure quality
Defers to others in decision-making and intervention	Takes initiative in developing and implementing interventions
Assumes partial responsibility	Assumes full responsibility
Bases work on theory and academic preparation	Bases work on academic preparation as well as accumulated experience and practice wisdom
May take client feedback personally and react emotionally	Sees client feedback as crucial to professional growth

As you move from the role of **student to professional**, evaluate yourself honestly in terms of where you are on the continuum between the two. Push yourself to leave a passive and partial student role behind, choosing to do whatever you can to assume the roles and responsibilities of a professional. Do not wait until you are in your first social work position to make this transition. Your future clients deserve the highest level of professionalism you can offer when you are a student as much as they will when you have finished your education and training.

A primary purpose of the practicum is to help you develop a **professional identity** as a social worker. To achieve this identity means that you have a clear understanding of the purpose of the profession, your roles and responsibilities as a social worker, the profession's core values and ethical guidelines, and the skills and knowledge needed to perform social work tasks and activities. You can begin developing a professional identity by observing other social workers and reflecting on their behavior, decisions, and attitudes. You will notice all of the professional social work roles that you learned about in the classroom being played out in real-life situations. Tables 13.2, 13.3, and 13.4 illustrate the **social work roles** played at the micro, mezzo, and macro levels of social work practice, accompanied by the major **social work skills** required at each level of practice.

Read the job description for social workers in your agency and determine if it is consistent with the profession's stated purposes, values, and practice roles. Watch for variation between how social workers define their own roles and responsibilities and how their roles may be defined by administrators or funding sources. Ask your field instructor or other social workers how they attempt to meet the expectations of high-level administrators and fiscal managers while still adhering to the mission and purpose of the profession and fulfilling their obligations to their clients.

You will begin to notice how the values, knowledge base, and approach of the social work professional are different from those of other helping professionals such as clinical psychologists, nurses, school counselors, physicians,

Table 13.2   Microlevel Practice: Social Work Roles and Skills

Microlevel Roles ↓	Microlevel Skills ↓
Advocate	• Assesses client need • Identifies resources and gaps • Understands social policy • Speaks on behalf of vulnerable clients
Broker	• Knows resources and gaps • Links clients to resources • Makes appropriate referrals
Case manager	• Identifies resources and gaps • Secures services for clients with multiple needs • Monitors and manage services
Counselor	• Assesses psychosocial needs of client or family • Understands orienting/explanatory theories • Understands practice theories/models • Utilizes psychotherapeutic techniques to address psychosocial needs
Educator	• Designs curricula to address educational needs of clients and families • Uses teaching techniques to promote social functioning
Mediator	• Understands dynamics of interpersonal conflict • Utilizes techniques to resolve conflicts that promote social functioning of parties
Networker	• Understands dynamics of social systems • Uses techniques to promote linkages between individuals and/or social systems

Table 13.3   Mezzolevel Practice: Social Work Roles and Skills

Mezzolevel Roles ↓	Mezzolevel Skills ↓
Administrator	• Understands organizational structure, dynamics, and development • Utilizes techniques of supervision and administration
Facilitator	• Understands interactions of social systems and stakeholders in a practice situation • Utilizes techniques that promote communication within social systems and progress toward mutual goals
Mediator	• Understands dynamics of conflict between groups and organizations • Utilizes conflict resolution techniques that promote interests of involved parties
Program developer	• Knows how to assess need for program development • Matches community needs to program development • Utilizes organizational skills to design and develop programs to address social needs

Table 13.4   Macrolevel Practice: Social Work Roles and Skills

Macrolevel Roles ↓	Macrolevel Skills ↓
Community developer	• Assesses conditions within communities that need to be addressed to build capacity and strengthen social bonds • Utilizes techniques to support community goals and address community needs
Community organizer	• Identifies community needs and community motivation for social change • Utilizes techniques to promote social change that focuses on an identified social need or problem
Policy analyst/ developer	• Understands impact of social policy on clients and client systems and the process for forming and influencing social policy • Utilizes approaches that build coalitions, mobilize resources, and effect social change through policy formation
Researcher	• Understands research approaches, methodology, and ethics • Conducts research that is designed to build knowledge base about social conditions and problems • Conducts research that evaluates effectiveness of programs, practice models, and social policies
Social planner	• Understands the nature and dynamics of macrolevel social change • Understands social movements and planned social change • Utilizes techniques to systematically influence societal attitudes, policies, programs, and institutions

and vocational counselors. The uniqueness of the social work profession will become apparent if you truly understand the profession's core values and ethical principles, as well as the concept of social functioning. The **uniqueness of the social work profession** lies in its commitment to the overall social functioning of people as well as its commitment to working for social change and social justice. However, contrary to the beliefs of many social work students, social work is not unique because it pays attention to the whole person, the client's environment, and the ecological perspective. These are ideas also commonly discussed in textbooks for nursing, education, counseling, and occupational therapy. The distinctive identity of social work comes from its commitment to both enhancing the social functioning of clients and creating social environments, conditions, and social policies that promote positive social functioning.

In addition to those professionals and clients who understand and value the social work profession, at times you are likely to encounter **stereotypes** and **misconceptions** about social workers and the social work profession, just as you would for other professions. This is likely to be challenging, and you may need to inform others about the profession's real purposes and values, as well as about the level of education required for professional social work.

You might also ask yourself where these perceptions of social work originated, and consider whether some social workers may speak or behave in ways that perpetuate the stereotypes. Hopefully you will commit to challenging these stereotypes and promoting the status of the profession.

Negative images of the profession are often based on limited information about social work and sometimes on experiences with ineffective or unethical social workers. They could also be based on negative experiences with persons who are assumed to be social workers but who do not have a degree in social work. Give careful thought to whether social workers are recognized and respected as true professionals. Consider why social workers in certain agencies are viewed as professionals, whereas in other agencies they are not treated as professionals. Do what you can to enhance the image of the profession by purposefully using the title social worker to describe your work, by committing to practicing in the most competent and ethical manner possible, and by taking opportunities to inform the public about the profession.

Finally, you will probably find it helpful to remember that for all the emphasis on social work knowledge, theory, and research, you will not be effective if you do not pay close attention to what many consider the "art" of social work. As Sheafor and Horejsi (2012, 25–30) note, the "***social worker as artist***" has several components:

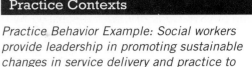

Practice Contexts

Practice Behavior Example: Social workers provide leadership in promoting sustainable changes in service delivery and practice to improve the quality of social services.

Critical Thinking Question: What responsibility does a social worker have to monitor, evaluate and improve services to clients?

- **Compassion and courage.** You will daily confront the pain of others and must join with them in a compassionate manner. You must also develop the inner strength to repeatedly face human suffering and frustration without being consumed by it.
- **Professional relationship.** Your most fundamental tool in practice is the capacity to build meaningful and productive professional relationships, which is rooted in your capacity for demonstrating empathy, genuineness, and nonpossessive warmth.

Ethical Practice

Practice Behavior Example: Social workers make ethical decisions by applying standards of the National Association of Social Workers Code of Ethics.

Critical Thinking Question: Upon what values and ethics of the profession is the concept of generalist practice based?

- **Creativity.** You must be innovative, imaginative, flexible, and persistent as you work to overcome barriers to change.
- **Hopefulness and energy.** You will need to believe in the basic goodness and ability of people, to continue working without becoming discouraged, and to bounce back from failures and mistakes.
- **Judgment.** You will need to develop sound judgment, critical thinking skills, thoughtful decision-making abilities, and the ability to reflect on and learn from successes and failures.
- **Personal values.** Your personal values must be compatible with the core values of social work, including respect for basic rights, a sense of social responsibility, commitment to individual freedom, and support for self-determination.
- **Professional style.** Because you are the instrument of change in practice, you will need to develop your own professional style, which is a combination of professional knowledge and your own personality and personal gifts.

Professional Social Work in Your Agency: A Workbook Activity

It is important to examine the impact of the profession's values, ethical code, practice principles, and knowledge base on the behavior and performance of the social workers in your practicum agency. In light of this, respond to the following questions.

1. Is the NASW *Code of Ethics* discussed by the social workers in your practicum agency?

_____

_____

_____

2. Does the NASW *Code of Ethics* appear to have a significant impact on decision making and practices within your practicum agency? If yes, in what ways? If no, why not?

_____

_____

_____

3. Do agency challenges (e.g., conflicts between personal and professional values, political pressures, or efforts to hold down operating costs) compromise good social work practice and basic principles of the NASW *Code of Ethics*?

_____

_____

_____

4. Which of the core values of social work are most apparent in your agency? Which are most lacking?

_____

_____

_____

5. Which of the core social work values are most consistent with your own personal values?

_____

_____

_____

6. Which of the following social work roles assumed by the social workers in your agency do you wish to experience?

_____	Administrator/manager/supervisor	_____	Group leader/facilitator
_____	Advocate	_____	Networker
_____	Broker of services	_____	Program planner
_____	Case manager	_____	Researcher/program evaluator
_____	Community developer	_____	Social activist
_____	Community organizer	_____	Social planner
_____	Counselor/therapist	_____	Social policy analyst/practitioner
_____	Educator/trainer	_____	Other (specify)

7. What are the requirements for obtaining and retaining a social work license in your state at the BSW and MSW levels (e.g., degree required, examination, years of experience, and hours of supervised practice)? What state agency is responsible for licensing?

_____

_____

_____

8. What percentage of the social workers in your agency have a social work degree? A social work license?

_____

_____

9. Does your agency require a specific social work degree (BSW or MSW) as preparation for certain positions or jobs? If yes, for what jobs?

_____

_____

10. What is the public image of social workers in your community? What forces and experiences have shaped this image?

_____

_____

11. What agency policies, procedures, and expectations reinforce and encourage social work professionalism within your agency or undermine it (e.g., continuing education is expected or not, workers are expected to take personal responsibility for decisions and actions or political concerns influence decisions, attention is given or not given to professional ethics)?

_____

_____

_____

12. What other professionals do you work with in or outside of your agency? How do you perceive your role and code of ethics to be similar to or different from theirs?

_____

_____

_____

Suggested Learning Activities

- Attend local chapter meetings of NASW or the meetings of other social work–related professional organizations and decide what issues are of greatest concern to the social workers in your community.
- Review announcements of social work conferences and workshops to determine what topics are of interest to social workers.
- Watch for media portrayals of social workers in newspapers, magazines, on television, or on the Internet to determine how social work is described and whether it is usually presented in a positive or negative light.

- Join the National Association of Social Workers as a student member, which will allow you to keep abreast of professional social work issues and programs and support its work.
- In Sheafor and Horejsi (2012), read and discuss the section titled "Improving the Social Work Image" (453–454).
- Investigate a variety of social work membership organizations, such as Association for Community Organization and Administration, the National Association of Black Social Workers, the Association of Oncology Social Workers, the National Association of Puerto Rican/Hispanic Social Workers, the Clinical Social Work Federation, the National Indian Child Welfare Association, the Rural Social Work Caucus, the Society for Spirituality in Social Work Practice, the North American Association of Christians in Social Work, International Federation of Social Workers, and the Social Welfare Action Alliance.

References

Barker, Robert L. *The Social Work Dictionary.* 5th ed. Washington, DC: NASW Press, 2003.

Commission on Accreditation. *Educational Policy and Accreditation Standards.* Alexandria, VA: CSWE, 2008.

DuBois, Brenda, and Karla Miley. *Social Work: An Empowering Profession.* 5th ed. Boston: Allyn and Bacon, 2008.

Finn, Janet L., and Maxine Jacobson. *Just Practice: A Social Justice Approach to Social Work.* 2nd ed. Peosta, IA: Eddie Bowers Publishing, 2008.

Gambrill, Eileen. *Social Work Practice. A Critical Thinker's Guide.* 2nd ed. New York: Oxford University Press, 2006.

Haynes, Karen, and Mickelson, James. *Affecting Change: Social Workers in the Political Arena.* 4th ed. Boston: Allyn and Bacon, 2000.

Hokenstad, Merl C., and James Midgley. *Lessons from Abroad: Adapting International Social Welfare Innovations.* Washington, DC: NASW Press, 2004.

LeCroy, Craig. *The Call to Social Work: Life Stories.* 2nd ed. Thousand Oaks, CA: Sage Publishing Company, 2011.

National Association of Social Workers. *Code of Ethics.* Washington, DC: NASW Press, 1999.

Payne, Malcolm. *Modern Social Work Theory.* 3rd ed. Chicago: Lyceum, 2005.

Sheafor, Bradford, and Charles Horejsi. *Techniques and Guidelines for Social Work Practice.* 9th ed. Boston: Allyn and Bacon, 2012.

Sheppard, Michael. *Social Work and Social Exclusion: The Idea of Practice.* Burlington, VT: Ashgate Publishing, 2006.

PRACTICE TEST

The following questions will test your knowledge of the content found within this chapter.

1. A body of knowledge, theory base, public sanction, code of ethics, and professional regulation are the main characteristics of a
   a. profession
   b. minority group
   c. social work school
   d. licensing body

2. The NASW definition of social work includes an emphasis on
   a. clinical practice
   b. micro- and macrolevel practice and the interaction between them
   c. political action
   d. continuing education

3. In comparison to other helping professions, the unique focus of social work is on
   a. psychological aspects of life
   b. spiritual aspects of life
   c. social functioning of individuals, families, and groups
   d. ethical standards for practice

4. Service, social justice, dignity and worth of the person, importance of human relationships, integrity, and competence are
   a. continuing education standards
   b. the core principles of the profession
   c. to be measured in each intervention
   d. the human rights values on which the profession is based

5. The social worker's duty to clients as the highest professional value is an example of
   a. a professional orientation to practice
   b. a social worker's individual moral code
   c. licensing requirements
   d. state law

6. Social workers are held accountable ethically and clinically through
   a. the use of standardized assessment tools
   b. the use of evidence-based practice
   c. the use of standardized evaluation tools
   d. the use of individualized treatment plans

7. In what ways is the social work role of advocate similar and different at the micro, mezzo, and macro levels of practice?

14

Social Work Ethics

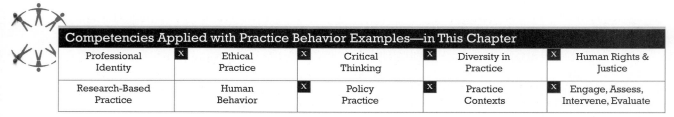

Competencies Applied with Practice Behavior Examples—in This Chapter									
Professional Identity		Ethical Practice	X	Critical Thinking	X	Diversity in Practice	X	Human Rights & Justice	X
Research-Based Practice		Human Behavior		Policy Practice	X	Practice Contexts		Engage, Assess, Intervene, Evaluate	X

CHAPTER PREVIEW

This chapter presents a description of professional values and ethics, and describes the ways in which professional codes of ethics can guide practice. It describes ethical competencies, ethical decision making, and a process for resolving ethical dilemmas. Tools are provided that demonstrate how primary social work values can be promoted through the use of specific agency practices and policies. The use of an ethics audit is also discussed as an organizational technique to monitor and maintain ethical service provision.

Every day, social workers make decisions and take actions based on ethical principles. These principles have a profound and far-reaching impact on practice. They also have a significant impact on a student's social work practicum. Prior to beginning your social work practicum, you have studied the **National Association of Social Workers** *Code of Ethics* and devoted classroom time to the discussion of ethical questions and issues. Up to this point, the topic of professional ethics may have seemed rather abstract, but in your practicum you will meet these questions and dilemmas face to face.

This chapter briefly reviews the nature of professional values and ethics, discusses a number of ethical issues common to social work, and offers guidance on identifying ethical issues and resolving ethical dilemmas. The workbook activity will heighten your awareness of ethical concerns within your practicum setting.

BACKGROUND AND CONTEXT

Each profession has a code of ethics that provides an ethical base for practice. These codes usually focus on professionals' responsibilities to those they serve, to the organizations for which they work, and to society at large. This is true for social work ethics, which you will be asked to apply daily in your practicum. Social work ethics are built upon a set of values that are central to the profession and give general guidance to social workers engaged in ethical decision making. *Ethical decision making* is the process of incorporating ethics into the decisions made at all phases of the planned change process, into organizational development, and into larger-scale efforts such as research and social justice efforts.

The term *ethical dilemma* describes a situation in which the social worker has two or more ethical obligations (e.g., to take action to protect the client from imminent harm and also to protect the client's right to privacy) but cannot adhere to one principle without violating another because of their conflicting and mutually exclusive nature. Rather than providing clear-cut guidance on each dilemma, the **NASW** *Code of Ethics* provides general principles that the social worker uses to make ethical decisions.

The standards for ethical conduct by social workers may be described as *ethical competencies*.

- The ethical social worker understands *definitions of ethics and values*, both personal and professional.
- The ethical social worker becomes familiar with the *NASW Code of Ethics*, including its purposes, uses, and limitations.

Practice Contexts

Practice Behavior Example: Social workers continuously discover, appraise, and attend to changing locales, populations, scientific and technological development, and emerging societal trends to provide relevant services.

Critical Thinking Question: In what ways might a social worker's responsibilities to clients conflict with his or her responsibilities to society at large?

- The ethical social worker develops the ability to *identify ethical issues* and situations.
- The ethical social worker develops and uses a *model of ethical decision making*.
- The ethical social worker develops the ability to examine, explore, and resolve *ethical dilemmas.*
- The ethical social worker understands connections between *ethical and legal issues* in practice.
- The ethical social worker *applies NASW Code of Ethics* to all levels of practice.
- The ethical social worker understands *potential ethical violations* and their consequences.
- The ethical social worker *applies critical thinking skills* to ethics in practice.
- The ethical social worker understands the importance of *supervision and continuing education.*

Your practicum agency's process or procedures for resolving ethical issues and dilemmas may be written or informal. Your agency may use ethics committees, staff discussions, and outside legal and ethics consultations to help staff members make difficult decisions. Hopefully you will be able to participate in such meetings as often as possible, because this will help you develop awareness of and skill in identifying and resolving ethical dilemmas. Each situation is unique to some degree, and there is seldom only one right way to deal with it, which is the nature of an ethical dilemma. Over time, you will become more comfortable with this uncertainty and be better able to sort out the competing values and potential consequences of each decision.

Professional Identity

Practice Behavior Example: Social workers use supervision and consultation.

Critical Thinking Question: Who can you ask to help you sort through ethical decisions and dilemmas?

When you encounter an ethical dilemma, consider the *ethical decision-making guidelines* offered by Sheafor and Horejsi (2012, 121) and begin by seeking answers to questions such as the following:

- Who is your *primary client* (i.e., usually the person, group, or organization that requested the social worker's services and expects to benefit from them)?
- What aspects of the *agency's activity or worker's roles* and duties give rise to the dilemma (e.g., legal mandates, job requirements, agency policy, questions of efficient use of resources, possible harm caused by an intervention)?
- *Who can or should resolve* this dilemma? Is it rightfully a decision to be made by the client? Other family members? The worker? The agency administrator?
- For each decision possible, what are the *short-term and long-term consequences* for the client, family, worker, agency, and community?
- *Who stands to gain and who stands to lose* from each possible choice or action? Are those who stand to gain or lose of equal or unequal power (e.g., child vs. adult)? Do those who are most vulnerable or those with little power require special consideration?
- When harm to someone cannot be avoided, what decision will cause the *least harm* or a type of harm with fewest long-term consequences? Of those who might be harmed, who is least able to recover from the harm?

- Will a particular resolution to this dilemma set an **undesirable precedent** for future decision making concerning other clients?
- What **ethical principles and obligations** apply in this situation?
- Which, if any, **ethical principles are in conflict** in this situation and therefore create an ethical dilemma?
- In this situation, are **certain ethical obligations more important than others**?

GUIDANCE AND DIRECTION

It is likely that you will encounter some very troublesome situations in which all available choices or options are to some degree harmful and destructive to your client and other people. In such cases you must decide which option is the **least harmful**. Essentially, you are forced to choose the lesser of two or more evils. Although this is hard for even the seasoned social worker, it is a reality you will learn how to address.

An ethical area that may be confusing for you is the question of limits to **client confidentiality**. Clients have a **right to privacy**. However, this right is not absolute. There are limits and exceptions to a client's right to confidentiality, including situations in which social workers are considered to be **mandated reporters**. You may need to release client information without your client's permission when your client is abusing another person, is planning or has committed a serious and dangerous illegal act that places others in danger, or is threatening harm to himself or herself or to another person. Confidentiality also may not apply when you receive a court order requiring you to release client information or when a contract requires you to share information with a third party or when your client is a minor.

Be certain that you understand the federal and state laws which apply to confidentiality as well as related agency policy on dealing with confidentiality. Make sure that you understand the concept of **privileged communication**, which refers to the principle that clients can expect that their social worker cannot or will not share information without their consent because information shared with a profession social worker is protected by law.

Social agencies are guided by professional values and ethics, all of which can be addressed in multiple ways through **agency policies and guidelines**. Table 14.1 lists the primary social work values and shows how agencies can uphold these values through comprehensive and creative agency policies for ethical professional behavior. Review it and ask your field instructor if these agency practices are used in your agency. If some of these agency practices are not used in your agency, consider whether they would be helpful in promoting ethical professional care.

A recommended practice for agencies who wish to monitor their performance in terms of adherence to and use of practices that are ethical is an **ethics audit**. Such a review of an agency's compliance with its own policies and ethical stances can be done at various time intervals with information gathered from a number of sources, and used to assess the ethical operation of an agency. A sample ethics audit which uses the same agency practices and policies as Table 14.1 is shown in Table 14.2, "Agency Ethics Audit."

Ethical Practice

Practice Behavior Example: Social workers apply strategies of ethical reasoning to arrive at principled decisions.

Critical Thinking Question: How will you balance the values of client self-determination and the protection of vulnerable populations?

Table 14.1   **Social Work Values and Agency Practices to Support Them**

Agency Practices	Social Work Values							
	Dignity and Respect	Safety and Protection	Equality	Autonomy and Self-Determination	Privacy and Confidentiality	Service	Quality and Competency	Cultural Competency
Advisory Board	✓	✓	✓	✓		✓	✓	✓
Best Practices Policy	✓	✓	✓	✓	✓	✓	✓	✓
Bill of Rights	✓	✓	✓	✓	✓	✓	✓	✓
Choice and Right to Refuse	✓			✓		✓		✓
Code of Ethics	✓	✓	✓	✓	✓	✓	✓	✓
Confidentiality Statement	✓	✓		✓	✓	✓		
Conflict of Interest Policy		✓					✓	
Consultation		✓		✓	✓		✓	✓
Credential Verification		✓					✓	✓
Documentation	✓	✓	✓		✓		✓	✓
Ethical Decision-Making Process	✓	✓	✓	✓	✓	✓	✓	✓
Ethics Committee	✓	✓	✓	✓	✓		✓	✓
Grievance Policy	✓	✓		✓	✓	✓	✓	✓
Informed Consent Policy	✓	✓	✓	✓	✓		✓	✓
Length of Service Policy		✓	✓			✓	✓	✓
Payment Policy	✓	✓	✓		✓	✓	✓	✓
Privileged Communication Policy		✓		✓				✓
Release of Information	✓	✓			✓			
Staff Development	✓	✓	✓	✓	✓	✓	✓	✓
Supervision	✓	✓	✓	✓	✓	✓	✓	✓

"List of Ethical Competencies" from BSW Competency Catalogue. Copyright © 2008 by the University of Montana. Reprinted with permission.

Agency Ethics Audit

Agency Processes and Policies	Levels of Compliance			
	In Compliance (*Minimal risk*)	**Minor Noncompliance** (*Low risk*)	**Major Noncompliance** (*High risk*)	**Source of Data** 1. Record review 2. Staff interviews 3. Advisory board 4. Client input 5. Outside party input 6. Other
Advisory Board				
Best Practices Policy				
Bill of Rights				
Choice and Right to Refuse				
Code of Ethics				
Confidentiality Statement				
Conflict of Interest Policy				
Consultation				
Credential Verification				
Documentation of Services				
Ethical Decision-Making Process				
Ethics Committee				
Ethical Violation Policy				
Grievance Policy				
Informed Consent Policy				
Length of Service Policy				
Payment Policy				
Privileged Communication Policy				
Release of Information				
Staff Development and Training				
Supervision				

Instructions: This instrument will assist an agency to assess its own level of compliance with self-designed agency processes and policies that ensure ethical professional behavior. **Low levels of agency compliance are related to high levels of risk to clients and client systems. High levels of agency compliance are related to low levels of risk to clients and client systems.** Check the agency's level of compliance with each of its own internal processes and policies governing ethical practice. In the right-hand column, indicate what source of agency-related data was used to determine level of compliance with ethical agency processes and policies. Use this tool to identify agency strengths and weaknesses in ethical agency operations, both of which can be incorporated into organizational development efforts.

It is important to know how violations of ethical codes sometimes result in client complaints and lawsuits so that you can avoid such unprofessional behavior while in practicum. Alleged violations of ethics may include breach of confidentiality, lack of informed consent, dual relationships, incompetence, defamation of character, termination of services, lack of cultural competence, inequitable access or service, and violation of client self-determination. Not only do these behaviors on the part of a social worker raise the risk of malpractice claims, but they can undermine services and potentially bring harm to clients, some of whom may be in vulnerable situations.

In order to function effectively as a social worker, you must be able to distinguish between your ***personal values and morals*** and those of the client. As a general principle, you should not impose your values and beliefs on the client. However, this is a challenging principle of practice because the social work profession and social agencies are built on and represent a set of values and beliefs about what is good for people and desirable in human relationships. Moreover, some clients engage in behaviors that are clearly wrong and a danger to themselves and others (e.g., assault, rape, robbery, child neglect). In such situations, attempting to be value-free or value-neutral can be extremely dangerous, irresponsible, and possibly unethical.

Policy Practice

Practice Behavior Example: Social workers analyze, formulate, and advocate for policies that advance social well-being

Critical Thinking Question: What laws and social policies regulate the ethical decisions of social workers in your agency?

You may find that your personal moral code conflicts with the values of your clients, your field instructor, your agency, or even the NASW *Code of Ethics.* When you encounter such conflicts, do not ignore them. They are important questions and dilemmas that must be faced honestly and squarely. You will need to decide when you can and cannot suspend your personal moral code.

There may be times when you conclude that your agency violates certain ethical principles or the rights of certain clients. If this occurs, discuss your concerns with your field instructor or faculty supervisor in order to sort out the issues and determine whether an ethical principle is being violated and what choices you have.

Finally, think about the NASW *Code of Ethics* as a minimum baseline for ethical conduct and professional behavior. Find ways to do more than the minimum required, as or that will help to prevent complaints or allegations of negligence or misconduct. If the welfare of clients is always the primary focus of your work, it will be easy to provide ethical and competent services, document their provision, and give clients and client systems the services they deserve.

Values and Ethics in Your Practicum: A Workbook Activity

1. What ethical concerns or dilemmas are most frequently encountered in your practicum setting, according to your field instructor?

_____

_____

2. How do the social workers in your agency deal with ethical questions and resolve ethical dilemmas (e.g., discussions at a staff meeting, presentations to an ethics committee, consultation with experts)?

_____

_____

_____

3. To what degree and in what way does the NASW *Code of Ethics* influence the decisions and behavior of the social workers employed by your agency (e.g., referred to during case conferences and staff meetings and available to social workers)?

_____

_____

4. Does your agency have its own code of ethics or a code of conduct for its employees? If yes, how is it similar to and different from the NASW *Code of Ethics*?

_____

_____

5. Does your agency have policies that, in your opinion, are in violation of the NASW *Code of Ethics*? If yes, describe how these policies are in conflict with specific provisions of the NASW *Code of Ethics*.

_____

_____

6. How does your agency handle reports of ethics violations on the part of its staff (e.g., written incident reports, temporary suspensions of staff, formal investigations, grievance policies, reports to state licensing bodies)?

_____

_____

7. Have any agency social workers or other agency personnel been dismissed or reprimanded for ethics violations? If so, what was the nature and type of misconduct?

_____

_____

8. What ethical principles in the NASW *Code of Ethics* do you feel most strongly about? Why?

_____

_____

9. Does your agency have policies that are in conflict with your personal moral code? If yes, how will you handle or resolve these conflicts?

_____

_____

10. Are there statements or sections in the NASW *Code of Ethics* that are in conflict with your personal moral and ethical standards? If yes, how will you attempt to resolve these conflicts?

11. What is the name of the agency in your state responsible for handling formal complaints about ethics violations by licensed social workers? What process is used to investigate possible ethics violations?

12. What are the possible sanctions in your state for social workers who commit ethics violations (e.g., loss of license, civil action for monetary damages, criminal prosecution, sanctions by the NASW)?

Suggested Learning Activities

- Read and study the NASW *Code of Ethics*. It can be downloaded from the NASW's website (http://www.naswdc.org).
- If members of other professions (e.g., psychologists, nurses, or teachers) work in your practicum setting, secure a copy of their profession's code of ethics and compare it to the NASW *Code of Ethics*.
- Interview experienced social workers and ask them to describe the ethical issues they most often encounter and the issues that are especially difficult for them to resolve.
- Review your agency's policy manual and identify policy principles that are very similar to the NASW *Code of Ethics*. Identify policies that appear to be in opposition to the NASW *Code of Ethics*.
- In Sheafor and Horejsi (2012), read the section titled "Making Ethical Decisions" (120–123).

References

Baird, Brian N. *The Internship, Practicum, and Field Placement Handbook: A Guide for the Helping Professions*. 5th ed. Upper Saddle River, NJ: Prentice Hall, 2011.

Banks, Sarah. *Ethics and Values in Social Work*. 3rd ed. New York: Palgrave Macmillan, 2008.

Barnard, Adam, Nigel Horner, and Jim Wild, eds. *The Value Base of Social Work and Social Care*. New York: Open University Press, 2008.

Corey, Gerald, Marianne Schneider, and Patrick Callahan. *Issues and Ethics in the Helping Professions*. 6th ed. Florence, KY: Brooks/Cole, 2003.

Hartsell, Thomas L., and Barton E. Bernstein. *The Portable Ethicist for Mental Health Professionals: An A-Z Guide to Responsible Practice*. New York: John Wiley and Sons, 2000.

Houser, Rick, and Stephen Thoma. *Ethics in Counseling and Therapy: Developing an Ethical Identity*. Thousand Oaks, CA: Sage Publications, 2012.

National Association of Social Workers. *Code of Ethics*. Washington, DC: NASW Press, 1999.

Payne, Malcolm. *What Is Professional Social Work?* 2nd ed. Chicago: Lyceum Books, 2007.

Reamer, Frederick. *Ethical Standards in Social Work: A Review of the NASW Code of Ethics.* 2nd ed. Washington DC: NASW Press, 2006.

Sheafor, Bradford, and Charles Horejsi. *Techniques and Guidelines for Social Work Practice.* 9th ed. Boston: Allyn and Bacon, 2012.

Somers Flanagan, Rita, and John Somers Flanagan. *Becoming an Ethical Helping Professional: Cultural and Philosophical Foundations.* Thousand Oaks, CA: Sage Publications, 2007.

Strom-Gottfried, Kim. *Straight Talk about Professional Ethics.* Chicago: Lyceum Books, 2007.

Thomlison, Barbara, and Kevin Corcoran, ed. *The Evidence-Based Internship: A Field Manual.* New York: Oxford University Press, 2008.

CHAPTER 14 REVIEW

PRACTICE TEST

The following questions will test your knowledge of the content found within this chapter.

1. A practice situation in which two ethical standards are in conflict is
   a. a values conflict
   b. an ethical dilemma
   c. an ethical violation
   d. malpractice

2. Social workers who find their moral code in conflict with legal codes should do what to reconcile the conflict?
   a. consult with a supervisor for help
   b. consult with an attorney for help
   c. consult with a spiritual advisor for help
   d. consult with a coworker for help

3. The NASW *Code of Ethics* provides
   a. a clear guide for every potential ethical situation or conflict
   b. a general guideline of ethical principles that professionals use to make decisions
   c. a standard for client behavior
   d. a description of legal standards for social work

4. Clarifying who the primary client is in a potential intervention is helpful in
   a. resolving ethical dilemmas
   b. setting ethical standards for practice
   c. abiding by state laws regulations practice
   d. understanding clients' points of view

5. An ethical dilemma means that
   a. social workers are empowered to make decisions about clients' lives
   b. clients are empowered to make the choices about their lives
   c. legal codes take precedence over ethical codes
   d. choosing one value will result in another value being violated

6. Violations of professional ethics can lead to
   a. allegations of abuse
   b. agency support
   c. licensing and legal sanctions
   d. practice wisdom

7. Maintaining dignity and respect is one of the primary social work values upon which agencies build their policies. Describe two agency policies which can promote that value, and explain how the policy can do so.

© Vladek/Dreamstime

15

Legal Concerns

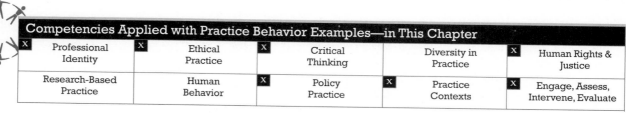

Competencies Applied with Practice Behavior Examples—in This Chapter				
x Professional Identity	x Ethical Practice	x Critical Thinking	Diversity in Practice	x Human Rights & Justice
Research-Based Practice	Human Behavior	x Policy Practice	x Practice Contexts	x Engage, Assess, Intervene, Evaluate

CHAPTER PREVIEW

This chapter provides an overview of the legal context of the practicum and social work practice. This includes basic legal terminology, examples of laws that impact clients and social workers, guidelines for functioning within the laws impacting social work practice, and suggestions for avoiding malpractice situations.

Social work, like all professions, is guided and impacted greatly by the law. Every social services agency is shaped and guided by specific codes or legal considerations. Some agencies were formed in response to a law requiring states or the federal government to provide specific programs and services. In some agencies, a client's eligibility for services is defined by law. In many instances, a social worker's actions are dictated by law, as in the case of mandated reporting of child abuse. Many social workers are licensed by state law and must practice in keeping with the provisions of that law and its provisions.

As a practicum student, you must understand the legal context of your professional practice. You must be alert to potential actions of yours and your agency that may violate the law and to the types of situations that might give rise to a lawsuit against an agency, a professional social worker, and even a social work student. You also need to understand which laws require you to take a specific action or which preclude you from certain actions. Because the legal context directly impacts social workers and clients, social workers must acquire a basic understanding of the laws and legal procedures that most directly impact their practice setting and clients served. They must become familiar with specific laws related to their practice roles, duties, and job description.

BACKGROUND AND CONTEXT

Social workers are often involved in helping their clients, groups, or organizations negotiate or utilize the legal system. This may involve advocating for and supporting individual clients and families, securing protections and reparations for clients, and securing various legal services for clients in need. Social workers may also become involved in macrolevel legal proceedings and legislative efforts such as promoting new laws, providing testimony on the impact of social policies on clients, or assisting groups involved in class action suits. In these cases of macro practice, the social worker must be skilled in the following:

- Preparing clients or groups to provide legislative testimony
- Drafting legislation to establish or amend current social policies
- Providing expert testimony at legislative hearings
- Encouraging client involvement in social policies which impact their lives
- Promoting voter registration efforts
- Engaging in efforts to empower clients and groups to advocate for themselves

Although it is not common for social work students to be sued for **negligence** or **malpractice**, it is possible. Because practicum students are acting in the capacity of social workers, they are held to the same standards of practice and ethical behavior that social workers are, and therefore it is vital to understand as much of the legal context of your agency as possible. It is also important to

Engage, Assess, Intervene, Evaluate

Practice Behavior Example: Social workers substantively and effectively prepare for action with individuals, families, groups, organizations, and communities.

Critical Thinking Question: Select an intervention in which you are involved and identify the precautions you need to take to prevent allegations of negligence and malpractice.

act in accordance with agency policy, professional standards, university policy, and the NASW *Code of Ethics* in order to provide the highest quality services to clients while also avoiding the possibility of malpractice allegations or lawsuits. It is recommended that you secure student professional liability and malpractice insurance through your university, the agency, the National Association of Social Workers, or independently.

Laws impacting both social work and clients are based on certain professional and societal values. They may have been enacted to promote social justice or to protect and ensure human rights. Such values include the following:

- Protection and safety of individuals
- Equality in access to or level of services
- Autonomy and freedom
- Least harm
- Quality of life
- Privacy and confidentiality
- Full disclosure
- Empowerment of vulnerable and oppressed populations.

As you learn about the laws specific to your agency and your clients, consider which of these social values underlie the laws you will be following or working to change.

BACKGROUND AND CONTEXT

Three broad categories of laws serve to guide, direct, and sometimes mandate the actions of social workers and agencies. Table 15.1 lists and describes these categories.

Table 15.1	**Laws Impacting Social Work Practice**
Category of Law	Impact on Social Work Practice
Laws regulating services or actions related to a specific client	Such laws may determine whether a client is eligible to receive a certain service or benefit, whether a specific client can be forced to accept intervention (e.g., involuntary hospitalization), or whether a particular family situation can be defined as suspected abuse or neglect that must be reported to the authorities because social workers are mandated reporters.
Laws regulating a field of practice or type of social services program	Specific social work arenas may have laws that affect the services provided by agencies in this arena. For example, if an agency provides service to youth, many of its policies and procedures for dealing with young clients will be shaped by laws related to the notification of parents regarding services to be provided to their children. In hospitals, laws related to informed consent, release of patient records, and durable power of attorney for health care are daily concerns to a medical social worker.

(continued)

Table 15.1   **Continued**

Category of Law	Impact on Social Work Practice
Laws regulating the professional practice of social work	Laws guiding professional social work practice such as state licensing laws for social workers dictate how social workers must conduct themselves in order to practice competently. These laws may deal with matters such as confidentiality, privileged communication, informed consent, responsibilities to clients, duty to warn, and requirements for obtaining a social work license. They set standards for professional conduct, provide procedures for dealing with allegations of misconduct, and specify disciplinary actions against social workers who violate laws or the ethics of the profession.

Practitioners and social work students must operate on the assumption that any of their professional records, case notes, reports, and correspondence may eventually become the target of a subpoena, gathered and reviewed by attorneys, and read in court. They need to be thoughtful and cautious about what they put into a written record and how they write it, for at some point they may be asked to explain and defend their statements.

Because a growing number of social workers are being sued for malpractice, this possibility must be considered daily, even as a practicum student. Malpractice and professional negligence fall under a category of law known as tort law. A **tort** is a private or civil wrong or injury that results from actions other than the breach of a formal legal contract and the commission of a crime. In order for the plaintiff (e.g., a social worker's client or former client) to be successful in this type of lawsuit alleging malpractice against a defendant (e.g., the social worker or practicum student), the plaintiff's attorney must prove four points:

1. The social worker had a **professional obligation** or duty to provide the plaintiff with a certain level of service, a certain standard of care, or a certain manner of professional conduct.

2. The social worker was **negligent or derelict** in his or her professional role because he or she did not live up to this recognized obligation or duty, standard of care, or expected professional conduct.

3. The plaintiff suffered **injury or harm** (e.g., physical, mental, emotional, or financial) as a result of what the social worker did (act) or did not do (omission) and this act or omission had a foreseeable harmful consequence for the plaintiff.

4. The social worker's act or omission was a **direct or proximate cause** of the harm experienced by the plaintiff.

A wide variety of **acts or omissions** can place social workers or the agencies for which they work at risk of being sued and held liable for causing harm to their clients or to individuals harmed by their clients. Such acts or omissions on the part of the social work might include the following:

- Failure to clearly outline duties of social worker and client
- Sexual or romantic involvement with a current or former client so that both parties understand and agree
- Failure to warn others when a client discloses clear intent to inflict serious physical harm on someone

- Failure to alert others when a client discloses intent to harm self
- Failure to attempt to prevent a client's suicide
- Failure to provide needed treatment and services to a client or premature release, termination, or abandonment of a client
- Failure to maintain and protect confidentiality
- Failure to maintain accurate professional records and a proper accounting of client fees, payments, and reimbursements
- Misrepresentation of professional training, experience, and credentials
- Breach of client civil rights
- Failure to refer clients to other services or professionals when indicated
- Misdiagnosis or use of harmful, inappropriate, or ineffective interventions
- Failure to protect a client from harm caused by other clients in a group, program, or facility
- Failure to report suspected child or elder abuse, neglect, or exploitation
- Treating clients without consent

Human Rights and Justice

Practice Behavior Example: Social workers understand the forms and mechanisms of oppression and discrimination.

Critical Thinking Question: How do the concepts of social work effectiveness and negligence relate to the concepts of human rights and social justice?

Certain clients and practice situations place social workers and agencies at a higher risk of being sued. These clients and situations may include the following:

- Clients who are a real physical danger to others
- Clients who have been separated from their children because of actions taken by the social worker or agency (e.g., foster care placement and custody evaluations)
- Clients with complex and intense needs requiring social workers to provide highly technical and competent services
- Clients at risk to commit suicide
- Clients who are very suspicious of others and quick to blame and accuse others of some wrongdoing
- Clients with a history of alleging malpractice and negligence and bringing suits against various professionals
- Clients who are very manipulative and deceptive

GUIDANCE AND DIRECTION

Make a special effort to become familiar with the laws relevant to your practicum setting, including the laws that regulate the services your agency provides and the laws that regulate professional social work practice. Depending on the nature and purpose of your agency, you will need to become familiar with federal and state codes, and sometimes local ordinances, that apply to your clients and the services your agency provides. Your clients' lives are affected directly and indirectly by such laws. For example, you may need to understand laws pertaining to the following areas when you engage in ***microlevel practice with individuals and families***

- Marriage, parenthood, divorce, and child custody
- Child or elder abuse and neglect
- Partner violence and abuse

- Termination of parental rights, foster care, and adoption
- Guardianship, conservatorship, power of attorney, durable power of attorney for health care
- Involuntary hospitalization of persons with mental illness
- Involuntary hospitalization of persons who are suicidal or a threat to others
- Parental notification regarding services provided to minors
- Adult and juvenile adjudication, probation, and parole
- Crime victim assistance
- Immigration and refugee status
- Buying and selling of illegal drugs
- Family planning, reproductive rights, and abortion
- Education of children with disabilities
- Discrimination in employment and housing
- Confidentiality in health and mental health settings
- Reporting of contagious diseases and public health hazards
- Personal debt and bankruptcy
- Disability accommodation
- Restorative justice

Diversity in Practice

Practice Behavior Example: Social workers recognize and communicate their understanding of the importance of difference in shaping life experiences.

Critical Thinking Question: In what ways might the experiences of diverse clients lead them to view the legal aspects of intervention differently?

Social work supervisors and administrators working at the ***mezzo or macro level of practice with organizations and communities*** will need a basic understanding of laws related to employee matters, financial management, and the like. Although as a practicum student, it is not likely you will be engaged in administration, laws that impact your agency are an important part of the context of providing quality services and of maintaining good employees and employee relations. Watch for opportunities to learn about laws pertaining to the following:

- Contracts, leases, and rental agreements
- Property and liability insurance
- Employee compensation and benefits
- Workers compensation and unemployment insurance
- Hiring and dismissal of employees
- Employee unions
- Financial recordkeeping
- Accessibility for persons with disabilities
- Restrictions on political action and lobbying by public employees
- Sexual harassment
- Drug-free workplaces
- Affirmative action
- Whistle-blowing in cases of alleged ethics violations or mistreatment of clients
- Mediation processes for individuals, groups, and organizations

In some settings, social workers are commonly required to appear in court. If social workers in your agency commonly appear in court, request the opportunity to observe their testimony. Determine their role and function in court, how they prepare for a court appearance, what types of questions they are asked by attorneys, what written documents they provide the court, and if their recommendations tend to be followed by judges. Give special thought to legal

Table 15.2 Guidelines for Testifying in Court

Stages of Providing Court Testimony	Guidelines
Preparation for Court Testimony	• Understand laws impacting intervention. • Read client files and understand history and prior legal proceedings. • Anticipate questions from attorneys and presiding judges. • Rehearse testimony, including providing your credentials, describing your intervention, answering questions, and making recommendations. • Be ready to provide professional and objective rationale for recommendations. • Request supervisor observation of court testimony.
Providing Court Testimony	• Dress professionally and in accordance with court requirements. • Demonstrate a calm, professional, and respectful demeanor. • Answer what is being asked. • Use professional terminology. • Explain the meaning of testimony when needed. • Provide factual, objective, and documented information.
Post-testimony Review	• Solicit feedback and constructive instruction on professional testimony. • Learn from preparing testimony. • Learn from questions resulting from testimony or mistakes made. • Incorporate the experience into preparation for subsequent testimony.

and ethical issues that may arise when social workers advocate for their clients, when they are asked to participate in involuntary treatment of clients, or when they must testify on behalf of one client and against another. Identify the social work interventions that follow those documents and orders. Learn about social workers who testify as expert witnesses and what is required of them.

If possible, read the case records of clients whose cases are heard in court. Read the petitions and other legal documents filed on behalf of or against your agency's clients. Read the court orders found in client records. If you have questions about what these records mean, ask your field instructor to explain their significance and what is expected of social workers in these situations. The process of becoming skilled in providing court testimony can be enhanced by separating the stages of court testimony into those described in Table. 15.2.

An agency policy and procedures manual generally describes a standard of care and service owed to, and expected by, the client. Thus, in a malpractice lawsuit, a social worker's failure to follow agency policy may be used as evidence of **professional negligence**. An agency places itself at higher legal risk when it has an official policy that is not or cannot be regularly followed by its employees. Agency policies will not protect social workers who do not abide by them. The best way to avoid becoming involved in a malpractice lawsuit is to be proactive in learning about and acting on the following guidelines:

- Read the **NASW Code of Ethics** regularly and abide by its guidelines.
- Adhere to **agency policy**, procedure, and protocol.
- Make every effort to **practice competently** and avoid situations beyond your level of competence.

- Utilize **supervision** regularly to ensure that your techniques are legal, ethical, and therapeutically sound.
- Recognize situations of **high legal risk**.
- Consult with your agency's **legal counsel** whenever confronted with troublesome or confusing legal issues or questions.
- Obtain **malpractice insurance** if your agency does not provide it for you.
- Avoid **dual relationships** with clients.
- Protect **client confidentiality** and inform clients about the limits of confidentiality.
- Maintain up-to-date, accurate, and complete **client records** that are free of hearsay and judgmental language.
- Obtain written permission from clients to **release information** about them to others.
- Document any **client complaints or grievances**, and the steps you took to resolve them.
- Understand and abide by laws pertaining to **privileged communication** for social workers in your state.
- Abide by all **mandatory reporting laws** requiring you to report suspected abuse or neglect.
- Abide by **duty to warn** principles when third parties are threatened.
- **Refer** clients to other professionals and programs when you are unable to provide the services they require and document your efforts to make a referral.

You are not likely to become entangled in a malpractice lawsuit if you follow the guidelines described above, so do not let concerns over legal risk and malpractice keep you from learning or acting in the best interests of your clients. However, it is important to be careful to avoid legal consequences. Adhere to what would be considered reasonable, customary, and prudent practice by an average citizen, a jury, or a judge. The actions you take on behalf of clients must be fair, in good faith, and in keeping with how other professionals would tend to act. If you need clarification in any particular area, seek guidance and consultation from your social work supervisor and/or agency legal counsel.

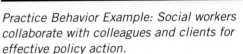

Policy Practice

Practice Behavior Example: Social workers collaborate with colleagues and clients for effective policy action.

Critical Thinking Question: What social policies are in need of change in order to serve your clients more effectively?

Legal Issues and Concerns: A Workbook Activity

The following questions are designed to heighten your awareness of the legal context of social work practice and the legal considerations that are relevant to your practicum agency. Discuss these questions and issues with your field instructor and with experienced social workers in your agency. Your agency may also have a legal department and staff attorneys who can respond to your questions and explain legal principles.

1. Is eligibility for your agency's services in any way defined by law? If so, what statutes, legal rules, and regulations are used to determine who is eligible and who is not?

   _____

   _____

2. Are certain individuals legally required or mandated to obtain services from your agency (e.g., those on probation and subject to court-ordered treatment or those whose children are in foster care)? If so, what specific statutes apply to these individuals and situations?

   _____

   _____

3. Do those individuals who are pressured to make use of your agency have a right to refuse to participate? If so, do they face any consequences for that action?

   _____

   _____

4. Is your agency licensed by the state (e.g., a child placing agency, and residential center for youth)? If yes, identify the specific license(s) and the laws and regulations that apply to these licensures.

   _____

   _____

5. What outside agencies or organizations (e.g., governmental agencies, accrediting bodies, and citizen review boards) are authorized to interview staff about their practices and review the records kept by your agency (e.g., client records, client services, and financial records)?

   _____

   _____

6. Does your agency have malpractice insurance that provides employees with legal defense against allegations of wrongdoing and/or pay the assessed damages if found guilty? If so, what limitations and restrictions apply (e.g., must the employee be following agency policy and behave in an ethical manner before he or she be covered the insurance policy)?

   _____

   _____

7. What are the possible legal consequences for a social worker who takes action that conflicts with or violates the agency's written policy?

   _____

   _____

8. Has the agency or any staff member been sued for negligence or malpractice? If yes, what was the nature of the allegation(s) and the outcome of the lawsuit(s)?

   _____

   _____

9. What agency policies apply in the following client situations which may have legal ramifications?

Practice Situations	Agency Policy
A client who may not be mentally competent to make legal, medical, or financial decisions	
A client who is a minor in need of services and whose parents may or may not be informed	
A client who puts himself or herself at risk by refusing or withdrawing from treatment	
A client known to have or suspected of having committed a serious crime	
A client who has been ordered to receive services from your agency	
A client who has lied, withheld information, or falsified an application in order to become eligible for benefits or services	
A client who states that he or she intends to bring a lawsuit against a social worker or agency	
How to proceed when a client asks to read or copy the records in his or her case file	
How to obtain a client's permission to release records to your agency or another one	
When and how to report suspected child or elder abuse or neglect	
How to obtain a client's informed consent to participate in programs and receive services	
How to handle and record the receipt of gifts from a client	
How to respond to a subpoena for client records or to be a witness in a trial or court action	

Suggested Learning Activities

- Examine your agency's policy manual and identify policies that refer to the need for staff to conform to specific legal codes or requirements.
- Identify situations in which there might be a conflict between what is required by the NASW *Code of Ethics* and the requirements of a specific state or federal law.
- Observe court proceedings, especially ones in which your agency is involved.
- Determine whether your agency has a staff attorney. If so, familiarize yourself with the legal services provided by the attorney to staff social workers.
- In Sheafor and Horejsi (2012), read the sections titled "Avoiding Malpractice Suits" (433–436) and "Testifying in Court" (437–438).

References

Albert, Raymond. *Law and Social Work Practice: A Legal Systems Approach.* 2nd ed. New York: Springer Publishing Company, 2000.

Baird, Brian N. *The Internship, Practicum, and Field Placement Handbook: A Guide for the Helping Professions.* 5th ed. Upper Saddle River, NJ: Prentice Hall, 2011.

Bernstein, Barton E., and Thomas L. Hartsell, Jr. *The Portable Guide to Testifying in Court for Mental Health Professionals: An A–Z Guide to Being an Effective Witness.* Hoboken, NJ: John Wiley and Sons, 2005.

Birkenmaier, Julie, and Marla Berg-Weger. *The Practicum Companion for Social Work: Integrating Class and Field Work.* 3rd ed. Boston: Allyn and Bacon, 2011.

Bullis, Ronald. *Clinical Social Worker Misconduct: Law, Ethics, and Interpersonal Dynamics.* Chicago: Nelson-Hall, 1995.

Houston-Vega, Mary K., Elane M. Nuehring, and Elizabeth R. Daguio. *Prudent Practice: A Guide for Managing Malpractice Risk.* Washington, DC: NASW Press, 1997.

Israel, Andrew. *Using the Law: Practical Decision Making in Mental Health.* Chicago: Lyceum Books, 2011.

National Association of Social Workers. *Code of Ethics.* Washington, DC: NASW Press, 1997.

Reamer, Frederic. *Social Work Malpractice and Liability.* New York: Columbia University Press, 1994.

Reamer, Frederic. *Social Work Malpractice and Liability.* 2nd ed. New York: Columbia University Press, 2003.

Sheafor, Bradford, and Charles Horejsi. *Techniques and Guidelines for Social Work Practice.* 8th ed. Boston: Allyn and Bacon, 2012.

Slater, Lyn. *Social Work Practice and the Law.* New York: Springer Publishing Company, 2011.

CHAPTER 15 REVIEW

PRACTICE TEST

The following questions will test your knowledge of the content found within this chapter.

1. Social workers must inform themselves of the laws regulating their practice because
   a. malpractice can be easily proven
   b. ignorance of the law is not considered a legal defense
   c. professional liability policies require it
   d. clinical practice is based on legal issues

2. Breaking confidentiality, dual relationships with clients, and use of ineffective treatment are examples of
   a. common reasons for lawsuits
   b. state laws regulating social work
   c. agency guidelines for practice
   d. moral codes

3. The obligation to notify authorities of a client's threat to harm others is
   a. a violation of client confidentiality
   b. an ethical dilemma
   c. the concept of duty to warn
   d. always a clear-cut decision

4. Which is true?
   a. There are limits in client rights to confidentiality.
   b. Client rights to confidentiality are limited when clients do not understand.
   c. Limits to client confidentiality may be based on payment issues.
   d. Social workers can decide on client rights to confidentiality.

5. In a malpractice suit, the plaintiff must prove
  a. he or she suffered harm because of what the social worker did or did not do
  b. the social worker violated the NASW *Code of Ethics*
  c. the agency was derelict in its duty
  d. the social work supervisor was negligent

6. Social workers may be found negligent
  a. only for what they did
  b. only for what they failed to do
  c. acts and omissions
  d. only in clinical situations

7. Define professional negligence and how professional malpractice insurance protects social workers, including how negligence by the social worker impacts such insurance coverage.

16

Planned Change Process

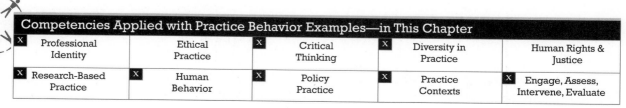

Competencies Applied with Practice Behavior Examples—in This Chapter				
X Professional Identity	Ethical Practice	X Critical Thinking	X Diversity in Practice	Human Rights & Justice
X Research-Based Practice	X Human Behavior	X Policy Practice	X Practice Contexts	X Engage, Assess, Intervene, Evaluate

CHAPTER PREVIEW

This chapter presents the planned change process as the central approach of social work at the micro, mezzo, and macro levels of practice. Guidelines and considerations for engaging in planned change are offered. The phases of the planned change process are described. Conceptual frameworks guiding social work practice are defined and described, including professional perspectives, explanatory/orienting theories, and practice theories/models.

Fundamentally, the practice of social work is about the ***process of planned change***. In the practice of social work, the worker takes deliberate and specific steps to encourage and facilitate movement toward a certain goal. Your practicum offers an excellent opportunity to observe and critically examine the values, beliefs, ethical principles, theories, and knowledge base that guide a social worker's efforts to bring about a desired change.

All social agencies are committed to and structured around deep-seated beliefs about how clients, communities, or broad social conditions change. Strive to identify the assumptions about change that are embedded in your agency's programs and policies as well as in its various approaches to practice. Identify your own beliefs about how, why, and under what circumstances desirable change by individuals, families, small groups, organizations, and communities is possible and probable. In addition, work to integrate the theories and models you learned in the classroom into your practicum experiences, guided by the content of this chapter.

BACKGROUND AND CONTEXT

As explained in Chapter 13 (Professional Social Work), social work is often seen as the profession that supports and promotes the social functioning of individuals, groups, and communities and also works to establish societal structures and policies that support that social functioning. ***Planned change*** at all levels, including the micro, mezzo, and macro levels, is the central focus of social work. Social workers assist clients, families, and communities to make changes that will improve their lives or change the conditions and social policies which impact their lives.

Social workers engaged in planned change see the connections and mutual interactions between people and the social environments of which they are a part. In order to be truly effective, social workers need to be skilled in and committed to interventions that reflect the ways in which people's lives are influenced by societal conditions and social policies. They must believe in clients' abilities not only to address their own needs and goals but also to empower themselves as they change and enhance their social environment. The following ***considerations for engaging in planned change*** provide guidance for this process.

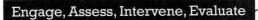

Engage, Assess, Intervene, Evaluate

Practice Behavior Example: Social workers select appropriate interventions.

Critical Thinking Question: What practice theories and models are most commonly used with the clients of your agency?

- Planned change is built on ***hypotheses*** that certain interventions will produce certain outcomes.
- Planned change is built on ***professional perspectives, orienting/ explanatory theories,*** and ***practice theories/models***.

- Planned change is effective when built upon **good assessments**.
- Planned change is effective when **assessment is ongoing** throughout interventions.
- Planned change is always based on **incomplete information**.
- Planned change is effective when **interventions are amended** as needed.
- Planned change may lead to **partial success**.
- Planned change may be impacted by **unexpected and unforeseen factors** and barriers.
- Planned change is most effective when based on **client input and goals**.
- Planned change is guided and limited by **agency programs and protocol**.
- Planned change is impacted by **client/client system characteristics**.

Planned change efforts do not take place in a social vacuum. In fact, such efforts are greatly impacted by a wide variety of external factors. For interventions to be effective, these contextual considerations must be taken into account, integrated into the plans, and factored into the overall success of the intervention (Table 16.1).

Table 16.1   Contextual Considerations for Planned Change

Context	Considerations for Planned Change
Client/client context	• Client definition of and meaning assigned to situation • Client goals • Client level of motivation • Client self-awareness and insight • Client characteristics • Social support available • Meaning of problem and potential solution • Voluntary or involuntary client • Diversity factors
Social worker context	• Skill level • Knowledge base • Training and preparation • Professional values • Personal values • Quality of assessment completed • Level of rapport and engagement
Agency context	• Agency mission • Agency programs and services available • Agency resources available • Agency priorities • Best practices • Timeliness of services
Community context	• Attitudes toward clients • Attitudes toward agency • Positive community characteristics • Negative community characteristics • Informal resources available

(continued)

Table 16.1	**Continued**
Social policy context	• Laws regulating practice • Laws mandating services • Laws limiting services • Political climate • Effectiveness of social policies • Value base of social policies
Ethical context	• Ethical base of intervention • Values base of client/client system • Values base of agency • Ethical dilemmas

The social worker and client may seek change and formulate interventions at one or more of three levels: micro, mezzo, and macro. The ***micro*** level of social work practice refers to interventions that focus on personal, individual, or family concerns such as relationships, communication problems, emotional or psychological problems, and issues related to individual social functioning. The ***mezzo*** level of social work practice refers to improving social functioning at the level of the neighborhood, the group, or the organization. This may include interventions through the use of support groups, neighborhood development projects, and organizational growth and development. The ***macro*** level of social work practice refers to interventions aimed at changes in communities, societies, and social policies. These interventions focus on community capacity building, community organization, and large-scale social change efforts.

Although these three levels of intervention may have different targets for change, they are all built on the same ***process of planned change***. In addition, social workers often practice at multiple levels simultaneously, recognizing the connections between them and moving between levels as the situation requires. Social work at all of these levels, whether the client is an individual or a community, typically moves through the ***phases of planned change***, which are listed below.

Practice Contexts

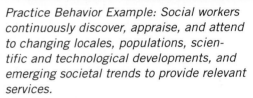
Practice Behavior Example: Social workers continuously discover, appraise, and attend to changing locales, populations, scientific and technological developments, and emerging societal trends to provide relevant services.

Critical Thinking Question: In what ways do societal trends and scientific evidence regarding social problems impact the types of interventions used in your agency?

1. **Engagement Phase of Planned Change:**

   Social workers at all levels of practice engage with clients and client systems in order to establish effective working relationships that form the basis for effective assessment, intervention, and evaluation of planned change.

2. **Assessment Phase of Planned Change:**

   Social workers gather, sort, and interpret information related to client or client system functioning (including strengths and needs), identify goals and objectives, and develop intervention plans based on client input and an understanding of orienting/explanatory theories prior to and during intervention.

3. **Intervention Phase of Planned Change:**

   Social workers implement intervention plans, monitor progress of planned change efforts, and adapt intervention plans as necessary to achieve desired change.

4. **Evaluation Phase of Planned Change:**

   Social workers evaluate effectiveness of intervention plans toward desired change using a variety of measures, terminate planned change process when appropriate, and incorporate results into future planned change processes.

This list of phases gives the impression that the change process is quite orderly and linear, but that is seldom the case. Typically, the client and worker move back and forth between these phases several times during the intervention process. In addition, others involved in the intervention, such as extended family members, may not move through the intervention process at the same pace or with the same goals in mind. This can make the change process more complex and unpredictable, and needs to be taken into account.

Social workers use what are called conceptual frameworks to guide practice. A ***conceptual framework*** is a way of organizing ideas about social work practice, and includes practice perspectives, orienting theories, practice theories, and practice models. A ***professional perspective*** is an intentional viewing of a practice situation using a certain professional lens, which helps to clarify and magnify a particular facet of the person-in-environment. Using these lenses helps us to examine and draw attention to what needs attention in any given situation. A situation may require a generalist perspective because it needs to be addressed at multiple levels, using a variety of theories and models.

Ethical Practice

Practice Behavior Example: Social workers apply strategies of ethical reasoning to arrive at principled decisions.

Critical Thinking Question: What ethical principles do you believe to be most central to the choice of an intervention? Would your clients agree?

All practice situations require a ***strengths perspective*** in order to highlight strengths and resources upon which to build an intervention. An ***ecosystems perspective*** prompts us to consider the impact of the social environment on our clients, as well as the interaction between our clients and their social environments. A ***diversity perspective*** ensures that we consider the ways in which diversity of all kinds impacts a client's experience and view of that experience. Depending on the situation, a social worker may use one perspective more than another to understand the unique features of that situation.

Orienting/explanatory theories are those that contribute to a social worker's body of knowledge about how individuals, families, groups, communities, and societies develop and change over time. They often build on and synthesize the social and behavioral sciences such as psychology, sociology, economics, and political science. Such theories attempt to explain human behavior; human development; social forces that shape human experiences, and political and economic systems which impact individuals, families, and communities. Although necessary to good practice because they help us understand what might be happening and why, these theories are limited because they do not provide guidance on how to facilitate planned change. Examples of orienting theories include social systems theory, human

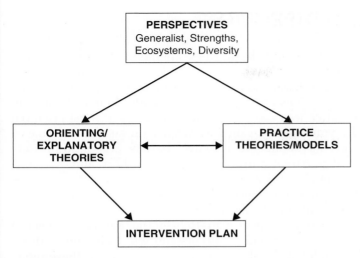

Figure 16.1

Conceptual Frameworks: Guides for Social Work Practice

development theory, group dynamics theory, organizational theory, and community development theory.

Practice theories/models are those that offer general guidelines about how to intervene at various levels of practice. They build on orienting/explanatory theories and suggest that certain situations call for specific practice theories. They are the actual approaches and techniques chosen to use in real interventions.

Figure 16.1 shows the relationship between the conceptual frameworks defined above, including professional perspectives, orienting/explanatory theories, practice theories/models, and actual interventions. The blending of these conceptual frameworks and others is done in any effective planned change process that is based on social work knowledge, theory, evidence-based practice, best practices, and social work values.

Based on this diagrammatic representation of how conceptual frameworks are used to design effective, theory-based, and individualized intervention plans, a number of practice examples are included in the Appendix. The following examples are included in the appendix:

- Micro Level Practice Examples
  - Intervention with individuals
  - Intervention with families
- Mezzo Level Practice Examples
  - Intervention with groups
  - Intervention with organizations
- Macro Level Practice Examples
  - Intervention with communities
  - Intervention with social policy

Refer to the examples in the appendix so that you can see in a visual way how conceptual frameworks are linked in the planned change process to elicit positive outcomes.

GUIDANCE AND DIRECTION

It is important to identify the practice frameworks (perspectives, explanatory/orienting theories, and practice theories/and models) used in your agency. Whether implicit or explicit, these frameworks influence how your agency designs its programs and services and how it works with clients. Determine why these particular practice frameworks are appropriate and most effective for the clients served by your agency. Consider what your agency's choice of practice frameworks reveals about the agency's beliefs and assumptions concerning the causes of personal and social problems, how and why clients and client systems change, and what actions are most likely to facilitate change. Learn about how success is measured and ask about the importance placed on identifying and using client strengths.

Your practicum agency will expect you to use the regularly selected forms of intervention used by other social workers and will train you in these approaches. Do your best to learn the skills required to implement these interventions, remembering that many of these skills can be transferred to another setting even if that organization takes a different approach to intervention. Over time you will see how interventions, even though they may seem similar for several clients, are customized based on different needs and goals. You will begin to see how your own interventions will be tailored for those reasons as well. As you grow in experience and confidence, your ability to craft appropriate interventions will increase.

Recognize that your practicum experience is limited to one setting and that other agencies and programs may be quite different from the one you know best. There are significant differences between programs, even when they have similar goals and serve the same types of clients. Try to learn how and why other agencies have adopted forms of intervention, practice perspectives, and theories and models that are different from the ones used in your practicum setting.

During your practicum, try to gain experience in as many practice roles as possible in order to understand the nature of these roles and better understand your own abilities. Do not limit yourself to the performance of only a few practice roles. Most likely your career in social work will require that you assume many different practice roles and perform a wide range of tasks and activities. This variety of roles is also one of the most attractive aspects of the social work profession because social workers can move between roles, creatively addressing needs in a variety of ways and at a variety of levels.

As you become involved in the ***engagement*** phase of planned change, it is incumbent on you to use the skills of rapport-building, active listening, and partnering to build a strong initial professional relationship. This phase requires that you and the client or client system understand the problem or need, task at hand, and perspectives of all those involved. This first phase of planned change will require you to learn how to use yourself as the tool for change, since the next three stages of planned change hinge on your ability to connect in a meaningful way with your client.

In the ***assessment*** phase of planned change, whether you are assessing a client, a community's capacity to serve its citizens, an organization's ability to provide services, or a social policy's ability to address the needs of a group of people, there are general guidelines that can help you do a thorough and effective assessment. When assessing client situations, make sure to assess for strengths as well as problems and use assessment tools that are effective and appropriate. Include the client in the assessment process. Prioritize the identified needs in order to maximize your effectiveness. Consider the impact of diversity on your interventions. Pay attention to any ethical and legal issues related to assessment. Ask yourself what value judgments you might be making. Consider the sociohistorical context of your client or client system. Continually ask yourself what else you might need to know in order to have a comprehensive assessment upon which an effective intervention can be built.

As you design ***interventions*** from the micro level to the macro level, follow these guidelines for effective interventions. The intervention plan must address both strengths and needs, be built on as comprehensive an assessment as possible, and be feasible and reasonable for both the client and social worker. The plan should be mutually developed by the client and social worker, based on a theory of change that matches the client's needs, and within your knowledge base and skill level. Remember that your intervention may need to be modified at some point. Make sure that the plan has incremental steps and reasonable goals. Do what you can to minimize negative effects on clients, avoid being overly intrusive into your clients' lives, address important issues of diversity, and include a timeline and termination plan.

Diversity in Practice
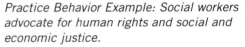

Practice Behavior Example: Social workers advocate for human rights and social and economic justice.

Critical Thinking Question: What NASW cultural competence standards should be met when developing intervention plans?

As you enter the ***evaluation*** phase of the planned change process, consider how to design ***evaluations*** for your interventions. Remember to measure the outcomes of the intervention in relation to the goals and objectives which were identified. The profession of social work is rightfully asked to hold itself accountable and to demonstrate its ability to address social issues in effective and efficient ways. Social workers are asked to use what is commonly called ***evidence-based practice,*** which means that they need to base their interventions on some form of empirical evidence whenever possible and engage in proactive program evaluation to determine effectiveness of services provided. Such research on practice often leads to what is termed ***best practices.*** This refers to what the profession considers to be ideal approaches based on its values and its research on what is effective, what is in the best interests of clients, and what clients wish for themselves. Learn to research the best practices in your field so that you can pattern your work after them, knowing that as your career proceeds, you may be involved in the development of best practices.

Drawing upon your classroom learning about the theories that guide social work practice, and combining those with the sample orienting/explanatory theories and practice theories/models, consider how your practicum learning experiences at the micro, mezzo, and macro levels will help you design interventions with a solid theoretical base. Figure 16.2 illustrates a number of the commonly used theories at all three levels.

Commonly Used Orienting/Explanatory Theories for Micro Level Practice (for use with individuals and families)		
• Behavioral	• Biopsychosocial	• Crisis
• Cycle of change	• Medical model	• Psychosocial development
• Moral development	• Hierarchy of needs	• Object relations
• Cognitive development	• Psychodynamic	• Psychological learning
• Social exchange	• Social systems	• Social behavioral
Commonly Used Practice Theories/Models for Micro Level Practice		
• Behavioral	• Client-centered	• Cognitive behavioral
• Crisis intervention	• Empowerment	• Family preservation
• Family reunification	• Harm reduction	• Motivational interviewing
• Solution-focused	• Strategic family therapy	• Structural family therapy
• Task-centered		

Commonly Used Orienting/Explanatory Theories for Mezzo Level Practice (for use with groups and organizations)		
• Chaos	• Family life cycle	• Family systems
• Group development	• Group dynamics	• Multicausal
• Organizational development	• Role	• Social exchange Social learning
• Social systems	• Social systems	• Subculture
Commonly Used Practice Theories/Models for Mezzo Level Practice		
• Empowerment	• Harm reduction	• Mutual aid group
• Organizational development	• Program development	• Psychoeducational group
• Self-help group		

Commonly Used Orienting/Explanatory Theories for Macro Level Practice (for use with communities, societies, and social policy)		
• Conflict	• Multicausal	• Political economy
• Social exchange	• Social learning	• Social movement theory
• Social systems	• Strain	• Structure
• Subculture		
Commonly Used Practice Theories/Models for Macro Level Practice		
• Community development	• Community organization	• Harm reduction
• Policy practice	• Research practice	• Social change
• Social development	• Social justice effort	• Social planning
• Structural		

Figure 16.2

Orienting/Explanatory Theories and Practice Theories/Models

Social Work as Planned Change: A Workbook Activity

This workbook activity asks that you examine the conceptual frameworks (perspectives, theories, and models) used in your practicum agency. In order to analyze these frameworks, consider these questions.

1. What types of problems, needs, or concerns are typically addressed by your agency?

_____

_____

_____

2. What conceptual frameworks (perspectives, theories, or models) are typically used to guide assessment and interventions?

_____

_____

_____

3. At what level of practice (micro, mezzo, or macro) are interventions typically implemented?

_____

_____

_____

4. How is a particular practice model chosen for a specific client?

_____

_____

_____

5. Are social workers in your agency regularly trained in new intervention approaches?

_____

_____

_____

6. Are interventions tailored to diverse clients (i.e., culture, age, gender)?

_____

_____

_____

7. What evaluation tools does your agency use to evaluate the effectiveness of its interventions?

_____

_____

_____

8. Does your agency adapt its strategies based on the result of its self-evaluation?

_____

_____

_____

9. What recommendations do you have for improved effectiveness in your agency?

_____

_____

_____

Suggested Learning Activities

- Examine the data-gathering and assessment tools and instruments used in your agency.
- Ask social workers or other professionals in your agency to identify the perspectives and theories that guide their practice. Ask why those frameworks are preferred over other possibilities.
- Identify the beliefs, values, and assumptions implicit in the perspectives, theories, and models used in your agency.
- Ask social workers or other professionals in your agency to describe how they and the agency determine whether they are being effective in their work with clients.
- In the *Encyclopedia of Social Work* (Mizrahi, 2010), read chapters on the various practice frameworks used in your agency and by social work professionals.
- In Payne (2005), read descriptions of social work theories and models.
- Refer to the *Social Work Desk Reference* to see what interventions are recommended in certain situations.

References

Coady, Nick, and Peter Lehmann, eds. *Theoretical Perspectives for Direct Social Work Practice.* 2nd ed. New York: Springer Publishing Company, 2001.

Corcoran, Jacqueline, and Joseph Walsh. *Clinical Assessment and Diagnosis in Social Work Practice.* 2nd ed. New York: Oxford University Press, 2010.

Cournoyer, Barry R. *The Evidence-Based Social Work Skills Book.* Boston: Pearson Education, 2005.

Finn, Janet L., and Maxine Jacobson. *Just Practice: A Social Justice Approach to Social Work.* 2nd ed. Peosta, IA: Eddie Bowers Publishing, 2007.

Gambrill, Eileen. *Social Work Practice: A Critical Thinker's Guide.* 2nd ed. Cary, NC: Oxford University Press, 2006.

Hull, Grafton. *Understanding Generalist Practice with Families.* Pacific Grove, CA: Brooks/Cole, 2006.

Jordan, Catheleen, and Cynthia Franklin. *Clinical Assessment for Social Workers: Qualitative and Quantitative Methods.* 3rd ed. Chicago: Lyceum Books, 2011.

Karls, James M., and Maura O'Keefe. *Person-in-Environment System Manual.* 2nd ed. Washington, DC: NASW Press, 2008.

Lister, Pam. *Integrating Social Work Theory and Practice.* Clifton, NJ: Routledge, 2011.

McKenzie, Fred. *Understanding and Managing the Therapeutic Relationships.* Chicago: Lyceum, 2011.

Miller, William R., Stephen Rollnick, and Kelly Conforti. *Motivational Interviewing: Preparing People for Change.* 2nd ed. New York: Guilford Press, 2002.

Mizrahi, Terry, ed. *Encyclopedia of Social Work.* 20th ed. New York: Oxford University Press, 2010.

Mizrahi, Terry, and Larry E. Davis. *Encyclopedia of Social Work.* 20th ed. Washington, DC: NASW Press and Oxford University Press, 2010.

Netting, F. Ellen, Peter McKettner, and Steven L. McMurty. *Social Work Macro Practice.* Boston: Allyn and Bacon, 2004.

O'Hare, Thomas. *Evidence-based Practices for Social Workers: An Interdisciplinary Approach.* Chicago: Lyceum Books, 2005.

Payne, Malcolm. *Modern Social Work Theory.* 3rd ed. Chicago: Lyceum Press, 2005.

Roberts, Albert R. *Social Workers' Desk Reference.* 2nd ed. New York: Oxford University Press, 2009.

Saleeby, Dennis, ed. *The Strengths Perspective in Social Work Practice.* 4th ed. Boston: Allyn and Bacon, 2006.

Sheafor, Bradford, and Charles Horejsi. *Techniques and Guidelines for Social Work Practice.* 9th ed. Boston: Allyn and Bacon, 2011.

Schweitzer, H. Fredrick, and Mary King. *The Successful Internship: Personal, Professional, and Civic Development.* Florence, KY: Brooks/Cole, 2009.

Turner, Francis. *Social Work Treatment: Interlocking Theoretical Approaches.* 5th ed. New York: Oxford University Press, 2011.

CHAPTER 16 REVIEW

PRACTICE TEST

The following questions will test your knowledge of the content found within this chapter.

1. Each step of the planned change process
   a. is distinct and unrelated to the others
   b. is related to and builds upon the others
   c. legally requires social work supervision
   d. should utilize valid instruments

2. The conceptual frameworks that offer a professional lens through which to view clients are
   a. professional ethics
   b. practice theories
   c. professional perspectives
   d. methodology

3. The theories which attempt to describe the development of human behavior and social problems are
   a. practice theories
   b. professional theories
   c. social functioning theories
   d. orienting/explanatory theories

4. Orienting/explanatory theories are used primarily at what stage of the planned change process?
   a. all phases
   b. termination phase
   c. assessment phase
   d. planning phase

5. Evidence-based practices in social work are
   a. required by funding sources
   b. those which have been empirically shown to be effective
   c. pilot programs
   d. program evaluations

6. The evaluation phase of planned change efforts is vital because
   a. social workers are accountable for their work for performance evaluations
   b. evaluation efforts can be used to improve services
   c. clients are vulnerable
   d. grant-funded programs will not be funded without evaluation

7. Using a client or client system from your practicum agency, write about how orienting/explanatory theories and practice theories/models are used in combination to design an effective evaluation.

©Akinshin/Dreamstime

17

Evaluating Your Practice

Competencies Applied with Practice Behavior Examples—in This Chapter				
Professional Identity	Ethical Practice	X Critical Thinking	Diversity in Practice	Human Rights & Justice
X Research-Based Practice	Human Behavior	Policy Practice	X Practice Contexts	X Engage, Assess, Intervene, Evaluate

CHAPTER PREVIEW

This chapter will provide basic information on the process of student evaluation used by programs of social work education, and encourage you to examine and evaluate your own performance so you can make the best possible use of the practicum as a learning opportunity. It will also describe types of evaluation commonly used in social work practice, the purposes of practice evaluations, and the concepts of best practices and culture of evaluation. Also contained in this chapter is a discussion of ways in which evaluation of client growth, social work performance, program evaluation, and policy analysis are interrelated.

The evaluation component of social work practice, both in the practicum setting and in the subsequent practice, is a vital phase of intervention, both for the client and the practitioner. Clients expect and deserve competent social workers, and ethical social work practice requires that the best interests of vulnerable clients take center stage. A successful practicum prepares you for competent and responsible practice. Your competence as a practicum student is developed over time when classroom knowledge and practicum experiences are integrated through real social work experiences. Ongoing monitoring and frequent evaluations of your performance are necessary to determine whether you are making progress, document learning, identify strengths, and identify areas of performance that may need special attention and remediation. It is important to understand the role of practicum evaluation as a tool for professional growth, and to think ahead about how evaluation, including self-evaluation, can be incorporated into your professional practice.

BACKGROUND AND CONTEXT

Every school of social work education uses some type of rating scale or evaluation tool to monitor and evaluate student progress, with the ultimate question being asked as to whether a student's performance meets the standards expected of the entry-level social work practitioner. The evaluation process compares the student's performance to standards and criteria established by schools and required by the Educational Policy and Accreditation Standards of the Council on Social Work Education, and also to the learning goals, objectives, and activities outlined in the student's learning agreement (see Chapter 3, Developing a Learning Plan).

Evaluations of student performance are of two types: formal and informal. An ***informal evaluation*** consists of the ongoing feedback and suggestions offered by the field instructor. This type of evaluation takes place on a weekly or even a daily basis, and is provided both in scheduled meetings and as needed in practice situations. A ***formal evaluation*** is a detailed review, rating, and comparison of the student's performance with agreed-upon evaluation criteria, standards, and learning objectives for the practicum. It occurs at the end of each academic term or more often, depending on school policy or special circumstances.

Formal evaluations are based on a school's specific evaluation criteria and placed in a written report. This report typically consists of the ratings assigned to the various items on the school's evaluation tool and a few paragraphs of narrative that describe special strengths and abilities and/or special problems and deficiencies in performance. The report may also describe how needed learning experiences will be secured or deficiencies corrected prior to the next formal evaluation.

Some practicum programs and field instructors may ask students to prepare for this evaluation by compiling a portfolio that includes various reports and documents that describe the student's practicum activities and achievements, and serves to illustrate his or her level of performance. Students may be asked to evaluate their own performance using the evaluation instrument provided by their university and then compare their self-ratings with those of their supervisor.

A variety of agency staff members with knowledge about student assignments and work may be asked to comment on student learning and performance based on their observations of student professional growth. The faculty supervisor will also participate in the formal evaluation. In some cases, other agency staff may be asked to join in the evaluation if they have worked closely with the student and observed the student's performance.

The areas addressed in the practicum evaluation are usually very similar to those addressed in the performance evaluation of social workers employed by an agency. In order to ensure high-quality performance and reduce their exposure to lawsuits and employee grievances, agencies strive to make their expectations of employees and students as clear as possible and to use personnel evaluation tools (i.e., rating scales) that are as objective as possible. These same forces have prompted programs of social work education to develop evaluation tools that are as valid and reliable as possible.

A practicum evaluation tool should be both clear and specific in its descriptions of standards and criteria, and also flexible enough to accurately and fairly evaluate the practice of social work, which is complex and difficult to observe directly. An evaluation should be objective to the degree possible, but even a well-designed procedure will require judgments by the field instructor. For example, ratings of a student's level of cooperation, motivation, adaptability, and use of supervision are difficult to assess except when in an extreme form (i.e., very high or very low motivation). Consequently, there will be times when the field instructor and practicum student disagree on the actual ratings given on a formal evaluation.

An evaluation can be considered fair and relevant when

- The *evaluation criteria*, *standards*, and the agency's preferred practices and outcomes are *made known to the student* at the beginning of the practicum or at the beginning of the time period to be evaluated
- It addresses the *areas of performance or competency* that are truly important to professional social work and to the agency's mission and goals
- The criteria used to evaluate the student are *clear and objective*
- The student's performance is compared to *written standards* rather than to unstated or implied standards
- The student has been given *adequate orientation and training*
- The student has been given *ongoing feedback on professional growth*
- The student has been given ongoing feedback and *warnings of unsatisfactory performance* prior to the formal evaluation
- The performance *criteria and standards are realistic* given the student's level (e.g., first semester versus second semester, BSW versus MSW)
- The evaluation can cite *examples of performance* that form the basis of the ratings
- The evaluation gives *consideration to extenuating circumstances* that may influence the evaluation (e.g., the student had limited opportunity to learn or demonstrate certain skills and the supervisor had limited time to observe the student's performance)

- The evaluation takes into consideration the ***nature and complexity*** of the assignments given to the student
- The evaluation ***recognizes student growth*** and good performance as well as ***student problems*** or need for continued learning

An inaccurate or unfair evaluation exists when

- The ***student did not understand*** what was expected of him or her, or did not understand the criteria to be used for evaluation
- The rules, standards, and criteria used to evaluate the student are ***changed without the student's knowledge***
- The student was ***not given ongoing feedback***, guidance, and suggestions prior to the evaluation
- Student performance has ***not been observed*** and evaluations are not based on actual knowledge of student abilities
- The student receives ***low ratings without being given a description*** and explanation of the poor performance that resulted in the low ratings
- The ***criteria or standards are unrealistically high*** or not relevant to the student's performance as a social worker
- Several students receive essentially the same ratings when there were ***clear differences*** in their performances
- ***Interpersonal factors*** such as personality conflicts between the student and the field instructor influence student ratings

Both the field instructor and the student must be alert to certain pitfalls that exist whenever one person attempts to rate another person's performance. These are as follows:

- The ***halo effect***—the tendency to rate a person the same on all items based on the observed performance in only a few areas
- The ***attraction of the average***—the tendency to evaluate every student or employee about the same or about average regardless of real differences in their performance
- The ***leniency bias***—the tendency to evaluate all students or employees as outstanding or to assign inflated ratings so as to avoid arguments or conflict or to avoid hurting their feelings
- The ***strictness bias***—the tendency to evaluate and rate all students or employees on the low side because the evaluator has unrealistically high expectations or holds the belief that low ratings will motivate them toward even higher levels of performance

In some instances the field instructor or the practicum coordinator may conclude that the practicum arrangement is unworkable and unsatisfactory for the student, the field instructor, or both. This may happen when it becomes apparent that the agency cannot meet the student's learning needs or because the student's performance is irresponsible, unethical, or far short of expectations. Examples of student behaviors or performance problems that may prompt the field instructor or the school to consider terminating the practicum include the following:

- The student's ***behavior is harmful*** to clients, agency staff, or the agency's reputation
- The student's ***behavior is irresponsible and unprofessional*** (e.g., late for work, missing scheduled appointments, unable to spend the required hours in the practicum setting)

- The student is **unable to communicate** adequately, either verbally or in writing
- The student is **hostile toward supervision** and resistant to learning
- The student displays **inappropriate behavior or cannot manage emotions** in a manner that interferes with work (e.g., bizarre behavior, inability to concentrate, aggressiveness, withdrawal, inappropriate emotional expression)
- The student **inappropriately shares personal views**, experiences, and problems with clients after being made aware of this unacceptable behavior
- The student enters into **dual relationships** with a client (e.g., dates a client, sells a product to a client)

Some behaviors by the student are considered so serious that they may result in the student's immediate dismissal from the practicum. These include the following:

- Clear and serious **violations of the NASW Code of Ethics**
- Clear and repeated **insubordination**
- **Theft or the clear misuse** of agency money, equipment, or property
- **Concealing, consuming, or selling** drugs on agency premises
- Being intoxicated or **under the influence of drugs or alcohol** when at work
- **Reckless or threatening actions** that place clients and staff at risk of serious harm
- Deliberately **withholding information** from a supervisor or from agency personnel that they need to know in order to properly serve clients and maintain the integrity and reputation of the agency and its programs
- **Falsifying agency records** and reports
- **Soliciting or accepting gifts** or favors from clients in exchange for preferential treatment
- **Sexual or romantic relationships** with clients
- Clear **violations of strict agency** policy
- **Failure to correct or improve** inadequate performance
- **Inability to deal with the emotional and stressful aspects** of practice

As mentioned earlier, evaluation of practice is an essential component not only of practicum learning but of social work practice in all arenas and at all levels. Even though students are understandably most interested in the evaluation of their practicum performance, it is important to understand the purposes, types, processes, and uses of evaluation in social work practice. Evaluation is done to protect clients, ensure that quality services are provided, measure the impact of services and programs on client functioning, demonstrate effectiveness to funding sources, and contribute to the professional body of knowledge of the social work profession.

Research-Based Practice

Practice Behavior Example: Social workers use practice experience to inform scientific inquiry.

Critical Thinking Question: Based on your practicum experiences, what research project would answer the questions you have about practice?

To accomplish this, the profession has committed to evidence-based practice that is measured through the use of a variety of evaluation tools and approaches that measure both client progress and social work effectiveness. Each of these approaches is done to meet a certain evaluative goal, and each one

Table 17.1   Categories of Social Work Evaluation: What We Are Measuring and Why

Quantitative Evaluation	Qualitative Evaluation
Purpose:	*Purpose:*
To measure intervention outcomes in a numeric manner that allows for quantification of results, analysis of success, and demonstrated level of change	To measure intervention outcomes using a non-numeric approach that allows for the description of outcomes in subjective, individual, and nonquantifiable ways
Examples:	*Examples:*
Pre- and post-tests, standardized instruments, surveys, questionnaires, external review	Interviews, client satisfaction instruments, narrative evaluation tools, self-evaluation, and report by client/client system.
Process Evaluation	**Outcome Evaluation**
Purpose:	*Purpose:*
To measure the intervention process in terms of fidelity, stages of planned change, monitoring and adapting of objectives, and completion of intervention effort	To measure the results of the intervention process in terms of level of success, achievement of goals and objectives, and changes over time
Examples:	*Examples:*
Completion rates, assessment of fidelity to intervention model, process recordings	Pre- and post-tests, standardized instruments, surveys, questionnaires, goal attainment scaling, logic model, and longitudinal studies
Evaluation of Social Work Performance	**Evaluation of Client/Client System Progress**
Purpose:	*Purpose:*
To measure the quality and level of performance of a social worker, organization, or social program in achieving intervention goals and objectives	To measure the quality and level of progress of a client/client system, which is the target of change in terms of the achievement of intervention goals and objectives
Examples:	*Examples:*
Supervisory feedback, self-assessment, quality assurance, peer review, external review, agency compliance with standards, program evaluation, client satisfaction instruments, advisory board input	Pre- and post-tests, standardized instruments, achievement of goals and objectives, goal attainment scaling, self-evaluation and report of client/client system, observation, level of functioning scales

results in information that can be used to continually inform the profession and improve practices. Table 17.1 illustrates three categories of evaluation approaches commonly used in social agencies, and includes both definition of terms and examples of these categories of evaluation approaches. Consider how these approaches are used in both practicum evaluations and evaluations of social workers in your agency. Pay attention to the ways in which these categories could help you organize your thinking about what needs to be evaluated, why it should be measured, and how such measurements are made.

Think about how practice evaluations are actually one way of **testing hypotheses**, as described in Chapter 8 (The Agency Context of Practice). Even if based on empirical evidence of previous effectiveness, interventions can be seen in every client case as a hypothesis that a particular intervention will be effective with a specific client or client system. Refer to Table 8.1, which provides samples of practice hypotheses at the micro, mezzo, and macro levels and apply them to your agency. Your agency no doubt makes hypotheses about its services and programs and must find ways to test these hypotheses in meaningful and effective ways. Consider what hypotheses you have proposed in your interventions, reflecting on how your evaluation approaches support these hypotheses or do not.

It is commonly said about social work practice that not everything social workers do is measurable and not everything about clients' social functioning is measurable. This is true, and even though there are limits to evaluating practice, it cannot be underestimated in terms of importance. Not everything is quantifiable, but that does not mean that we do not evaluate our practice. Other limitations of evaluation are related to time and money constraints in agency settings, lack of commitment to evaluating practice, limited knowledge of program evaluation techniques, lack of rigor in design of evaluation tools, use of inappropriate evaluation tools, and lack of connection between those doing practice research and those engaged in practice. Other ways in which evaluation procedures may be flawed include lack of clarity in goals and objectives, which makes it difficult to measure their achievement; unclear vision of what exactly is being measured; and a misunderstanding about whether success or failure is related to the characteristics of the social worker or the client.

Professional Identity

Practice Behavior Example: Social workers engage in lifelong learning.

Critical Thinking Question: How can the licensing requirements for continuing education be used to enhance the quality of services provided to clients?

Contemporary agencies wishing to provide quality services that can be demonstrated to be effective develop a *culture of evaluation*. This means that the agency considers evaluation of its services to be as important as the provision of its services. Such a culture would encourage the following:

- Commitment to achieving *mission* of agency
- Allocation of *time and resources* to evaluation
- *Training of staff* in evaluation philosophy, processes, and uses of evaluation to improve practice
- Commitment to *developing empirical knowledge* upon which to base services
- Commitment to *innovation* in addressing current and emerging social issues
- Commitment to *measuring effectiveness*
- Creative combining of evaluation techniques to *measure in multiple ways*
- Protocol for *sharing results* of evaluation, dissemination of knowledge gained, and utilizing results for program improvement and growth

Contemporary social work is also committed to a set of evaluation concepts which are based upon social work values related to the provision of quality care and services. Table 17.2 lists and defines a number of evaluation concepts commonly used in social work agencies.

Table 17.2   **Evaluation Concepts Which Guide Practice**

Evaluation Concept	Definition	Uses
Standard of care	Generally agreed-upon minimum standard for provision and quality of services	Provides basic level of expectation for services as understood by practitioners, agencies, and professional organizations
Accepted practice	Generally agreed-upon approach to the provision of services to clients with specific needs and resources	Provides common, standardized approach for services to clients with similar needs and resources
Emerging practice	Innovative and promising approaches based on advances in orienting/explanatory theories and the practice models associated with them, but which are not yet fully evaluated empirically	Promotes the development of improved services and outcomes for specific populations, allows for adaptations of accepted practice, and incorporates emerging knowledge into existing practice
Evidence-based practice	Empirically tested and affirmed approaches which are based on accepted orienting/explanatory theories and which have demonstrated effectiveness over time	Provides standardized and effective services based on empirical testing and allows for ongoing testing of innovative approaches
Best practice	Recommended practice approaches found to be most effective and of highest quality, combined with guidelines for incorporation into practice at the individual, agency, social policy, or research level	Promotes highest standards for service provision, provides criteria upon which to build intervention, and ensures quality of practice at all levels

GUIDANCE AND DIRECTION

In all phases of your practicum and your subsequent practice, you will be observed, guided, encouraged, assigned tasks, given feedback, and evaluated. In your practicum, your field instructor should provide an informal and ongoing critique so that you know how you are doing from week to week. You will be evaluated in a more formal and systematic manner at the end of each academic term.

When conducting the formal evaluation, your field instructor will most likely use an evaluation tool provided by your school. This tool will rate you on the specific values, attitudes, knowledge, and skills your school defines as important to your professional development. Obtain a copy of this evaluation tool early in your practicum and construct your learning agreement so that you will have opportunities to learn and grow in each of the areas of performance to be evaluated. You may also be evaluated on the completion of the tasks, projects, and activities you planned at the beginning of your practicum. Review your learning goals for the practicum regularly to determine if you are making satisfactory progress (see Chapter 3, Developing a Learning Plan).

Your field instructor and your faculty supervisor will ask you how the practicum is proceeding, as well as hear any suggestions or questions you might have. You may be asked the following questions as they evaluate you and continue to structure your learning:

- Are the ***tasks and activities*** that you are performing different from what you were expecting?
- What aspects of your practicum do you consider to be of ***highest priority***? ***Lowest priority***?
- Are the ***demands on your time*** reasonable?
- What do you ***hope to learn and accomplish*** in the next month? By the time you complete your practicum?
- Do you get ***enough supervision***?
- Is this the ***right type of social work practice*** and practicum setting for you?
- What aspects of practice in this agency are ***most and least appealing***?
- What new or ***additional learning experiences*** do you want or need?
- How well do you ***get along with agency staff***?
- Which practicum tasks have you ***completed most and least successfully***?
- Have you been able to strike a ***workable balance*** between the demands of the practicum, your other academic work, and your personal life and responsibilities?
- Do you have other ***comments, complaints, observations, or questions***?
- What can be done to ***improve the learning experience*** for the next practicum student?

When reviewing and thinking about your performance in the practicum, your field instructor may also ask himself or herself questions such as these:

- Has this student demonstrated ***dependability and professionally responsible*** behavior?
- Can this individual be ***counted on*** in a stressful and demanding situation?
- Would this student be able to ***handle a social work position*** in this agency?
- Would I ***hire this person*** for a social work job?
- Would I want this person to be a ***social worker for my mother***? For my child? For a good friend of mine?
- Would I be willing to write a strong ***letter of recommendation*** for this student?

Behaviors and personal qualities that impress a field instructor include the following: initiative, dependability, honesty, punctuality, capacity to meet deadlines, perseverance, ability to handle conflict in interpersonal relations, sensitivity to others, ability to achieve goals and objectives, ability to plan and organize work, clear writing, motivation and willingness to work hard, receptivity to new learning, self-awareness and openness to examining personal values and attitudes, capacity to work under pressure, personal maturity, emotional stability, respect for clients and other students, fairness in decision making, and professionalism.

Behaviors and qualities that cause a field instructor to doubt a student's ability to perform as a social worker include the opposite of the above listed behaviors, especially dishonesty, missing deadlines, disrespect for others, manipulation and efforts to bend rules and requirements, attempts to secure special concessions or privileges, not informing supervisors of problems, and inability to keep personal problems from interfering with professional tasks and activities.

In order to prepare for a formal evaluation, review your learning agreement and its stated goals and activities, as well as the practicum evaluation tool used by your school. Give careful thought to the question of how well you have carried out your various responsibilities and completed assigned tasks. Prepare a list of your assigned tasks and responsibilities and assemble documentation of your work and accomplishments so they can easily be reviewed by your field instructor. Prior to meeting with your field instructor for the formal evaluation, you may be asked to complete a self-evaluation using your school's evaluation tool. You can also prepare for your evaluation by completing the workbook activity of this chapter.

Think of the evaluation as a learning experience that can help you become more self-aware, insightful, and skilled. Become aware of any feelings of inadequacy or any emotional triggers that might be activated during the process of evaluation. If you know what they are, you are more likely to benefit from supervision and suggestions for improvement than if you lack this level of self-awareness.

Prepare yourself emotionally for the formal evaluation session so that you will be open to hearing feedback about your performance. When receiving feedback on your performance, strive to maintain openness toward what you are hearing. Refer to the parallel processes of student and client in regard to intervention and evaluation described in Chapter 5 (Learning from Supervision), which highlight the similarities between students and clients in terms of ambivalent feelings toward being observed and evaluated. Understanding these parallels will help you become more empathetic with your clients. Although it may be difficult to hear a frank appraisal of your work, avoid being defensive. Consider this feedback carefully and work to improve in the areas noted, knowing that feedback is actually a gift to you that will make you a better practitioner.

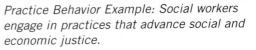

Human Rights and Justice

Practice Behavior Example: Social workers engage in practices that advance social and economic justice.

Critical Thinking Question: What is the relationship between the evaluation of social work practice and social justice?

In addition to constructive criticism, you will receive positive feedback related to areas in which you are doing well. Take note of what your field instructor sees as your skills and gifts. If you want more specific feedback about what you have done well so that you know what your skills or abilities are, ask for it. Review the Student Self-Assessment of Practicum Strengths in Chapter 1, and complete the assessment again as a post-test. Compare your self-assessment with the one you did at the outset of your practicum to determine if the strengths you identified there have been demonstrated in your performance and if the ones you did not identify earlier have been demonstrated over time. It will be helpful to see your professional growth to this point in practicum. This will underscore the fact that throughout your career you will continue to develop the strengths needed for professional practice. Build on your strengths because they will form the basis of your professional knowledge and abilities.

Strive to understand what your field instructor observed in your performance that led them to a particular conclusion concerning your work. Seek descriptions and examples of any poor performance and ask for specific suggestions on how it can be improved. Request descriptions of performances that were rated higher than most others. Reflect on these descriptions and determine

Human Behavior

Practice Behavior Example: Social workers critique and apply knowledge to understand person and environment.

Critical Thinking Question: What additional human behavior theories could be used to better understand and provide services to the clients of your agency?

why you perform some tasks and activities better than others. If you and your field instructor disagree on the adequacy of your performance, prepare factual documentation supporting your point of view. However, if you agree that your performance is deficient, it is best to acknowledge the problem rather than entering into a pointless argument that can only leave you looking dishonest or lacking in self-awareness.

Remember that although you are just beginning your practice as a social worker, you have much to offer. Build on those gifts, attributes, values, and skills over time, knowing that professional growth is your responsibility. Continue to evaluate your own growth, expecting yourself to continuously acquire new learning, exhibit new skills, and advance practice.

Finally, reflect on the ways in which your performance in practicum needs improvement in order for future interventions to be successful. Consider the connection between your competence, the effectiveness of your interventions, and the level of successful outcomes. There are many explanations for the level of success in interventions. Lack of desired success or disappointment in the outcomes of an intervention can be traced to a variety of factors, including those described in Table 17.3.

Use the information in this table to help you reflect upon and discuss with your field instructor or faculty supervisor the ways in which your success or the success of your clients could be explained through a combination of these factors. Consider in retrospect how your work could have been better with this knowledge, as well as how future interventions could be enhanced as you learn about what contributes to and detracts from successful interventions.

Table 17.3   When Interventions Do Not Go as Planned

Level of Practice	Potential Explanations	
	Client	Social Worker
Individual client	• Lack of ability and capacity • Lack of motivation • Little social support • Lack of self-efficacy • Multiproblem situation	• Lack of skill • Lack of knowledge • Lack of rapport • Insufficient assessment • Inappropriate intervention
Family	• Lack of ability • Lack of motivation • Lack of unity • Dysfunction • Multiproblem situation	• Lack of skill • Lack of knowledge • Lack of rapport • Insufficient assessment • Inappropriate intervention
Group	• Lack of cohesion • Lack of participation • Disruptive members • Lack of motivation • Involuntary membership	• Lack of skill • Lack of knowledge • Lack of rapport • Insufficient assessment • Inappropriate intervention

(continued)

Table 17.3	**Continued**	
Organization	• Lack of mission • Insufficient funding • Political factors • Inaccessibility • Culturally insensitive	• Lack of skill • Lack of knowledge • Lack of rapport • Insufficient assessment • Inappropriate intervention
Community	• Factions • Negative social indicators • Lack of resources • Political factors • Varying priorities	• Lack of skill • Lack of knowledge • Lack of rapport • Insufficient assessment • Inappropriate intervention

Student Self-Assessment of Practicum Strengths (Post-Test): A Workbook Activity

Refer to the Student Self-Assessment of Practicum Strengths in Chapter 1 (The Purpose of a Practicum). You completed this at the outset of your practicum as a pretest measure of your strengths for practicum. Complete it again now that your practicum is completed, and analyze the areas in which you have shown significant professional growth as well as the areas in which you still need development.

Suggested Learning Activities

* Compare the practicum evaluation instrument used by your school with the evaluation tool used to evaluate the performance of social workers in your agency. This will help you see what is expected of social workers that is not expected of practicum students.
* Evaluate yourself using both your school's evaluation instrument and the sample tool in the learning agreement/evaluation tool for generalist social work in Chapter 3 (Developing a Learning Plan).
* Identify fears you may have about being evaluated and discuss them with your supervisor.
* Talk with other practicum students about their experiences with the evaluation process.
* In Sheafor and Horejsi (2012), read the sections titled "Developing Self-Awareness" (427–429) and "Worker Performance Evaluation" (342–343).

References

Baird, Brian N. *The Internship, Practicum, and Field Placement Handbook*. 5th ed. Upper Saddle River, NJ: Prentice Hall, 2011.

Brun, Carl F. *A Practical Guide to Social Service Evaluation*. Chicago: Lyceum Books, 2005.

Courneyer, Barry R., and Mary J. Stanley. *The Social Work Portfolio: Planning, Assessing and Documenting Lifelong Learning in a Dynamic Profession*. Pacific Grove, CA: Brooks/Cole, 2002.

Drake, Robert E., Matthew R. Merrens, and David W. Lynde, eds. *Evidence-Based Mental Health Practice: A Textbook*. New York: W. W. Norton, 2005.

Ellis, Rodney A., Kimberly Crane, Misty Y. Gould, and Suzanne Shatila. *The Macro Practitioner's Workbook: A Step-by-Step Guide to Effectiveness of Organizations and Communities*. Florence, KY: Brooks Cole, 2008.

Grinnel, Richard, and Yvonne Unrau. *Social Work Research and Evaluation*. 9th ed. New York: Oxford University Press, 2011.

Kapp, Stephen, and Gary Anderson. *Agency-Based Program Evaluation: Lessons from Practice*. Los Angeles: Sage Publications, 2010.

Magnabosco, Jennifer, and Ronald Manderscheid. *Outcomes Measurement in the Human Services: Cross-Cultural Issues of Methods in the Era of Health Reform*. 2nd ed. Washington, DC: NASW Press, 2011.

National Association of Social Workers. *Code of Ethics.* Washington, DC: NASW Press, 1999.

Roberts-DeGennaro, Maria, and Sondra Fogel. *Using Evidence to Inform Practice for Community and Organizational Change.* Chicago: Lyceum Books, 2010.

Rzepnicki, Tina, Stanley McCracken, and Harold Briggs. *From Task-Centered Social Work to Evidence-Based and Integrative Practice: Reflections on History and Implementation.* Chicago: Lyceum Books, 2012.

Shaw, Ian. *Practice and Research: Contemporary Social Work Studies.* Williston, VT: Ashgate, 2012.

Sheafor, Bradford, and Charles Horejsi. *Techniques and Guidelines for Social Work Practice.* 9th ed. Boston: Allyn and Bacon, 2012.

Westerfelt, Alex, and Tracy Dietz. *Planning and Conducting Agency-Based Research.* 4th ed. Boston: Pearson Education, 2010.

CHAPTER 17 REVIEW

PRACTICE TEST

The following questions will test your knowledge of the content found within this chapter.

1. In regard to the success of an intervention, the most important opinion on this is that of the
   a. funding source
   b. agency
   c. social worker
   d. client

2. The reason that intervention evaluations are often not done well is that
   a. social workers are not trained to do evaluations
   b. it is impossible to measure the outcome of most evaluations
   c. time is limited and agencies do not value them enough
   d. clients do not insist upon them

3. Although it is important to evaluate the process of intervention, it is also important to
   a. evaluate client input
   b. evaluate outcomes
   c. evaluate expenditures
   d. evaluate agency policies

4. There are many approaches to social work research. Which is true about this research?
   a. Quantitative research is preferable to qualitative research.
   b. Quanlitative research is preferable to qualitative research.
   c. Both are important and useful.
   d. Clients prefer quantitative research.

5. The NASW *Code of Ethics*
   a. does not speak about the process of evaluation of practice
   b. provides detailed guidelines for evaluation of practice
   c. is often in conflict with agency evaluation guidelines of practice
   d. provides support for the importance of evaluation of practice

6. Client involvement in evaluation of interventions is
   a. only necessary in client-centered casework
   b. important in all interventions
   c. optional and at the discretion of the social worker
   d. ethical only if clients agree

7. Describe the ways in which process/outcome evaluations and quantitative/qualitative evaluations can be combined to achieve an overall and comprehensive measure of effectiveness in ways that only one form of evaluation cannot.

©Stocksnapper/Fotolia

18

Merging Self and Profession

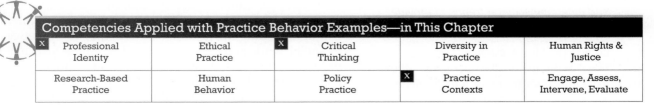

Competencies Applied with Practice Behavior Examples—in This Chapter				
X Professional Identity	Ethical Practice	X Critical Thinking	Diversity in Practice	Human Rights & Justice
Research-Based Practice	Human Behavior	Policy Practice	X Practice Contexts	Engage, Assess, Intervene, Evaluate

CHAPTER PREVIEW

This chapter provides content on the integration of the personal and professional aspects of social work as a profession, including effective ways to engage in a personally meaningful profession while also promoting balance through effective self-care strategies. Information on burnout, compassion fatigue and vicarious trauma is offered, as are reflective questions designed to stimulate critical thinking about the personal challenges of social work as a profession.

Your choice of social work as a profession was very likely an outgrowth of your commitment to helping others, facilitating social change, and contributing to social justice. Hopefully your practicum experience has reaffirmed your commitment to the profession and enhanced your knowledge and skills as well. Your commitment to ensuring the welfare of others, making a significant difference in the world, and promoting social justice has hopefully been reinforced up to this point, and reflecting on the integration of you as a person with you as a professional will help you consider the relationship between the two.

Previous chapters have asked you to consider separate but interrelated aspects of your practicum learning experiences and the profession of social, and each of them is important. This includes the topics of learning, personal safety, communication, the various contexts of practice (i.e., agency, community, social problem, and social policy), diversity, professionalism, ethics, legal concerns, the planned change process, and evaluation of practice. Although these topics have been presented in classroom settings and in this book as individual topics, they are also inextricably linked and must be purposefully integrated into your practice. Consider how best to do that as you proceed through this chapter.

BACKGROUND AND CONTEXT

Each of us is an individual with a unique personality and set of abilities and interests that are brought to the choice of a profession. In addition, each profession has a discreet set of demands and required skills. For you to be satisfied and effective as a social worker, there must be a good match between you and the profession as well as a good balance between your personal and professional selves. Selecting a career or occupation is one of the most important decisions you will ever make. That decision will have far-reaching implications for your basic contentment in life as well as the level of satisfaction you find in your work. Your clients will be best served if you understand how to use yourself as a professional tool which is built upon self-awareness, commitment to professional values, and ongoing professional growth.

Most social workers describe themselves as called to the profession of social work because they are committed to and passionate about helping others and they find the profession's values compatible with their own. They want to make a positive contribution to their community and world and they see that the practice of social work is a way of doing that. Some also feel drawn to the profession because events and experiences in their lives have opened their eyes to certain problems and to the needs of other people. Others are attracted to social work because they have the natural

Practice Contexts

Practice Behavior Example: Social workers continuously discover, appraise, and attend to changing locales, populations, scientific and technological developments, and emerging societal trends to provide relevant services.

Critical Thinking Question: What organizational and societal characteristics will be most important to you as a professional as you enter the profession?

skills and abilities necessary to the profession and see social work education as a formal way of acquiring the ability to make even more impact in terms of social justice. Most are drawn to social work by virtue of the way they think the world should be, the responsibility they feel to act on behalf of others, and the belief that they are compelled to become involved in social justice efforts.

It is important for those preparing for such a rewarding and challenging career to become skilled in ***merging the personal and professional aspects of practice.*** They must have a high level of self-awareness so they can make good choices in relation to the type of job they seek, practice self-care and stress management, and balance personal and professional responsibilities. Social workers must be aware of their unique gifts, their values, and their biases. A high level of self-awareness is critical to becoming a professional who is effective in his or her use of self in engaging with clients. Social workers must understand how their particular style and manner of interacting is perceived by others, especially by clients. Those planning to enter social work must be emotionally healthy, skilled in communication, able to build and maintain relationships, able to manage stress, and willing to continually learn and grow, both personally and professionally.

Choosing a helping profession as one's life's work means that you care deeply about those you serve. This commitment to others may take a toll on your personal life unless you learn to find a healthy balance between work and personal life. It is not possible to make a complete separation between our personal and professional lives. Our work affects our personal lives and our personal lives affect our work. Our personal experiences and life circumstances have the potential to impact our work both positively and negatively, and we must learn to manage the impact of our personal life for the benefit of our clients. We also must take care to protect the quality of our personal lives in light of the demands of the profession in terms of time, emotional energy, and the potential personal toll of dealing with the painful experiences of clients and injustices in society. Of course, this is no easy task, but it is necessary if we are to be effective as professionals and healthy as individuals.

It is important to find this balance because it is easy to allow your concern for clients to overtake you. You may worry about them or take more responsibility for them than is healthy for you. It is important to set clear boundaries between your personal and professional selves early in your career because this will help you retain your energy, enthusiasm, and optimism while also preventing discouragement and burnout. Ask your field instructor for suggestions on how to do this.

The relationship between career satisfaction and one's overall satisfaction with oneself and life is a close and intertwined one. Those who are satisfied with their careers and who maintain their overall well-being in a challenging profession tend to exhibit a variety of individual characteristics, abilities, and attitudes. Contextual and organizational factors also contribute to career satisfaction and longevity among social workers committed to the profession. Finally, societal factors also contribute in very important ways to the context that either supports or undermines professional satisfaction and success. Those three categories of contributing factors are highlighted in the Table 18.1, which lists specific contributions in each area.

Professional Identity

Practice Behavior Example: Social workers practice personal reflection and self-correction to assure continual professional development.

Critical Thinking Question: How can you continue to engage in self-reflection and professional growth so that you maintain a strengths perspective on clients and your work?

Table 18.1   **Contributing Factors to Professional Satisfaction**

Individual Factors

- Knowledge and skill
- Values consistent with professional goals
- Balance of collaborative and autonomous approach to work
- Optimism, enthusiasm, self-efficacy, belief in possibilities
- Ability to manage stress
- Flexibility, openness, and commitment to professional growth

Organizational Factors

- Reasonable workload and adequate funding
- Agency support and training
- Opportunity for professional growth and creativity
- Inclusion in agency mission and program development
- Collegiality, sharing of responsibility, and empowerment
- Invited participation in agency visioning

Societal Factors

- Political economy supportive of social justice efforts
- Positive societal attitudes toward clients and profession
- Social policy effectiveness that supports social work efforts
- Societal commitment to prevention of social problems
- Societal commitment to promotion of social justice
- Societal support of social work mission

Keep these factors in mind as you begin the search for a professional position in the field of social work. The work itself will be both challenging and rewarding, so the work environment should also contribute to your overall well-being as a professional. This is an example of the ways in which the social work profession and the social systems surrounding it interact over time, ultimately impacting both clients and the professionals serving them.

GUIDANCE AND DIRECTION

Social work requires an integration of professional knowledge, ethics, and self-awareness. It is not enough to know about people, to have skills, to know theories, or to understand models and techniques. You as a person must merge with you as a professional. Remember that all the skills and knowledge in the world are not enough to make you an effective social worker. You also need to bring your personal gifts, strengths, creativity, passion, and commitment to the social work profession. It is in the unique blending of your personal qualities and your professional education that you will become a truly skilled and qualified social worker.

Who you are as a person is just as important as what you know or what you can do. View your practicum as an opportunity to grow both personally and professionally, and to blend your unique personality and professional style with the requirements of your chosen profession. Over time the two parts of you will blend so that you will bring everything that is unique about you to your personal way of being a social worker.

Seek opportunities to continuously enhance your professional growth. For example, read professional books and journals, attend workshops and in-service training, try out new skills and techniques, think critically about intervention strategies, carefully observe the behavior and practice of social workers in your agency, and spend time talking with knowledgeable and skilled practitioners. Engage in critical self-reflection, asking yourself and trusted colleagues what you can do to continue growing. Open yourself to feedback so that you see yourself as others do. You will certainly see your own growth over time, and this will not only reinforce your choice of social work as a profession but also remind you of the importance of self-awareness as a tool for helping others.

Ask for feedback from coworkers, your field instructor, and clients. Use this information to better understand who you are, what you have to offer, and what you may need to change in order to become a skilled and effective social worker. You are certain to see that you have grown over time, your questions have become more probing, and your reflections are more sophisticated. This will reinforce the fact that you are growing as a professional. Your practicum is truly job-related experience. It is relevant preparation for practice and the job market. Do your best and remember that the skills you develop now, combined with favorable evaluations and recommendations from your field instructor, can help you obtain employment in the profession.

Observe how the social workers in your agency deal with challenges such as high caseloads, potentially modest salaries, unmotivated and difficult clients, seemingly intractable social problems, funding cuts, and the stress of dealing with deeply emotional and painful situations on a daily basis. Begin now to develop stress management skills and habits that will help you avoid excessive job-related stress or burnout. Learn how to set limits; define and keep ***personal and professional boundaries***, which will maintain your level of well-being; make time for your family and yourself; and maintain a positive outlook on clients and the work you do. Refer to Table 18.1, which highlights a number of contributing factors to professional satisfaction in social work, including individual, organizational, and societal factors.

Think about how you will deal with the stresses and challenges of professional social work. Learn how to avoid negative consequences for yourself and continue to maintain optimism and belief in possibility. You will need to find ways to avoid ***burnout***, which is the result of overworking, lack of support, and the inability to balance the demands of work with one's personal life. You also need to be aware of and avoid ***compassion fatigue***, to which social workers who care deeply about the welfare of others may fall prey if they are not able to manage the impact of extending oneself to benefit clients over time. Finally, make certain you understand the possibility of ***secondary or vicarious traumatic stress***, which is the negative impact on social workers of bearing witness to the pain and suffering of others.

To manage these challenges and maintain the quality of both your personal and professional life, refer to the tool called Holistic Self-Care Strategies and Areas of Stress for Social Workers in the workbook section of this chapter. It describes the challenges of social work

Research-Based Practice

Practice Behavior Example: Social workers use research evidence to inform practice.

Critical Thinking Question: What is the best way to become an evidence-based practitioner?

Engage, Assess, Intervene, Evaluate

Practice Behavior Example: Social workers use empathy and other interpersonal skills.

Critical Thinking Question: When social workers use themselves as tools for helping others, what professional attributes are most needed at each phase of the helping process?

as physical, intellectual, psychological, social, cultural, and spiritual stressors. It suggests that social workers who experience stress in these areas of their professional life design a holistic self-care strategy that employs approaches in a variety of areas. Social workers, like you, who are committed to their profession over time, will develop their own individual approach to self-care that maintains both personal and professional well-being.

Begin developing the habit of monitoring your own professional growth. Ask yourself these questions regularly:

- What is my **vision** for myself as a social worker?
- Do I feel a **calling** to the profession of social work?
- How can I maintain my **commitment** in the face of the challenges and stresses of the profession?
- What **social work values** are most important to me as I embark on this career?
- Am I **growing** as a person and a professional?
- Do I **know myself** better than I did last month? Last year?
- Am I **satisfied** with who I am and what I am doing?
- How can I **continue to grow** and change in a positive way?
- Do I continue to see the **potential, possibility, and strengths** of clients?
- Am I **optimistic** about social change?
- What **self-care activities** can I engage in to maintain energy and optimism?
- After **5, 10, or 15 years in the profession**, in what type of social work do I expect to be engaged?
- What **advice** would I give to social work students who are just starting practicum?
- What **impact** do I hope to make as a social worker?

Holistic Self-care Strategies and Areas of Stress for Social Workers: A Workbook Activity

This tool is designed to encourage you to thoughtfully identify the realms of your life in which you might potentially experience stress as a social worker. It also provides a way to identify individualized strategies to manage the stresses in these areas by engaging in self-care activities in these same realms of your life.

Apply this tool to yourself by identifying the stressors you have experienced during your practicum and designing and committing to self-care strategies that will help you manage this stress and keep you fresh, optimistic, and healthy.

Holistic Self-care Strategies and Areas of Stress Management for Social Workers

	Strategies					
Areas of Stress	Physical Self-care	Intellectual Self-care	Psychological Self-care	Social Self-care	Cultural Self-care	Spiritual Self-care
Physical Stressors Fatigue, overwork, neglected health and fitness						

(continued)

(*continued*)

Intellectual Stressors Continual need to learn new techniques and expand knowledge						
Psychological Stressors Worry, anxiety, stress, guilt, counter-transference, inadequate coping skills						
Social Stressors Impact of work on relationships, dealing with colleagues and supervisors						
Cultural Stressors Cross-cultural work, discomfort with diversity						
Spiritual Stressors Impact of work on values and belief system						

Suggested Learning Activities

- Interview experienced social workers in your agency and in other agencies. Ask about their level of job satisfaction, as well as their strategies for self care.
- Speak with social workers who have obtained advanced degrees (MSW, Ph.D., or DSW) and ask them to help you consider the possibility of further education.
- Observe the self-care practices of those around you and adopt those which match your needs.
- Determine the ways in which your agency supports its workers in terms of self-care, stress management, and critical incident debriefing in the face of very challenging situations.
- In Sheafor and Horejsi (2012), read the section titled "Getting a Social Work Job" (422–424).
- Examine the social work job openings advertised in local and regional newspapers, public agency bulletins, and in NASW news. (The NASW website is www.socialworkers.org.)

References

Birkenmaier, Julie, and Marla Berg-Weger. *The Practicum Companion for Social Work: Integrating Class and Field Work.* 3rd ed. Boston: Allyn and Bacon, 2011.

Rothman, Juliet Cassuto. *The Self-Awareness Workbook for Social Workers.* Boston: Allyn and Bacon, 1999.

Schon, Donald A., and Aleksandr Romanovich Luria. *The Reflective Practitioner: How Professionals Think in Action.* New York: Basic Books, 1990.

Seden, Janet, Sarah Matthews, Mick McCormick, and Alun Morgan. *Professional Development in Social Work: Complex Issues in Practice.* Clifton, NJ: Routledge, 2010.

Sheafor, Bradford, and Charles Horejsi. *Techniques and Guidelines for Social Work Practice.* 9th ed. Boston: Allyn and Bacon, 2012.

Skovholt, Thomas, and Michelle Trotter-Mathison. *The Resilient Practitioner: Burnout Prevention and Self-Care Strategies for Counselors, Therapist, Teachers, and Health Professionals.* 2nd ed. Clifton, NJ: Routledge, 2010.

CHAPTER 18 REVIEW

PRACTICE TEST

The following questions will test your knowledge of the content found within this chapter.

1. The personal values of social workers
   a. generally provide the motivation for their choice of profession
   b. are totally separate from their professional values
   c. are always secondary to those of the agency in which they work
   d. should override professional values in client situations

2. Self-awareness is an important part of social work practice because
   a. social workers represent the profession to society
   b. social workers use themselves as professional tools
   c. it will help prevent professional burnout
   d. professional growth is required in the profession

3. Social workers and their clients may have values conflicts, which should be resolved by
   a. having a mediator negotiate between them
   b. the social worker ensuring that his or her values do not negatively impact clients
   c. supervisors
   d. client advocates

4. Professional boundaries are important to maintain because
   a. social workers are vulnerable to client manipulation
   b. social workers tend to think they are unnecessary
   c. social workers need to protect themselves and clients
   d. agencies require them

5. The value of peer supervision is that
   a. it costs less than supervision by a trained supervisor
   b. it is less threatening to the social worker
   c. it allows for colleagues to share information not shared with supervisors
   d. it provides another perspective by an experienced colleague

6. Which term describes the vicarious traumatization that can happen to social workers based on their exposure to painful client experiences?
   a. burnout
   b. compassion fatigue
   c. secondary traumatic stress
   d. stress reaction

7. Articulate the relationship between personal and professional growth. What can a social agency do to address this relationship and promote both to continuously enhance social work effectiveness and satisfaction with one's position?

©Pixelfabrik/Dreamstime

19

Leadership for Social Justice

Competencies Applied with Practice Behavior Examples—in This Chapter				
X Professional Identity	X Ethical Practice	X Critical Thinking	Diversity in Practice	X Human Rights & Justice
Research-Based Practice	Human Behavior	X Policy Practice	X Practice Contexts	Engage, Assess, Intervene, Evaluate

CHAPTER PREVIEW

Now that your practicum is nearing its completion, you have nearly fulfilled all of the requirements necessary to obtain your degree. No doubt you are excited about job possibilities and thinking seriously about the personal satisfaction with and ramifications of entering the world of social work. This is a time of transition. What lies ahead for you? Where will you work? What will be expected of you? What kind of social worker do you hope to become? What contributions can you make to the welfare of others and to the profession of social work? Perhaps even more important, what kind of person do you want to become? This chapter invites you to reflect on these questions.

BACKGROUND AND CONTEXT

The mission of social work is always rooted in social change and social justice, and hopefully your practicum has reinforced the importance and centrality of that emphasis to your work. Whether your professional work finds you working at the micro, mezzo, or macro level, social justice is at the forefront. Because of the ongoing and challenging nature of the fight for social justice, social workers must embrace the role of leader in order to achieve the goals of social justice. Because of the personal and professional commitment to the welfare of others through the promotion of social justice, the practice of social work usually brings both challenges and rewards. Hopefully your journey as a social worker will involve a professional life filled with meaning and purpose, and that you will emerge as a leader within your community and your chosen profession.

It is both exciting and rather daunting to think about being a social worker. There are many problems to be addressed and numerous clients to be served. Injustices must be challenged and many programs need to be designed or redesigned. There is so much to be done and so few resources. There is also much more to learn as you move from the academic world of a practicum student to the real world of the professional social worker.

Because you have completed the requirements for a social work degree in a program accredited by the Council on Social Work Education, your professors and field instructor have concluded that you are ready to begin the practice of social work. Although you may still feel anxious and ill prepared to assume the full responsibilities of a social worker, your professors and supervisors believe that you possess the knowledge and basic skills needed to move into a social agency and apply what you have learned. You have been educated in an academic setting, trained in a social agency, and exposed to many social problems and various ways of addressing them. Do not underestimate what you have learned and what you are capable of doing. You are now a professional social worker by virtue of all you have learned and the ways in which you have demonstrated your competence and commitment to ethical practice.

Even though you are moving from the role of a student to that of a professional, it is important to reflect often on what you have learned about the unique mission of social work and its commitment to those in society considered most vulnerable and oppressed. Social work is a profession deeply committed, both by its history and current practice, to creating communities and a society that will nurture the well-being of individuals and families and to making sure that all people have access to the basic resources and opportunities necessary to live with dignity. You have entered a profession that is committed to challenging systems and institutional structures that do not treat people in a fair and humane manner. If you, as a social worker, do not speak out against and seek to correct a social or economic injustice, you are, in effect, giving your tacit approval to the current state of affairs.

Good generalist or integrated social work practitioners view the practice of social work as much more than the tasks and activities listed in their job description or suggested in their agency's mission statement. They work hard at whatever they are hired to do, but also assume the additional responsibility of becoming an advocate for those who are not able to speak for themselves. Social work, at its unique best, is about going beyond one's job description and acting on a commitment to social justice by weaving together the networks of people and resources that can bring about needed changes at the community, state, and national levels. In fact, a true leader sees what is possible and is not constrained by a job description or by limited resources. A leader develops a vision, knows what needs to be done, and makes things happen, building on acquired knowledge and skills, combined with the synergy generated by bringing committed people together.

You have no doubt been schooled in the person-in-environment perspective that is fundamental to the way social workers view people, assess human problems and concerns, and design interventions. Social workers, whether employed to work at the micro or macro level, must be cognizant of the wider societal context of the lives and problems of their clients and the context of the agencies, programs, and interventions that address these client concerns. For example, a social worker employed at the micro level as an advocate for those in poverty should question why poverty exists and take a macro level leadership role in addressing the myriad of macro level contributors to poverty. Conversely, social workers working on the macro level to change social policies must never forget the very serious impact of any social policy changes on the lives of individual people struggling with poverty. This is a very broad and demanding mission, but a crucial one that a leader will embrace.

The realities and time pressures associated with employment in an agency that has a particular mission and program tend to set in motion a number of forces that might narrow the range of your concerns, interests, and vision. You will feel very busy with all of the demands of your job, but it will be important that you find ways to remain involved in social issues beyond the scope of your work responsibilities. Doing so will help remind you that others care about their work as much as you and can serve as a source of inspiration for you. Strive to maintain a wide range of interests, involvements, and professional activities. Seek out new ideas, even when they are not immediately applicable in your everyday work.

As you enter into the work of a particular agency, you may discover that the agency uses an unfamiliar conceptual framework or rationale to guide its practice activities. As you are exposed to new practice theories, remember that each one needs to be examined in terms of its potential to enhance practice effectiveness, its appropriateness for use with particular types of clients in particular settings, evidence of its effectiveness, its stated or implied assumptions about clients and the process of change, and its compatibility with social work values.

Critically consider why you might prefer one approach over other possibilities. Most likely, you prefer a particular practice framework because it is the one most compatible with your beliefs about human behavior and human problems, and because it instructs you as a professional to perform those tasks and activities to which you are especially attracted. Although it is natural to pursue your own interests, seek to broaden and deepen your understanding of the various perspectives, theories, and models used in social work practice. Carefully examine the assumptions underlying each approach. Strive to understand the strengths and limitations of each one. Be open to gaining insights and guidance from several practice frameworks.

To know whether you are being effective over time, you will need to document your work and study the outcomes of your practice, both individually and in concert with other professionals and agencies. Be ready to change your approach if you are not being as effective as you had hoped or think is possible. Needless to say, much of what social workers do and much of what clients experience is difficult to measure, but resist the temptation to use this as an excuse for not making a genuine effort to evaluate your practice. You cannot improve your practice unless you are willing to look at it critically and allow others to offer constructive criticisms.

To the extent possible, build your knowledge base from empirical and scientific studies, but remember that there are many other sources of useful knowledge. Some are empirical and some are not. It is important to balance the **positivist view of knowledge building**, which rests primarily on the scientific method of understanding, with contributions from **practice wisdom**, which refers to the collective professional experiences and observations of practitioners and the **postmodern view of knowledge**, which values the contributions of alternative theories, qualitative research, and deconstruction of assumptions. Add to that the additional insights derived from study of the humanities, religion, and classic and modern literature. Finally, learn from your clients as you listen to their stories and experiences, and add their wisdom to yours.

As you use new research findings and theories drawn from the social and behavioral sciences, consider the observation by sociologists that such knowledge is **socially constructed**. Our knowledge of a social or psychological phenomenon or a particular human problem is shaped and limited by the context in which it was studied, by our positionality in relation to the problem, and by the language used to describe it. It is very much tied to culture, history, economics, and politics. Our knowledge is, at best, incomplete and only temporarily true. The awareness that knowledge is a social construction helps us put data and conclusions in perspective and realize that the concepts and theories used in practice, no matter how well conceived and impressive, are purely human inventions. It is your prerogative and responsibility to thoughtfully question all findings and claims, regardless of their source.

It is actually the job of critically reflective social workers to deconstruct their knowledge and what is being told to them. This means that you must examine what you know, question how you came to know it, ask yourself how this view might be inaccurate or limited, and become comfortable at times with not knowing everything you need to know. In a similar vein, recognize that the **concept of client** is a human invention or social construction that has arisen out of our cultural views and presumptions about who is in need of help, who is powerless to help himself or herself, and who is qualified to help another person. Always be sensitive to the possibility that agencies, social workers, and other professionals can misuse their power and authority to label a person, family, or group as troubled and in need of certain services or interventions. Remember also that the designation of one person as a client and another as a social worker does not mean that the social worker is more knowledgeable or more insightful than the client. Rather, the opposite could be true. The lines between social worker and client, although useful, are arbitrary and can limit our ability to relate to each other in significant ways.

Becoming involved in those professional organizations can support your work, challenge you intellectually, and remind you that others are also involved in the struggle to create a just society. Remember that you are expected to contribute to the ongoing development and shaping of the profession, and that social work educators need to hear your observations and suggestions as much as clients need your skills. You will be expected to voice your opinions about directions you believe the profession should take based on your observations and your projections of future needs. For example, you will need to speak up when you see your profession becoming focused too heavily on one aspect of social work to the detriment of its overall mission.

Living and working in the world of ideas and questions and committing to lifelong learning are important for social workers to remain effective over time. There are numerous approaches you can take to continue learning and growing, which will not only make you more effective but will also make you a better, more informed, and capable practitioner. The following professional growth responsibilities are often expected of social workers.

- Continuing to read professional literature and attending advanced training
- Joining or forming a group of professionals that takes seriously its commitment to continuing education and peer supervision
- Looking globally and internationally for possible solutions to nagging and serious social problems
- Learning from your clients who experience on a daily basis what you may only observe, read about, or imagine
- Identifying the connections between social conditions and the social problems resulting from them
- Staying connected to schools of social work through training and conferences, and by offering guest lectures
- Talking on a regular basis to those with whom you fundamentally disagree in order to retain an open mind and clarify your own beliefs and values
- Finding ways to come to know and understand yourself better over time
- Asking yourself regularly what your vision for the world is and determine what you need to learn to bring yourself closer to your goals
- Supervising practicum students, recalling what it was like to be a student

Recognizing your ability to be a ***catalyst for change*** will be important, which means that you can bring individuals and groups together, contribute your skills and knowledge, and stimulate positive movement or changes that would not have occurred without your intervention. Remember that you are not alone in your efforts to help others. There are many social workers who will support and encourage you in your efforts. Seek them out, offer your support in return, and find avenues of renewal for yourself, both personally and professionally.

You already know how important it will be to take care of yourself, recognize the good in the world as well as the problems, celebrate large and small successes, learn to laugh, and cultivate the sources of your passion and strength. It will be vital to use your family, friends, spiritual beliefs, and core values to guide you, and take pride in your chosen profession.

GUIDANCE AND DIRECTION

As a social worker you will encounter many situations of oppression and social and economic injustice. You will also encounter situations in which agency policies, programs, and practices are in need of revision to make them fairer and more effective. You will want to change these situations but may quickly discover that bringing about needed and meaningful change can be a difficult and slow process. In order to bring about change you must be willing and able to assume the role, tasks, and responsibilities of leadership. Desirable changes do not happen by accident. Rather, they are set in motion by individuals who assert themselves, articulate their beliefs, and step forward to take on the hard work of leading.

Although it may be true that a few leaders are the so-called born leaders, most had to learn the skills of leadership much like they learned any other skill. Aspiring leaders must consciously and continually cultivate the development of those qualities, ways of thinking, attitudes, and interpersonal skills that are associated with effective leadership.

Leadership is much more than having good ideas. It is not enough to know what needs to be done. Leadership is the ability to make things happen and to inspire others to join in the effort. Leaders must have a clear vision of what they want to accomplish. Equally important, they must be able to articulate this vision and explain it in words that others understand. The vision must be one that can be translated into action steps and programs that are inspiring but also feasible and realistic.

It is the leader's vision that gives him or her the critically important sense of purpose, direction, and self-confidence to make difficult decisions. This sense of purpose must be evident in all that the leader does. Indecisiveness and the unwillingness to take action when action is clearly necessary can deeply undermine confidence in a leader's ability. It is better for a leader to occasionally make a bad decision than to avoid making a critically important decision, so learn to be decisive and bold when necessary as well as thoughtful and well prepared.

Effective leaders lead by example. Followers are inspired and motivated by the passion, resolve, courage, hard work, and sacrifices of their leaders. Leaders must model the behaviors they want to see in others. They should not ask others to do what they are unwilling to do themselves. Leaders must demonstrate respect and genuine concern for the wishes, values, and abilities of those they lead. They must be willing to curtail some of their own preferences and plans in order to avoid moving too far ahead of those they lead. Leaders cannot lead unless there are people who choose to follow them.

Effective leaders must maintain open and honest communication with those they lead. This communication must keep everyone focused on the goal while attending to the concerns, fears, and ambivalence they may have about investing their time, energy, and money in working toward this goal. Good leaders anticipate possible conflicts and disagreements among those they lead. They are proactive in taking steps to prevent or resolve these conflicts before they can distract from goal achievement and splinter the followers into competing factions.

Critical Thinking

Practice Behavior Example: Social workers demonstrate effective oral and written communication in working with individuals, families, groups, organizations, communities, and colleagues.

Critical Thinking Question: What critical thinking skills are necessary for the leader committed to social justice to effectively communicate at all levels of practice?

Leaders must be skilled in the art of collaboration and building bridges between individuals and organizations. They must reward others for their cooperation and share the credit for success with others, even those with whom they may disagree. Leaders must be willing to compromise when this is a necessary step toward reaching the sought-after goal.

The exercise of leadership always occurs within a context of competing and conflicting forces. Leaders shape, guide, and redirect those forces, so they move in directions that produce the desired effect and move people toward the desired goal. Because leaders must function within environments and situations that are unpredictable and always changing, they must be willing to take necessary risks and cope with ambiguity and uncertainty.

Effective leaders possess a high level of self-awareness. They understand their own strengths and limitations and constantly examine their own motives and behavior. Some leaders destroy their capacity to lead by allowing feelings of self-importance and a need for recognition to dominate their decisions or by becoming arrogant and overly confident because of past successes. Decide now that you will never let that happen to you.

In addition to the factors mentioned previously, the following personal qualities and characteristics are important to the exercise of effective leadership. Identify which of these characteristics describe you right now and which might describe you in the near future as you head into leadership positions in the profession.

- Capacity to ***think critically*** and examine personal decisions and actions
- Capacity to speak and write clearly to ***articulate a vision*** and purpose in ways people can understand
- ***Perseverance*** when faced with difficulties and disappointments
- Ability to ***delegate responsibility*** and teach or ***empower others*** to perform as well as they can
- Ability to ***make difficult decisions*** in situations that are complex and fluid
- Willingness to ***assume personal responsibility*** for one's decisions and actions
- Personal flexibility, ***openness to new ideas***, and the ability to work with people with various abilities and from diverse backgrounds
- Ability to ***create a sense of belonging and community*** among those working toward the same goals
- Ability to ***make effective use of available time*** and get things done
- Willingness to ***assess one's own effectiveness*** in a nondefensive manner and to adopt approaches that will be more effective

Leaders in the social work profession find themselves in the midst of public debates, tensions, competing points of view, and value systems which are on the far ends of the spectrum. Each of these contemporary discussions highlights the challenges of leadership in bringing together varying opinions, values, and preferred approaches to preventing or dealing with social problems and issues. For example, social work leaders must lead their organizations through discussions such as the following ones. Think about how you as a leader will negotiate these conversations in a way that fulfills the social work mission.

Ethical Practice

Practice Behavior Example: Social workers make ethical decisions by applying standards of the National Association of Social Workers Code of Ethics.

Critical Thinking Question: Which ethical competencies are most closely related to the characteristics of an effective leader committed to social justice?

- What is the most effective combination of **private and public responses** to social problems?
- Are social services a **human right or a privilege**?
- What is the best balance between **universal entitlement and eligibility** criteria?
- How should **personal responsibility** be balanced with the **availability of social safety nets**?
- At what **level(s) of practice** are social problems best addressed, from **micro to macro**?
- Should a **scarcity of resources** guide and control what a leader attempts to accomplish?

Work hard to become what is commonly referred to as a **transformational leader**—someone who understands and embodies the interpersonal and moral aspects of leadership. Through their passion and vision, and their deeply held beliefs and strong moral values, transformational leaders inspire others. They are able to get others to join with them because they are enthusiastic and energetic. Their integrity leads others to trust them. Their genuine desire to see others succeed makes others more enthusiastic. This form of leadership, which is motivated by the welfare of everyone involved in a common effort, is markedly different from the form of leadership that only pays attention to the tasks at hand. Try to become the sort of leader who balances the work to be done with the professional and personal support of those working together.

Clearly, it is a challenge to be an effective leader in one's agency or profession. It is an even more difficult undertaking when the leader's goal is to promote social and economic justice. However, this is at the heart of social work. At a fundamental level, justice can be defined as fairness in social interactions. Although there are several categories or types of justice, social and economic justice are of special concern to social workers. **Social justice** refers to the basic fairness and moral rightness of the social arrangements and institutional structures that impact the people of a community or society. **Economic justice** (also called **distributive justice**) can be defined as that dimension of justice having to do with the material or the economic aspects of a community or society.

![Human Behavior icon]

Human Behavior

Practice Behavior Example: Social workers understand the forms and mechanisms of oppression and discrimination.

Critical Thinking Question: What beliefs about human behavior underlie various forms of oppression and social injustice?

Because social and economic injustices are, by definition, embedded in existing institutional arrangements and social policies, many political, economic, and cultural forces are at work maintaining the unjust conditions. Those who seek change will encounter many powerful individuals and groups who will want to maintain the status quo. In order to secure real change, a leader working for social justice must be willing to take substantial risks and make significant personal sacrifices as he or she engages in the phases of social justice work.

A helpful way to view the role of a leader in social justice work is to understand the distinction between **facilitating leadership tasks** and **blocking leadership tasks** required in various stages of social change efforts. **Facilitating leadership tasks** are those proactive, positive, and affirmative practices which promote planned social justice work. They build on and capitalize on existing forces for change, resources, and values. **Blocking leadership tasks** are those resistance, critiquing, and reframing practices which fight the status quo and block forces opposing social justice. Table 19.1 highlights the facilitating leadership **tasks** involved in social

Table 19.1   **Social Justice Efforts and Facilitating Leadership Tasks**

Phase of Social Justice Effort	Facilitating Leadership Tasks
Consciousness-raising and assessment	Learn Anticipate forces for and against change Recognize problems and resources Clarify values Promote use of ecosystems perspective Scan social environment Promote social justice
Building coalitions	Collaborate Identify common concerns Mentor Identify stakeholders Inspire participation Empower constituencies Focus on solidarity Model
Planning and Organizing	Envision Set goals and objectives Engage stakeholders Encourage innovation Staff development Build capacity for change Acquire political power
Implementation	Create change effort Influence target system Supervise Consult Support Maintain focus Deal with opposing forces
Evaluation	Sustain social change Leverage success Transfer power Evaluate effectiveness Share lessons learned Disseminate findings Contribute to body of knowledge Develop best practices

Table 19.2	**Social Justice Efforts and Blocking Leadership Tasks**
Phase of Social Justice Effort	Blocking Leadership Tasks
Consciousness-raising and assessment	Deconstruct myths
	Challenge easy answers
	Challenge surface-level changes
	Ask critical questions
	Resist status quo
	Critique forces against change
	Challenge injustice
Building coalitions	Resist efforts to separate stakeholders
	Avoid silo approach to change
	Challenge special interests
	Recognize resistance
	Block fragmentation of efforts
Planning and organizing	Block efforts to exclude stakeholders
	Avoid band-aid goals and objectives
	Reframe single-level change to multilevel
	Counter scarcity paradigm
	Block counterorganizing efforts
Implementation	Neutralize resistance
	Challenge pessimism
	Resist consolidation of power
	Address efforts to undermine change efforts
	Block cuts to funding
Evaluation	Address efforts to discredit intervention
	Address critiques of efforts
	Block efforts to return to status quo

justice work, and Table 19.2 illustrates the blocking leadership tasks involved in social justice work. Keep these lists as a resource to guide your thinking as you move into professional practice.

Keep informed of the ***emerging issues in social work leadership*** that will require vision, innovation, critical thinking, and a willingness to improve practice over time. Because of societal and global changes in the social environment, social work itself must change in order to address and embrace those changes. The use of technology in practice presents many advanced methods for providing services, but also involves a number of clinical and ethical issues such as quality of services, confidentiality, and adaptations to practice approaches. The limits of funding for social services demands that organizations commit to true interdisciplinary approaches that recognize the mutual interactions between professional perspectives, the contributions of a variety of professions to the solving of social problems, and the approaches to practice that are truly broad and comprehensive.

Additional emerging issues include the need to create knowledge through program evaluation and the development of best practices designated as such by empirical evidence and solicited client input. Future social work practice depends on the ability of leaders to create theories, both those that explain social phenomena (orienting and explanatory theories) and those that guide intervention plans at all levels (practice theories and models). This requires leaders and administrators who support social work professionals in their professional development. They help social workers develop the ability to rely on practice wisdom, empirical evidence, and what is commonly referred to as a learning edge that encourages professionals to lean into innovation and develop a learning culture within their organizations. Finally, social work leaders must recognize and incorporate an understanding of the impact of global conditions and cultural diversity into their work in creative and effective ways.

As you identify your leadership abilities and skills, and as you work to incorporate the characteristics listed above into your practice over time, also consider some very specific ways in which you can acquire the leadership abilities that will be required of you. Commit to lifelong professional learning that will keep you abreast of the social work world. Identify mentors for yourself who will help you develop needed skills, networking opportunities, and supervision. Engage in interdisciplinary work whenever possible to maintain a broad and inclusive view of social problems and solutions. Become a part of a community of practice, which includes mentors, colleagues, confidantes, and support persons from both social work and other professions. This community of practice will help you learn, grow, prioritize, focus, and maintain commitment in the midst of challenging practice situations.

A good leader remembers the history of the movement in which he or she is involved as well as the lessons of the past. Reflect in a critical and appreciative manner on the evolution of the social work profession and the many significant contributions of social workers to social justice and the building of a social welfare system. Educate yourself about the contributions of the social work profession in such areas as Social Security, civil rights, child labor laws, Medicaid, unemployment insurance, minimum wage, the peace movement, and many others. Consider the contributions made by those who developed theories of practice, those who assumed leadership in the academic preparation of professional social workers, and the countless clients whose lives and stories have provided the motivation and inspiration for such service.

Practice Contexts

Practice Behavior Example: Social workers continuously discover, appraise, and attend to changing locales, populations, scientific and technological developments, and emerging societal trends to provide relevant services.

Critical Thinking Question: What vision of the world do you have, that if achieved by you and others during your professional careers, would allow you to consider yourself successful in your helping career?

Many social workers say that social work is not what they do, but it is who they are. Their professional lives are guided by their personal beliefs, values, and spirituality, and they believe that being a social worker allows them to live out the beliefs and values they hold dear and about which they feel passionate. That notion indicates a compatible merger between person and the profession, as discussed in Chapter 18. However, always remember that you are now and will always be more than your profession and your job. If your whole identity is tied up in being a social worker, broaden your horizons and life experiences. You need to be healthy for your clients, but also for yourself, friends, and family.

Consider the idea of describing your practice through the use of metaphors. These are visual and personal ways of thinking about what social work is, especially in regard to the overall social justice mission of social work. Using a metaphor for your work can help you personalize your commitment and continue to view it as a creative endeavor. Table 19.3 lists several common metaphors for social work practice, with an accompanying description of how these metaphors for social justice work. Think about which of these metaphors, or another one that is not included here, can be useful to you as you enter the world of social work.

Your practicum will soon come to an end, and your professors and field instructors will tell you that you are ready for professional social work practice. You will have earned the designation of a professional social worker by virtue of your academic preparation, your practicum experience, your commitment to the National Association of Social Workers **Code of Ethics**, and your sense of calling to promote social justice. You have all of the tools needed to be a social worker, whether you are working with individual clients or whether your efforts are focused on large-scale social change. Those tools, including your knowledge, your commitment to helping others, and your helping skills, will all come together in a unique way as you become a professional social worker. In fact, you yourself are the tool by which clients will be served and social justice will be furthered. Welcome to the proactive, progressive, and visionary profession of social work.

Table 19.3   **Metaphors for Social Justice Practice**

Metaphorical for Practice	Correlation with Social Justice
Practice as journey	Achieving social justice is a journey, complete with road maps, detours, mergers, one way roads, traveling companions, and destinations.
Practice as tapestry	Achieving social justice is a tapestry woven of variegated elements, combined colors and textures, creative images and opposing threads.
Practice as story	Achieving social justice is a story including plot, surprises, an interesting cast of characters, a moral, and an ending.
Practice as art	Achieving social justice is art combining color, perspective, interpretation, creativity, and mixed methods.
Practice as vision	Achieving social justice is a vision based on values, possibilities, purpose, forward thinking and commitment to change.
Practice as dance	Achieving social justice is a dance involving background music, training, communication with an audience, and interpretation.
Practice as battle	Achieving social justice is a battle including commitment, enemies and allies, strategy, skirmishes, victory and defeat.
Practice as evolution	Achieving social justice is evolution including gradual changes, mutations, progress, ongoing development and shifts.
Practice as invention	Achieving social justice is invention based on creativity, recognition of an unmet need, trial and error, and innovation.

Suggested Learning Activities

- Subscribe to electronic listservs offered by professional organizations and advocacy groups to stay abreast of issues of importance to you, as well as legislative and social justice implications of their work.
- Search out websites that will expand your understanding of social work's responsibility to maintain global standards of practice. For example, read the United Nations Universal Declaration of Human Rights.
- Read Pablo Freire's works, which describe the relationship between education and political struggles.

References

Bertolino, Bob. *Advocacy Practice for Social Justice.* Boston: Pearson, 2010.

Bondi, Liz, David Carr, Chris Clark, and Cecelia Clegg, eds. *Towards Professional Wisdom: Political Deliberation in the People Professions.* Williston, VT: Ashgate, 2011.

Chung, Rita Chi-Ying, and Frederic Bemak. *Social Justice Counseling: The Next Steps beyond Multiculturalism.* Thousand Oaks, CA: Sage Publications Company, 2011.

Dolgoff, Ralph, and Donald Feldstein. *Understanding Social Welfare: A Search for Social Justice.* 9th ed. Boston: Allyn and Bacon, 2013.

Figueira-McConough, Josefina. *The Welfare State and Social Work: Pursuing Social Justice.* Thousand Oaks, CA: Sage Publications, 2007.

Finn, Janet, and Maxine Jacobson. *Just Practice: A Social Justice Approach to Social Work.* 2nd ed. Peosta, IA: Eddie Bowers Publishing, 2008.

Freire, Pablo. *Pedagogy of the Oppressed.* New York: Seabury, 1973.

Freire, Pablo. *Pedagogy of the Heart.* New York: Continuum, 1997.

Haynes, Karen S., and James S. Mickelson. *Affecting Change: Social Workers in the Political Arena.* 6th ed. Boston: Allyn and Bacon, 2006.

Hoefer, Richard. *Advocacy Practice for Social Justice.* 2nd ed. Chicago: Lyceum Books, 2012.

LaFosto, Frank, and Carl Larson. *The Humanitarian Leader in Each of Us: 7 Choices that Shape a Socially Responsible Life.* Thousand Oaks, CA: Sage Publications, 2011.

Lieberman, Alice A., and Cheryl B. Lester. *Social Work Practice with a Difference: Stories, Essays, Cases, and Commentaries.* Boston: McGraw Hill, 2004.

Lum, Doman. *Culturally Competent Practice: A Framework for Understanding Diverse Groups and Justice Issues.* 3rd ed. Florence, KY: Wadsworth Publishing, 2006.

Schillmeier, Michael. *New Technologies and Emerging Spaces of Care.* Williston, VT: Ashgate, 2010.

Thomlison, Barbara, and Kevin Corcoran, eds. *The Evidence-Based Internship: A Field Manual.* New York: Oxford University Press, 2008.

Wronka, Joseph. *Human Rights and Social Justice: Social Action and Service for the Helping and Health Professions.* Thousand Oaks, CA: Sage Publications, 2008.

PRACTICE TEST
The following questions will test your knowledge of the content found within this chapter.

1. Social workers in leadership positions should promote social justice by
   a. earning a masters degree in social work
   b. supervising and mentoring social work students
   c. critically challenging societal assumptions and creating a vision for social justice
   d. focusing primarily on macro level practice

2. The professional knowledge obtained by social workers through experience is considered
   a. continuing education
   b. practice wisdom
   c. self-awareness
   d. theory building

3. The critically reflective social worker must examine his or her assumptions and examine new possibilities for practice through
   a. deconstruction
   b. self-evaluation
   c. peer supervision
   d. evidence-based practice

4. Social workers wishing to become catalysts for social change can do so
   a. at any level of practice
   b. only at the macro level of practice
   c. through strategic planning in agency settings
   d. by engaging in counseling themselves

5. Social work leaders empower others by
   a. securing majority votes in client advocacy groups
   b. sharing power with social workers and clients
   c. teaching clients to become peer counselors
   d. diversifying the composition of their boards of directors

6. Which is true about the various forms of justice?
   a. Social and economic justice are the same
   b. Social and economic justice are mutually exclusive
   c. Social and economic justice are unrelated
   d. Economic justice is one form of social justice

7. Based on your practicum experiences in the area of social justice at any level of practice, articulate two vital leadership skills necessary for a social worker to be effective in achieving social justice. Evaluate the social work profession in terms of its position on social justice being part of its overall mission.

Appendix

LEARNING AGREEMENT AND PRACTICUM EVALUATION FOR GENERALIST SOCIAL WORK PRACTICUM

Based on CSWE Educational Policies and Accreditation Standards (2008, 3-7)

Student _____   Faculty Supervisor _____

Agency _____   Agency Field Instructor _____

INSTRUCTIONS: Student learning goals/competencies are listed in the left-hand column. Students (in consultation with their agency field instructor) are to list learning objectives (activities), timelines for completion, and learning outcomes (practice behaviors) that will be evaluated at the end of each academic term.

Evaluation Scale:

1. Excellent performance and demonstration of learning
2. Above-average performance and demonstration of learning
3. Average performance and demonstration of learning
4. Below-average performance and demonstration of learning
5. Unsatisfactory performance and demonstration of learning
6. No basis for judgment

Learning Goals (Competencies)	Learning Objectives (Activities)	Timeline	Learning Outcomes (Practice Behaviors)	Evaluation of Learning Outcomes (Practice Behaviors)
1. Identify as a professional social worker and conduct oneself accordingly	A.	A.	A.	A. 1 2 3 4 5 6
	B.	B.	B.	B. 1 2 3 4 5 6
	C.	C.	C.	C. 1 2 3 4 5 6

Learning Goals (Competencies)	Learning Objectives (Activities)	Timeline	Learning Outcomes (Practice Behaviors)	Evaluation of Learning Outcomes (Practice Behaviors)					
2. Apply social work ethical principles to guide professional practice	A.	A.	A.	A. 1	2	3	4	5	6
	B.	B.	B.	B. 1	2	3	4	5	6
	C.	C.	C.	C. 1	2	3	4	5	6
3. Apply critical thinking to inform and communicate professional judgments	A.	A.	A.	A. 1	2	3	4	5	6
	B.	B.	B.	B. 1	2	3	4	5	6
	C.	C.	C.	C. 1	2	3	4	5	6
4. Engage diversity and difference in practice	A.	A.	A.	A. 1	2	3	4	5	6
	B.	B.	B.	B. 1	2	3	4	5	6
	C.	C.	C.	C. 1	2	3	4	5	6
5. Advance human rights and social and economic justice	A.	A.	A.	A. 1	2	3	4	5	6
	B.	B.	B.	B. 1	2	3	4	5	6
	C.	C.	C.	C. 1	2	3	4	5	6

Learning Goals (Competencies)	Learning Objectives (Activities)	Timeline	Learning Outcomes (Practice Behaviors)	Evaluation of Learning Outcomes (Practice Behaviors)		
6. Engage in research-informed practice and practice-informed research	A.	A.	A.	A. 1 2 3 4 5 6		
	B.	B.	B.	B. 1 2 3 4 5 6		
	C.	C.	C.	C. 1 2 3 4 5 6		
7. Apply knowledge of human behavior and the social environment	A.	A.	A.	A. 1 2 3 4 5 6		
	B.	B.	B.	B. 1 2 3 4 5 6		
	C.	C.	C.	C. 1 2 3 4 5 6		
8. Engage in policy practice to advance social and economic well-being and to deliver effective social work services.	A.	A.	A.	A. 1 2 3 4 5 6		
	B.	B.	B.	B. 1 2 3 4 5 6		
	C.	C.	C.	C. 1 2 3 4 5 6		
9. Respond to contexts that shape practice.	A.	A.	A.	A. 1 2 3 4 5 6		
	B.	B.	B.	B. 1 2 3 4 5 6		
	C.	C.	C.	C. 1 2 3 4 5 6		

Learning Goals (Competencies)	Learning Objectives (Activities)	Timeline	Learning Outcomes (Practice Behaviors)	Evaluation of Learning Outcomes (Practice Behaviors)					
10. Engage, Assess, Intervene, Evaluate	A.	A.	A.	A. 1	2	3	4	5	6
	B.	B.	B.	B. 1	2	3	4	5	6
	C.	C.	C.	C. 1	2	3	4	5	6

Comments _____

_____

_____

_____

Overall Score _____

(Total number of points given _____ divided by number of items rated _____ = _____)

Student Signature/Date _____

Agency Field Instructor/Date _____

Faculty Supervisor/Date _____

MICRO LEVEL PRACTICE EXAMPLE WITH INDIVIDUAL CLIENT

(using conceptual frameworks to design intervention)

The client is a 17-year-old male who was kicked out of his family's home after disclosing that he is gay. He was living on the streets when contacted by a social worker doing outreach with homeless youth.

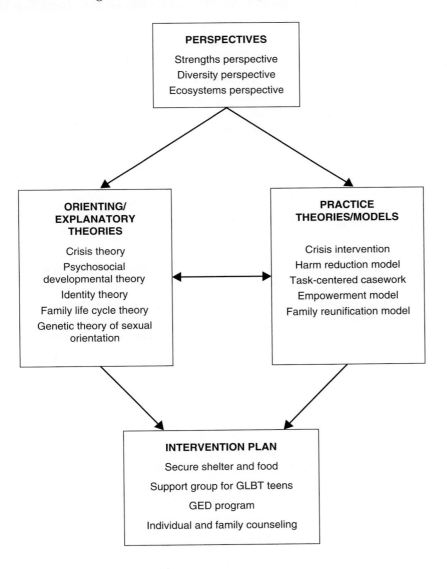

PERSPECTIVES

Strengths perspective
Diversity perspective
Ecosystems perspective

ORIENTING/ EXPLANATORY THEORIES

Crisis theory
Psychosocial developmental theory
Identity theory
Family life cycle theory
Genetic theory of sexual orientation

PRACTICE THEORIES/MODELS

Crisis intervention
Harm reduction model
Task-centered casework
Empowerment model
Family reunification model

INTERVENTION PLAN

Secure shelter and food
Support group for GLBT teens
GED program
Individual and family counseling

MICRO LEVEL PRACTICE EXAMPLE WITH FAMILY

(using conceptual frameworks to design intervention)

A family who has been caring for its 85-year-old widowed father and grandfather is no longer able to provide him with adequate care due to his health problems and dementia. They are considering placement in a nursing home and are working with a hospital social worker where the client has been admitted following a stroke.

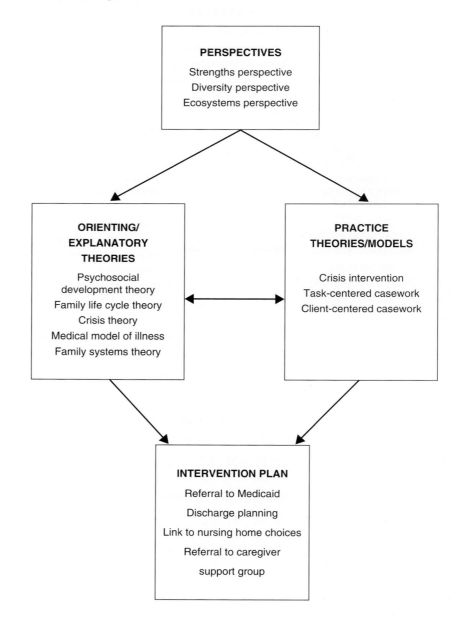

PERSPECTIVES

Strengths perspective
Diversity perspective
Ecosystems perspective

ORIENTING/ EXPLANATORY THEORIES

Psychosocial development theory
Family life cycle theory
Crisis theory
Medical model of illness
Family systems theory

PRACTICE THEORIES/MODELS

Crisis intervention
Task-centered casework
Client-centered casework

INTERVENTION PLAN

Referral to Medicaid
Discharge planning
Link to nursing home choices
Referral to caregiver
support group

MEZZO LEVEL PRACTICE EXAMPLE WITH GROUP

(using conceptual frameworks to design intervention)

A group for survivors of sexual assault is being designed by the YWCA sexual assault program.

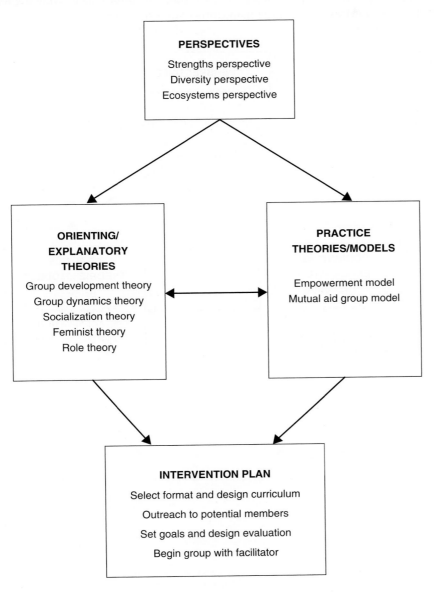

MEZZO LEVEL PRACTICE EXAMPLE WITH ORGANIZATION

(using conceptual frameworks to design intervention)

Two family counseling agencies with similar missions are considering a merger, but want to retain the unique programs each one offers.

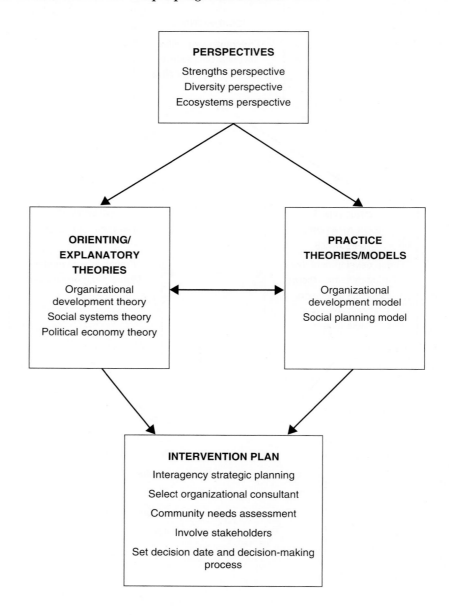

MACRO LEVEL PRACTICE EXAMPLE WITH COMMUNITY

(using conceptual frameworks to design intervention)

A factory employing 800 people threatens to close, which would put its workers into unemployment. The community has few job opportunities and a high rate of unemployment. The factory owners maintain that the community's antibusiness approach contributed to the potential closure. A community organization group is working to resolve conflicts and retain this factory in the community.

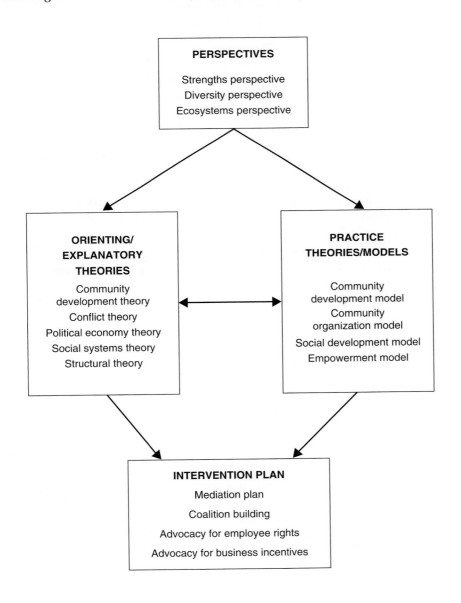

PERSPECTIVES

Strengths perspective
Diversity perspective
Ecosystems perspective

**ORIENTING/
EXPLANATORY
THEORIES**

Community development theory
Conflict theory
Political economy theory
Social systems theory
Structural theory

**PRACTICE
THEORIES/MODELS**

Community development model
Community organization model
Social development model
Empowerment model

INTERVENTION PLAN

Mediation plan
Coalition building
Advocacy for employee rights
Advocacy for business incentives

MACRO LEVEL PRACTICE EXAMPLE WITH SOCIAL POLICY

(using conceptual frameworks to design intervention)

A state coalition of mental health providers is sponsoring legislation regarding improved treatment of individuals with mental illness who are involved in the criminal justice system, including transport, mental health court, and treatment while incarcerated.

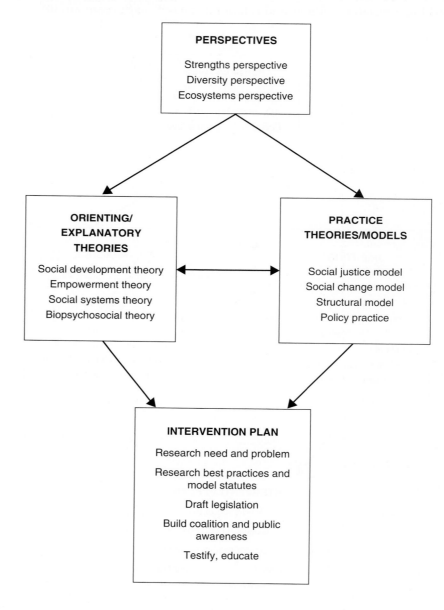

PERSPECTIVES

Strengths perspective
Diversity perspective
Ecosystems perspective

**ORIENTING/
EXPLANATORY
THEORIES**

Social development theory
Empowerment theory
Social systems theory
Biopsychosocial theory

**PRACTICE
THEORIES/MODELS**

Social justice model
Social change model
Structural model
Policy practice

INTERVENTION PLAN

Research need and problem

Research best practices and
model statutes

Draft legislation

Build coalition and public
awareness

Testify, educate

Index

Note: Locators followed by 'f' and 't' refer to figures and tables respectively.